THE BOOK OF TOP TEN HORROR LISTS

By "Cryptmaster Chucky" Charles F. Rosenay!!!

The Book of Top Ten Horror Lists

© 2021 Charles F. Rosenay!!! All Rights Reserved.

No part of this book may be reproduced or transmitted in any form or by means electronic or mechanical, including photocopying or information and retrieval system, without permission in writing from the publisher. Permission is granted to other publications or media to excerpt the contents contained for review purposes, provided that the correct credit and copyright information is included for any materials reproduced.

The images included in this book are © of their respective copyright holders and are presented as Fair Use to be illustrative for the text held. Photos are used by permission. All added material is © of their respective copyright holders. The material in this book is intended for historical purposes and literary criticism and review and is used by permission.

There is no affiliation, endorsement, or connection between any of the contributors and this book and its author.

Published in the USA by

BearManor Media
1317 Edgewater Dr. #110
Orlando, FL 32804
www.BearManorMedia.com

Softcover Edition
ISBN: 978-1-62933-764-7

Hard cover Edition
ISBN: 978-1-62933-765-4

Printed in the United States of America

TABLE OF CONTENTS

Dedication 5

Fang You 6

Introduction 7

Top 10 Lists 13

The "Cryptmaster Chucky" List 267

The Ultimate TERRORble Top 10 List 278

Index of Films 279

Index of Contributors 292

THE BOOK OF TOP TEN HORROR LISTS

DEDICATION

Dedicated to My Loved Ones in Two Chapters of My Life:

Chapter One of my life is my parents, the greatest and most loving and supportive parents ever…my Mom, Rose Rosenay, who made me watch my first monster movie, and my Dad, Harry Rosenay, who helped me make my childhood monster home movies.

Chapter Two of my life is my own family, who brings me more joy and simcha than anything else in the world (yes, even more than monsters, The Beatles, or baseball)…

My wife Melissa, for being the binding of our family, for all her hard work and support with my many projects, but, most importantly, for being my partner in creating our three greatest productions: our children Lauren, Harrison, and Ian.

May all your monsters be only like the fictional ones in this book.

FANG YOU

There are lots of people to say FANG YOU to…

Thank you to each and every celebrity and personality and friend who contributed their list to this book.

Thank you to **Janet Davis**, who is the best Assistant Editor on this planet. She's also the best Associate Editor!

Thank you to my daughter, **Lauren Rosenay**, for her layout of the book cover.

Thank you to three brilliant artists who brought some iconic images to life with their artwork gracing the book cover:

Robb Ortel, responsible for Boris Karloff's Frankenstein's Monster (with The Bride behind him), Bela Lugosi's Dracula, Lon Chaney Sr.'s London After Midnight Vampire and Phantom of the Opera, George Romero, and Pennywise from "It."

David R. Heywood, who supplied us with his Creature From The Black Lagoon and also Linda Blair's Regan in "The Exorcist."

John Sargent, rounding out this Unholy Trio of Artists, with Lon Chaney Jr's Wolfman, Boris Karloff as Ardeth Bay in "The Mummy," Janet Leigh from "Psycho," and King Kong.

Thank you to authors **Beverly Roberts, Stephen Spignesi, Debe Branning, Jude Southerland Kessler, Bruce Spizer, Mark Arnold**, and **Tony Renzoni** for their professional advice, and to **Dan Galli** of DGG Design for formatting assistance.

Thank you to **Ben Ohmart** of BearManor Media for believing in this project, and **Michael A. Ventrella** for his skill in laying out the book.

INTRODUCTION

I love horror. I always have.

Well, maybe not always.

I was an only child in a middle-class Bronx household, where my parents always had the radio and TV on, often at the same time. We'd be listening to AM radio and singing along with The Beatles, Four Seasons, The Supremes, and all the hits of the day, and I'd be watching cartoons, Bozo, Superman, or the Three Stooges during the day, while the news and usually a movie would be on after dinner. In those days, television was limited to the three networks plus local channels 5, 9, and 11. One of those local channels, WOR Channel 9, would show "The Million Dollar Movie" – screening a motion picture on Monday night and then repeating it every night through Friday. This was before videotaping, cable TV, DVRing, and streaming. It was before you could watch what you wanted, when you wanted.

My Mom, who loved monster movies, wanted to introduce me to a movie she loved all her life, **Frankenstein**. She kept checking *TV Guide*, but it wasn't airing. One week, "The Million Dollar Movie" was showing the next best, **The Bride of Frankenstein**. That Monday night, at age four or five, I watched a few minutes of the film before I begged to go to bed. Believe me, I never begged to go to bed. She turned off the TV and I went to bed a wreck. The next night, she tried again, adding Jiffy Pop popcorn and warm milk to the mix. I actually sat through the movie, but with my eyes closed tight the entire time. On Wednesday night, she tried again, and I half-watched it through my fingers. On Thursday, I sat mesmerized, not just watching it, but loving every second. By Friday, I couldn't think of anything else except seeing it again…and every possible monster movie that aired (I still see every possible monster movie, but now we call them horror films). I always say that seeing The Beatles on "The Ed Sullivan Show" was my first memory in life, but, admittedly, this may have come first.

In any case, I was hooked. I was a "Monster Kid." Along with baseball and The Beatles, it was all I obsessed about. I built every Aurora model kit, read though every issue of *Famous Monsters of Filmland*, and even made some 8mm silent monster movies with my Dad and friends. My Mom and I did watch the original **Frankenstein** together shortly thereafter, but one thing bothered her. She originally saw it in a movie theater, and swore that there was a scene where Frankenstein's Monster threw the little girl in the water. I told her it was probably her imagination, or she remembered wrong, but sure enough she was right: that scene was in fact cut from local broadcast TV showings. So many films were edited for TV, and not always for the better, but I digress.

THE BOOK OF TOP TEN HORROR LISTS

When I was 10, we moved out of the Bronx to Connecticut, and, fortunately, the monster mags, models, comics, baseball cards, and records all came with us. Yes, my parents were amazing!

I continued to love watching horror films but if I'm being honest, about nine out of 10 weren't very good. It was worth sifting through the junk to find the gems, though.

Me as a child playing with my monster models (with a Beatles poster on the wall behind me)

Fast forward to 1998. I was already in the entertainment business for about two decades. I'd been entertaining professionally as a mobile/ party DJ/ MC, producing Beatles fan conventions since 1978, publishing a Beatles magazine titled *Good Day Sunshine* since the early '80s, co-producing Monkees fan conventions, booking bands, and also organizing and hosting the "Magical History Tour," bringing fans to Liverpool and London since 1983. My best friend, Danny, encouraged me to branch out. He asked where else I thought people would want to go. I told him that I always wanted to visit Transylvania, and before you could say "Creatures of The Night," vampire vacationers were joining me on my "DraculaTour to Transylvania." These tours were recognized by the Romanian Tourism Office, written about in international horror and vampire magazines, and even attended by notables such as genre writer Joe R. Lansdale and Butch ("Eddie Munster") Patrick. Legendary Hammer horror scream queen Ingrid Pitt was a special guest on one of our spooktacular tours. My Dracula Tour was featured on the Travel

Channel (as was my Beatles Tour), Discovery Channel, and also BBC/ Granada Television.

Thanks to our itinerary, our phenomenal tour-guide Radu, and the amazing travelers who take the annual pilgrimage to the "un-holy land," there is no other Dracula Tour that is put on by fans, for fans, with both day and night activities, and is as much fun and highly-rated: www.DracTours.com.

Soon after, I branched out into producing "GHOSTour," week-long trips to other notoriously haunted locations worldwide. Over the years, I've brought groups of travelers to England, Ireland, Scotland, Eastern Germany (Frankenstein's Castle), Prague in the Czech Republic, Hungary, Cuba, and even the Middle East. Some travelers join me to every new, successive location, and many have become close friends (same with the Beatles tours): www.GHOSTours.com.

My love for monsters, similar to my passion for all things Beatles, somehow went from being a hobby to a part-time business. And what a joyous, satisfying part-time job! Because of my theme tours, I was invited to be a guest at horror conventions, even joining the celebrity panel some years at the Horrorfind Weekend shows, alongside the likes of Dee Wallace Stone, Ken Foree, Doug Bradley, Jack Ketchum, and others. But the whole monsters thing didn't stop with the tours.

In 2007, my wife of just a few years, Melissa, and my friends Danny Levine and Mark Kirschner helped me open the largest indoor haunted attraction in Connecticut, "Fright Haven," which was the perfect combination of scares and fun. After a hiatus, it was resurrected in a new location in 2016, with haunt impresario Bobby Arel, and is still the largest, scariest, and greatest indoor haunted house in the state. Beyond being the founder, I'm a proud "scaremaster" there, honing my acting and ad-libbing skills, and bringing chills and thrills to all who visit. I'm not only an actor at the haunt, but also in films and television. "Fright Haven" is a family affair in many ways: my wife was the box office manager, my daughter worked on helping with the design of the haunt, and also acted, along with both of my sons, as scare-monsters inside the haunt. The rest of the actors in the haunt are all considered our extended "fright family." Speaking of acting, you can read more about my on-camera roles inside, accompanying my personal Top 10 List. It's the very last list in the book, following the true celebrities herein.

For many moons, I was often asked if I would ever write a book on all my travels, encounters, adventures, and memories. I would explain that after about a quarter-century of publishing and editing the Beatles magazine *Good Day Sunshine*, which was 80 pages long and came out every other month, I felt like I was already putting out six books a year!

People always expected me to be a real life "paperback writer," and come up with a Beatles book of some sort. They thought I would possibly write a book containing all the interviews I've conducted at my conventions and for my magazine, or perhaps a book detailing my Beatles or tour encounters, or maybe even just a biography or memoir revealing all my unique stories and life experiences.

Who knows if I'll ever get to any of those projects, but this book you're holding in your hands really came about accidentally. As if I didn't have enough going on, for about five years I wrote/ edited/ published the "National Horror Happenings" column for an online news company, with daily reports, reviews, and updates. It promised "free online horror & monster alerts" and was read by thousands. Pictured is my "Horror Happenings" business card.

Most likely inspired by my admiration for David Letterman's Top 10 Lists, and as a lark, I started asking celebrities for Top 10 Lists of their favorite fear films, favorite genre actors, or 10 scenes that scared them the most. I figured that the readers of my column would enjoy these quickie lists. Who doesn't love lists? The first person I ever asked was Kevin Clement, producer of the incredible Chiller Theatre Expos. Kevin was a pioneer in the genre convention world, and an inspiration in so many ways. Soon, I was able to score lists from actors, authors, directors, athletes, and pop culture personalities, many of whom I now consider to be my friends. I was amazed when I'd get a list from someone you'd never think was a horror buff.

When the COVID-19/ Coronavirus hit in 2020, just like you, I was staying home and safely isolating. I had the good fortune of being able to be home with my wife, Melissa, and my three children, Lauren, Harry, and Ian. With no DJ gigs, no tours, no band bookings, no haunted house, and actually a little extra time on my hands, I mostly watched a lot of movies (yes, mostly horror!), played board games and lots of pinball, and went bicycling and hiking with my family when the weather was nice. But late at night, after my wife and kids went to sleep, I stayed up long past the witching hour, collecting and re-reading all these great lists I'd had on file for a while, and set out to procure even more. I didn't even realize that I was stockpiling these lists for about ten years, and that, sadly, some of the contributors had already passed away, and would never see their lists in a book. Thanks to my office manager, Kelley Adinolfi, those lists were saved.

In 2010, I produced an historic music event, "Rock Con: Weekend of 100 Stars," which was sort of a rock and roll version of Comic Con, and is referenced several times in this book. My goal was to finish this book when I hit that same magic number (100).

In July of 2020, I reached my goal: I compiled and edited one hundred celebrity lists. Some are quick one-word thoughts or just a few word comments, while others are longer, well-thought-out articles. Some are from pop culture icons, some are heroes of mine growing up, while some you may never have heard of. Most are Top 10 Lists of favorite horror movies, but others are more creative topics.

You'll see. Every single one of the one hundred lists deserved a place in here. With the help of my incredible assistant editor, Janet Davis, the book I never thought I had in me was completed.

I hope you'll enjoy reading the lists as much as I enjoyed getting them. Now that I have the finished book to show to celebrities, perhaps I'll eventually get another hundred and hopefully release a second volume someday. That's something I could sink my teeth into (sorry, obvious vampire pun). If you're reading this and know of a celeb or notable who might want to be included in the next book, let us both know! In fact, send me in YOUR Top 10 List. Maybe another volume could be the best Top 10 Lists from readers like yourself. I sincerely hope to publish more of this format – I was never one of those who disliked sequels! The email to write to is: BookofTop10HorrorLists@gmail.com.

While we're at it, the website is www.BookOfTop10HorrorLists.com.

The Instagram is @BookOfHorrorLists.

And please "LIKE" us on Facebook: www.facebook.com/bookofhorrorlists.

I know I personally don't always read bios at the beginning of a book, but rather go directly to the chapters. If you got this far, and didn't jump right to the lists, it's probably because you either know me personally, or you're a monster maven like me.

In any case, thank you for reading this, and for getting the book. If you enjoy it, write a review somewhere, get another copy for a friend as a gift, tell someone about it, or post about it on Facebook or anywhere online. Fang you (thank you) for that!

Better yet, come with me on one of my travel adventures!

Cheers and Chills, "Cryptmaster Chucky" Charles F. Rosenay!!!

www.DracTours.com
www.ParaConn.org
www.LiverpoolTours.com
www.GHOSTour.com
www.FrightHaven.com
www.ToursAndEvents.com
www.BookOfTop10HorrorLists.com

Enter freely and of your own free will. I bid you welcome.
And now, on to the lists…

FORREST ACKERMAN

Once upon a time there lived a man named Forrest Ackerman (November 24, 1916 – December 4, 2008). He was a hero to so many who shared his passion for all things monsterriffic. Friends called him "Forry," and he was the ultimate monster fan/ editor/ expert/ collector/ archivist/ affecionado/ ambassador. He was the heart and soul and punmaster of the fangtastic magazine *Famous Monsters of Filmland*. He even appeared in a few genre films, and was considered by some to be the Stan Lee of horror.

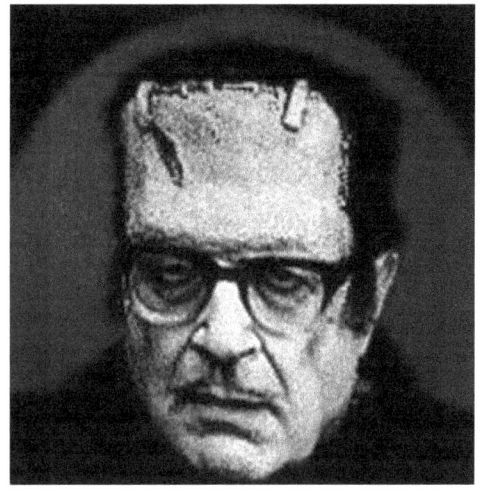

On his way to issue #115 of *Famous Monsters*, the Ackermonster offered his handful of horror films he liked best, probably because someone "axed for it."

Forrest Ackerman's TERRORble List of Horror Films He Liked Best

The Phantom of the Opera (1925): Forry loved the "consummate artistry of Lon Chaney (Sr.)."

Frankenstein (1931): "Sent authentic chills up and down" Forry's spine.

Dracula (1931): "The bats, the coffins, the cobwebs, the creatures of the night, the trio of women…" all contributed but ultimately, it was Bela Lugosi.

Dead of Night (1945): "The perfect multiple episode picture… plus the ending that knocks you for a loop."

King Kong (1933): Ackerman said that even the magnificent musical score "raises the hackles on your neck."

And if he was asked for a sixth choice, it was **The Mummy** (1932, original version, with Boris Karloff).

BIANCA ALLAINE
Dying a Horrible Death in the Woods

Bianca Allaine Kyne (born Bianca Allaine Evans) is better known as Bianca Allaine, but she has also gone under the names Bianca Abel or Bianca Barnett. At least she's consistent with her first name. She is an American actress, host, and model, who earned the Golden Cobb Award for Best Rising B-Movie Actress back in 2011.

At a young age, Bianca discovered the book *Scary Stories to Tell in the Dark*, which began her "love for macabre." She was scared so badly by the book that she told her mother, who tried to have it removed from the school library!

The book may have been her inspiration for future roles, including Pig Bitch in 2009's "Albino Farm."

Her most recent project was a starring role in "Zombienatrix," the zombie heavy metal horror movie she co-wrote and produced.

Bianca Barnett/Allaine wrote: "I have a fetish for obscure horror flicks, especially from the 1970-1980s, particularly those that combine the great out-

doors with horrifying deaths. Narrowing down this list to just ten was difficult, but here we go!"

My 10 Favorite "Dying a Horrible Death in the Woods" Films

Grizzly (1976): Watch this if you are stupid enough to think that bears, specifically those that stand 18 feet tall, are your friend.

Rituals (1977): Five doctors get more than they bargained for in the wilderness of the Great White North.

Night of the Demon (1980): I have a Sasquatch fetish, so this surprisingly gory (you know the scene) little ditty about Bigfoot hit the spot.

Motel Hell (1980): Won my heart by combining two of my favorite pastimes: farming and homicide. Filled with morbid humor and disturbing imagery, don't pass up the depravity.

Just Before Dawn (1981): You know the drill: go camping and croak, but it's worth watching for the ending alone.

Don't Go in the Woods (1981): Never one to listen to authority, I went – and loved it.

Madman (1982): Backwoods shenanigans abound in this picture with Madman Marz, who has his very own theme song.

The Forest (1983): Cool music, tight pants, and groovy dancing enhance this bizarre "stalker in the woods" flick.

Pumpkinhead (1988): This visually stunning, rural horror film is one of my very favorites and one of the reasons I pursued a career in movies. My dad used to sell Pumpkinhead model kits through his business, Lunar Models, and gave me one to paint as a tyke.

Albino Farm (2009): Hillbilly slasher flick set in the Ozark Mountains, worth seeing for a few bizarre and disturbing scenes. A gang of deformed mutants led by the grotesque, hookwielding, busty Pig Bitch (me) wreak havoc on stereotypes. It has played on the Movie Channel's "Splatterdays." Yes, I had to throw in some self-promotion. Kill me.

JOHN AMPLAS
Martin

What do all these horror films have in common: **Martin** (1977), **Dawn of the Dead** (1978), **Knightriders** (1981), **Creepshow** (1982), **Midnight** (1982), **Day of the Dead** (1985), and **Daddy Cool** (2002)? If you said George Romero, you were right about most of them. However, if you knew that the actor John Amplas was in all of them, you'd be right about all of them!

Pittsburgh's John Amplas has been a professor teaching acting at Point Park University's Conservatory of Performing Arts for decades, as well as being a founder and Associate Artistic Director of the professional theater organization The REP.

Through the years, John has embraced conventions and enjoys the interaction of meeting fans one-on-one, rekindling appreciation for John's genre film work among fans young and old. He has appeared at many of these horror cons, occasionally with co-stars from **Dawn of the Dead** and **Day of the Dead**. He also guests at the Living Dead Weekend inside the Monroeville Mall, original home of the Living Dead Museum. The Monroeville Mall was a location in Romero's first classic, **Night of the Living Dead**.

John Amplas' TERRORble Top 10 List for Horror Happenings

(which includes, he notes, "of course, anything George Romero")

Martin (1978): Hailed by critics as the most unique vampire film ever made! Filmed in 1976. Forty-five years later has become a cult classic! Must See!

Night of the Living Dead (1968): Frighteningly real! First in what became a trilogy! Made Romero the Godfather of the "ZOMBIE" film. Although George did not coin the phrase, he calls his creatures "the living dead."

Dawn of the Dead (1978): The living dead are taking over and evolving. Lots of adventure, with SWAT Team and the Dead doing battle in the Monroeville Mall. Oh, and bikers too!

Day of the Dead (1985): Military and scientist clash in an underground mine! The dead are learning, analogous to Mary Shelley's Frankenstein! Scientist, actor Richard Liberty, aids in the creation of Bub, played by actor Howard Sherman (the greatest characterization since Karloff's "Creature").

Creepshow (1982): Five episodes of scary fun, comic book-style, colorful and bold, written by Stephen King and directed by George Romero. Stay Scared!

The Last Winter (2006): Environmental horror! By filmmaker Larry Fessenden.

Wendigo (2001): Another extraordinary horror film by Mr. Fessenden, one of the most unique voices in modern horror!

The Hunchback of Notre Dame (1939): Who doesn't cry due to Charles Laughton's performance!

Frankenstein (1931): Karloff! Need I say more!?!

Dracula (1931): Bela Lugosi! Which reminds me I got to meet Martin Landau…

ED ASNER

Ed Asner. Period. A great actor who needs no introduction. The veteran television legend is perhaps best known as "Lou Grant" on "The Mary Tyler Moore Show" (1970-1977) and for playing the same character on the "Lou Grant" series (1977-1982). Animation fans know him as the voice of Carl Fredricksen in the 2009 Oscar-winning and Golden Globe-winning Pixar film **Up**.

Asner has won five Golden Globe Awards and a record seven Emmy Awards, more than any male actor in history. Now in his 90s, he has racked up about 400 film and television credits dating back to 1957.

His genre credits seem to be few and far between. They include "The Alfred Hitchcock Hour," "The Outer Limits," "Voyage to the Bottom of the Sea," and "The Invaders" on TV in the '60s, and movies such as **The Satan Bug** (1965) and **Death Scream** (1975).

Asner has appeared on Broadway and was formerly President of the Screen Actors Guild. He has written eight books including 2017's *The Grouchy Historian: An Old-Time Lefty Defends Our Constitution Against Right-Wing Hypocrites and Nutjobs*.

In a handwritten letter, along with a photo of himself staring and pointing menacingly, the seemingly-ornery actor confided that he's always avoided horror movies, but gave us a great short list. He was also impressed with how he was tracked down for the list, writing "Scotland Yard couldn't point an accusing finger at you better than I." He added, "You name 10 great horror films."

Ed Asner's TERRORble Top 4 Favorite Scares

Psycho (1960): Nothing equals its shock.

Alien (1979): John Hurt is tough enough to look at without a split stomach

Rebecca of Funny-Folk Farm ("Get Smart," Season 5: Episode 17, 1970): Actress Gale Sondergaard could creep me out even today.

Oliver Twist (1948): When the character popped out from behind that tombstone, I leaped into my date's lap.

TIM ATWOOD

With nominations for R.O.P.E. Entertainer of the Year and AWA Male Vocalist of the Year, Tim Atwood has performed in the spotlight's fringe, backing country music's elite as staff piano man on the most venerable stage in country music history – the Grand Ole Opry. Atwood has played the Opry stage more than 8,500 times.

Today, Tim performs center stage, where he belonged all along. He was featured artist on "Larry's Country Diner" and "Country Family Reunion's Another Wednesday Night Prayer Meeting." Atwood is the recipient of the 2017 Reunion of Professional Entertainers Musician of the Year Award. The Academy of Western Artists recently elected him AWA Instrumentalist of the Year, and the Genuine Country Music Association named him 2017 Fan Favorite.

Tim's TV credits include "Opry Live," "Nashville Now," "Hee Haw," "Church Street Station," "Country On The Gulf," "Pop Goes The Country," "Country Connection," "Late Night With David Letterman," "The Dailey & Vincent Show," and features on both CBS and NBC National News. Tim is a regular guest host on the iconic "Ernest Tubb Midnight Jamboree" on WSM Radio, and he continues to be a sought-after studio musician in Nashville.

Thanks to Publicity Manager Scott Sexton of 2911. Photo Credit: David Bailey.

Website: www.TimAtwood.com.

Tim Atwood's TERRORble Top 10 List of Favorite Horror Movies

The Exorcist (1973): This is the movie that ruined pea soup for millions of moviegoers forever – me included. A head executing a 360 degree spin atop its neck, a young girl crawling up a wall and ceiling, a physical body deteriorating from pure evil, and a voice summoned from Hell itself; this movie haunted my dreams for years. It was the quintessential battle between Catholic priests and demonic forces with a movie score that made every cell in my body scream with terror.

The Shining (1980): Jack Nicholson's deranged performance as the custodian of a haunted hotel in the mountains, isolated from civilization by months of inclement winter weather, was brilliant. I witnessed him spiral into insanity to the peril of his wife and son – the only other "living" residents in the hotel. Those long-ago murdered twin sisters eternally lurking in the hotel hallways gave me the heebie-jeebies, along with the woman/ corpse soaking in the bathtub in Room 237. Hide the knives and the baseball bats. Heeeeeeere's Johnny!

The Wizard of Oz (1939): Forget the Wicked Witch of the West! I know this is a child's movie at heart, but whoever thought of a battalion of evil flying monkeys wearing fez hats and tiny vests with the strength to kidnap and fly away with little girls and dogs was not a nice person.

Halloween (1978): This is the movie where I first fell in love with Jamie Lee Curtis. For that reason alone, this movie makes my top 5 on the list. However, my business is music, and the music in this armchair-gripper absolutely makes this stalk-and-slash thriller a horror classic. The score builds suspense and horrific anticipation with every eye-closing cringe.

Jaws (1975): I wish I had purchased stock in a swimming pool company BEFORE this movie was released because I know water lovers who never returned to the ocean for a swim once they saw this movie. **Jaws** never kept me away from the ocean, but I'd be lying if I said that, to this very day, my heart doesn't skip a beat every time something underwater brushes against my leg in the sea.

The Fly (1986): The Jeff Goldblum remake of the Vincent Price classic is a prime example of a metamorphosis to the grotesque. Yuck!

Aliens (1986): Someone should have warned me that a sharp-toothed, salivating creature from another planet was going to rip itself out of the chest of a human host. This has to be the ultimate in indigestion. I'd never seen anything like it.

Snakes On A Plane (2006): Snakes! Hundreds of them! On a plane. Nowhere to run or hide. Thousands of feet in the air. Slithering. Striking. Falling out of overhead luggage compartments onto the heads and shoulders of passengers below. No, thank you!

Anaconda (1997): I thought the movie's creative team fell short in their special effects for the anaconda for this movie. However, the thought of the snake itself is terrifying. It's just one snake, but it's one BIG A%# snake!

Cujo (1983): Sometimes pet St. Bernards aren't the large, cuddly dogs known for their rescues in the Alps. Sometimes they're downright demonic. This movie is a great reminder to make sure your pup's rabies shot is up to date.

JULIA BAIRD
John Lennon's Sister

Julia Baird is well-known to Beatles fans worldwide, as not only John's sister, but also as an ambassador to the City of Liverpool and a friend to so many who have visited this Beatles' city over the years. She is a Director of the legendary Cavern Club and has visited the U.S. on goodwill trips and special occasions. These include two events produced by the author of this book, Charles F. Rosenay!!!: the NY/ New England Beatles Convention and NYC FAB 50, the 50th Anniversary Gala, presented in New York City in 2014.

Julia is a younger sibling of John Lennon and the middle daughter of their Mother, Julia Lennon. A former language teacher, then Special Needs teacher, she has written three books: *In His Own Youth, In My Own Words*; *John Lennon, My Brother*; and *Imagine This: Growing Up With My Brother, John Lennon*. The latter publication inspired a film. It is hopeful that a more honest version of John and their family will someday be made.

The author, Charles F. Rosenay!!! ("Cryptmaster Chucky"), with Julia Baird in Liverpool during Beatleweek.

Currently, Julia is the Honorary President for the recently re-opened Strawberry Field, in Liverpool. This iconic former children's home is forever immortalized by John Lennon in his song, "Strawberry Fields Forever." It has been regenerated as a Training Programme for young people with mild-to-moderate Learning Difficulties, supported by a Gallery, a café, a shop, and beautiful gardens.

Please look at their website: https://www.strawberryfieldliverpool.com.

Julia's own website is to be found at www.JuliaBaird.eu. Be sure to check out her Strawberry Field blog.

Enjoy what may be the most literary Top 10 List in the book.

Julia Baird's Top 10 Horrors in Literature

Hamlet, William Shakespeare (1599-1601)

"Hamlet" is commonly agreed to be the best of Shakespeare's plays. It is my own personal favourite of Shakespeare's 4 tragedies. Transylvania and spooky castles have nothing on the terror of these plays. His first stab at this genre (forgive the pun) was "Hamlet." Every actor worth his salt wants to play this part. Indeed, Ian McKellen, at 81, has stated his intention to take on this role. I will be in the front row, ready to be scared witless…even though I can almost quote the lines. He, like all the rest, yearns to portray the tragedy, betrayal, horror, and rage of the black side of the human condition. It is a mesmerising reflection of the darkest crevices of human nature, hardly redeemed right to the end.

There is a tragic flaw in Hamlet, as in all Shakespeare's main tragic players. It is known as 'hamartia' and always leads to their downfall. It was a central philosophy in Greek tragedy. This writer excels in it.

A family conspiracy is the backdrop. Hamlet's father, the King, is killed by his own brother, to gain the throne. He then marries the murdered king's wife in an act of unspeakable villainy. Bloodshed, rage, lust, and betrayal then combine to ruin Hamlet's life. Murder after murder follows, stabbing, drowning, until in the final act, Hamlet and his opponent both die from poisoned rapiers. Mistrust within a family. Surely, there is no greater betrayal.

As always, this is based on some element of truth, documenting the rise and fall of the great kings of Denmark. It is thought that Hamlet is actually based on a king called Amleth (1200 AD).

Go and see this play, or watch online. Put the children to bed…this is no place for innocence.

Enjoy!

Macbeth, William Shakespeare (1606-1607)
A bell rings 'Macbeth' after Duncan's murder.
Who's there, what ho?
I heard the owl scream and the crickets cry.
Hark, more knocking.
I hear a knocking.
An owl shrieks.

Hark, peace!

A cry within, of a woman.

What is that noise?

Macbeth is a brave Scottish general. He receives a prophecy from three witches, that one day he will become King of Scotland. This fills him with wild ambition. His wife encourages him to realise this by killing the incumbent king, Duncan. Guilt and paranoia follow immediately. We then live in the terrors and horrors of his black soul. (See what I mean about Transylvania??? Chicken feed!) The atmosphere is one of fear and anxiety, of deepest, darkest, devilish foreboding. The characters are experiencing ambiguous strains of fear and dread…and if you are watching, you are right in the midst of that…and perched on the very edge of your seat. Macbeth's 'seated heart knocks at his ribs.' Yours will too.

James 1st of England (early 17th century), the King of England at the time of the play, was terrified of witches. All of Shakespeare's stories had that pearl of historical truth. This was hardly a hidden dig at the monarch. Everyone would know who it was aimed at. "Macbeth" contains a lot of supernatural elements, emphasised by gloomy moors, great, thick fogs, cauldrons of fire, and the wild wailing of the Three Witches. Brave Macbeth goes totally insane, tormented by his conscience, expressed vividly in animal imagery. You will recognise the first line following:

"Double, double, toil and trouble; Fire burn, and cauldron bubble.

Fillet of a fenny snake, in the cauldron, boil and bake;

Eye of newt and toe of frog, wool of bat and tongue of dog,

Adder's fork and blind worm's sting, lizard's leg and howlet's wing,

For a charm of powerful trouble,

Like a hell-broth boil and bubble."

Shakespearian audiences would have been horrified by all this. I think you would, too.

Once again…children disinvited!

Othello, William Shakespeare (1603-1604)

Shakespeare has been compared to Stephen King, in his portrayal of Othello. How much more horror do you want??? The play was written during what is known as Shakespeare's 'tragic period' (it can be hard to remember that he was also a master of romance and comedy!). It appeared in 1604, set against the backdrop of the wars between Turkey and Venice, which raged right throughout the latter part of the 16th century.

This is the story of an African general, a Moor, in the Venetian army, who is deceived into thinking that his wife, Desdemona, has been unfaithful, whilst he was at war. The poisoning whisperer is Iago, who was overlooked for promotion. This is his gratuitous revenge. The play rapidly descends into a mire of sexual jealousy and racial prejudice. Othello is consumed by bitterness and jealousy, leading him to murder Desdemona, then to kill himself. Iago himself, grovelling underneath the whole blackening plot, also kills two people. Never was there a more gory dog-eat-dog revenge. In fact, Othello eats Othello, slowly and painfully.

Shakespeare could be a sadistic so-and so. There are films. Watch the version with Judi Dench. It will make everything curl.

Recommended age group…100.

King Lear, William Shakespeare (1605-1606)

This play, this plot, drives me insane. It is the one Shakespeare that I avoid, having seen it one too many times. It is an old, old story.

An aging King…a stupid, demented old man, divides his kingdom up between the two daughters who flatter him and banishes the daughter who loves him, but refuses to play the flattery game. The two favoured daughters then will not entertain their father in their own homes and he is abandoned to make his way back through a wild storm. An actual weather storm and a storm in his broken heart.

There ensues an eye-gouging and two stabbings. The king accuses his older daughters of 'unnaturalness.' This would have had the Elizabethan audiences aghast. After some more gruesome murders, including a literal 'cliffhanger,' the youngest daughter and Lear reunite. The one sunspot in this show! The good girl then gets hung, before anyone can stop it. (Of course!) Lear carries her body, weeping…and dies (more of course, of course). A simple enough account. I jest. This whole plot is one long wrongdoing. It is a mental screw-up. It is as much an emotional murder of the soul as the physical carnage inflicted by an all-powerful man in his dotage. Demented.

But, for me, the anguish of watching this old fool rejecting love in favour of unperceived greed and wanton, undeserved flattery is gut-wrenching, mind-blowing, and head-twisting stuff. It is the horror of all horrors. A wild plot. A psycho's dream. I have vowed never to go near the damn play again. It carries on too long in the mind. Daunting and haunting.

You, however, may love Shakespeare's torturous replaying of this old European myth.

Again, remember…absolutely most definitely no children under the age of 50.

Dr. Jekyll and Mr. Hyde, Robert Louis Stevenson (1886)

Well, this is a dastardly plot, grown like a weed out of the complexities of science and the duplicity of human nature. There you are, you already have the beginnings of a horror story! A well-respected doctor performs (impossible, thank goodness) magic with the darker side of science, journeying to find his 'second nature.' I don't think most of us want to go in search of that one! He achieves this by transforming himself from the goodly Dr. Jekyll…into the mad, bad Mr. Hyde. This is his alter ego, who never repents his evil crimes. Initially, the power base stays with Jekyll…but before long, the main man becomes more and more Hyde…out of control of the good doctor. They (both) die…by suicide. Of course, it only needed one. Jekyll. But who made that decision?

This is a psycho drama as much as a brutal display of man's basest desires. It is the first work in English literature to describe what we now call a split personality. Interestingly, Stevenson was a consumptive (T.B.) and wrote the novel whilst hallucinating under the influence of mind-altering drugs. He was actually meeting a mental patient over this time, who was suffering from split personality disorder. The allegorical split can refer to Victorian Christian respectability (sanctimonious), opposed to, and in battle with, degradation, poverty, injustice, and debauchery. (All the makings of a good horror show.) It shines a strong spotlight on the hypocrisy of 19th century England. The very term 'Jekyll and Hyde' has morphed into the English language, to describe a contradictory, but universal facet of human personality.

The film is a great watch…utterly scary. You don't want to meet this psycho in a dark alley, or even under a street light.

Give it a go.

Again…NO chil……

Frankenstein, Mary Wollstonecraft Shelley (1818)

When you are locked on an island, trying to scare the bloody wits out of your friends, to see who can come up with the worst, most nightmarish story EVER…guess who wins that contest? Not the men, who assumed they would (of course)…but kind, gentle Mary Shelley, the young wife of the poet Percy Bysshe Shelley. His golden hour was 'Ozymandias'…his sonnet about a pyramid in the desert (do look it up…a poem of rare beauty and a three minute read…a glowing tribute to an Egyptian king, Rameses 11)…but sweet Mary wrote one of the most spine-chilling thrillers ever. It is recorded in film after film, with all the grisliest of horror actors desperate to play the part…the best/ worst is still probably Boris Karloff.

The storyline, which starts out in genteel fashion, soon unravels into a futurist nightmare. A gifted scientist becomes consumed by the insane desire to know the secret of life (so we all know how this is going to end, right now!). He makes a creature, resembling a human man…well, sort of…out of old body parts (remember the Body Snatchers…that was a real activity). Eventually comes the night to electrify this amalgamation of body bits. Life sizzles in front of him. Victor is instantly horrified by his own creation. The Monster escapes the apartment, finds and kills William, Victor's brother, but as no-one knows of his existence, Victor's adopted, innocent sister is tried and executed for the murder. In short (read it for yourself!), when Victor and The Monster finally do meet, Victor is idiotically persuaded to start fashioning an equally abhorrent female, as a companion to The Monster, who is lonely. A girlfriend! For The Monster…making two Monsters! What the hell was he thinking???? Of course, Victor begins the process before seeing the error of his ways…and he destroys her. The now manically-possessed and depressed (a very bad mix) Monster is always heading north, into the ice caps and at the end of the plot, he is still out there. Somewhere. Anywhere. Yikes!!!!!

Watch an old version, followed by a newer version.

For some reason, children love this…but I would start at 10, maybe, on the couch, snuggled by two parents and four grandparents, hot chocolate, and cookies.

The Pit and the Pendulum, Edgar Allan Poe (1842)

The very name of Edgar Allan Poe used to strike terror into me, as a child, before I even knew about "The Pit and the Pendulum." There is a darkness about the very name. He married his 13-year-old cousin, when he was 27. (See what I mean?) He was the first author to attempt to make a living out of writing. Initially, he wrote mainly poetry, but then branched out into many short stories. "The Pit and the Pendulum" is one of those, published in a Christmas review magazine!! Christmas…in that Pit!!!! With that Pendulum swinging!!! Poe was responsible for intertwining the genre of horror with psycho depth and insights, deliberately designed to give you a heart attack.

"The Pit and the Pendulum" takes place during one of the worst times in Europe…the Catholic Inquisition. The anonymous narrator is sentenced to death by 'robed judges' for the sin of heresy. Not living up to ideals. Scary ideology is a really dark art. Agree with me, or die. The naissance of trolling, perhaps. (Hmmmmm.) The courtroom scene is everyone's worst nightmare. The judges just vanish, tall candles peter out where there is no whisper of a breeze, leaving black of black dark as 'all sensations appeared swallowed up in a descent of the soul into Hades.'

(And you thought Bela Lugosi, with his nightcap and candle at the gloomy castle door freaked you out. Get a load of this.) A mental collapse follows. Even the water he is given is drugged. Next time he wakes up, he is strapped on a stretcher, in the company of fetid rats, lured by meat to his head. A picture of Father Time. A giant pendulum swinging towards him (maybe time to take a break). A razor-sharp scythe is lunging at him…towards him, away from him. People are watching his terror (that is part of the fun for them). You won't believe the next bit. He is saved from certain butcher's death. The prison has been taken over, by an army determined to end this vile Inquisition. (Are you disappointed?) (Relieved?)

Try the Vincent Price film version…watch with a friend. Watch with a gang of friends.

Not the children (sorry, young guys…this just ain't for you…not for a long time).

Dracula, Bram Stoker (1897)

(How many of these freaked-out psycho horror stories are rooted in the 19th century?!...Gothic Horror!!...not a good time!)

I was deliberately excluding *Dracula*, as too predictable as a choice. But then it is one of the blackest films of all time, so it cannot be avoided. Here we go. (Hang on…you are in for a rocky ride!).

Well, Transylvania gets a mention, finally!!!! (Eat your heart out, Shakespeare…did I really say that???!!!) Although the basis of this story is that Dracula is trying desperately to leave it. He wants to come to England, to give us the cult of the undead. Vampires. (Time to emigrate.) The English lawyer had only travelled to Transylvania to conclude a property transaction…at Castle Dracula (had nobody sent him a memo?!). Wouldn't you have scarpered when the wolves started howling??? (Maybe he wasn't really English…) Lawyer cuts his throat accidentally whilst shaving. Dracula lunges at said throat. LAWYER DOESN'T RUN LIKE SHIT OUT OF THERE. This is a mad horror story. Lawyer seduced (ah…now I get it…) by three vampires and now knows that Dracula is himself a vampire…and that his blood is on the menu. He is locked inside Castle Dracula, whilst the Count goes to England, sucks the lifeblood from an innocent, sleepwalking girl called Lucy, and despite copious sprigs of vampire-slaying garlic, Lucy dies…Well, that is what they thought. She is now a fully-fledged vampire herself and children are disappearing (I hope they are not reading this!). They have to dig up her corpse, stake her through the heart, slice off her head, and…yes, you've got it…stuff her mouth with garlic.

Now, to get Dracula. He is tramping round England with dirt from his Castle...this keeps him going, apparently. The assailants are after the dirt. Meanwhile, Mina, the lawyer's girlfriend, has been vampired and lunges at Dracula!!!!! (A very brave vampire.) He flees back to Transylvania (he obviously didn't like the bloodsucking treatment on himself). He finally gets the Lucy treatment...head off, heart stabbed.

Wow! This is not my idea of Saturday night in the cinema! Sunday might be traumatic.

It is suggested that Count Dracula is based on Vlad the Impaler, a 15th century oddbod. Also, that historically, there was anxiety about Eastern Europeans invading Western Europe...or another idea...it could suggest the inversion of stereotypical gender roles, through the sexual liberation of the female vampires. Contradictory explanations. You choose. However you see it, this is a Hammer House of Horrors spectacular.

A good film might be the version with Jack Palance. Apparently, they wanted to remake it, with him starring again. Presumably, the film moguls had dreamt up more foul deeds for him to commit. Interestingly, Mr. Palance refused, as he had felt himself BECOMING Dracula and was terrified...of himself!!!!!!! (Who knew???!!!!!)

I don't think I need to mention the no-children rule here. I would think it would be an imprisonable offence.

Animal Farm, George Orwell (1945)

George Orwell...the Prophet of Doom. Or maybe just The Prophet...because what seemed like doom and gloom is all coming true. Oh so true. Where is he now, to guide us out of this Silicon Valley orgiastic mess?? Dead, that's what. He's just left us to it. Finish the story yourselves. (Thanks, George.) He explains clearly (if allegorically) the results of distorting the truth. We have fallen for it, hook, line, and sinker. This is a greater horror story than any of the previous ones. Caveat Emptor (buyer beware). So, his two main horror stories are <u>1984</u>...just add 40 years on and he had almost cracked that one (and my name is Julia!!!!! eeeek!!!)...and the other vile diatribe is, of course, *Animal Farm*...Just what it says on the cover. Animals. On a farm. BUT THESE ANIMALS ARE KINGS AND QUEENS OF SOCIETY. Read on.

Bad farmer Jones neglects his animals (watch out bad farmers...don't turn your backs on those creatures. Come-uppance is just around the corner.). He is kicked out. For a short while, as in all rebellions, life is good. More freedom, less work, more food, better education. Good story so far. But Napoleon and Snowball decide they want the position of top bod. Also known as Ruler. King. Emperor. And ever upwards of course, to Heavenly Status.

Napoleon and Snowball are PIGS! Top Pig just doesn't sound right…but these two are about to up-end the whole farm to get this position. When he wins (the clue is in the name), Napoleon becomes Crowned Pig. Honest…it is in the book. And the films.

Napoleon ends up worse than Farmer Jones. This always happens with revolutions. Always. The pigs, the great controllers, decide they like clothes. Like, real, human clothes. They look like crazy hominoids, but no-one dares tell them (The Emperor's New Clothes). They have descended into the depths of depravity and no-one can say a word. Punishment is swift. (See what I mean about being worse than castles and bloodsuckers?)

Trivial stuff, that lot.

Maybe children (and their adults) should be made to watch this, so they won't put clothes on animals for fun. They have their own coats. They do not need anthropomorphing into mini-mes. Or move to warmer climes.

Animal Farm is an allegory of the rise of Stalinism, post the Russian October Revolution of 1917. This 20th century monster makes Dracula look like an adorable puppy. And this is real. Stalin happened. He really, really happened. The animals are all representations of Russian politicians, voters, and workers.

If you really want to freak out, have sleepless nights, tear your hair out from the roots, scream out loud, and count every hair on your body individually…read Solzhenitsyn's *The Gulag Archipelago* and James Clavell's *King Rat*. Watch the 'King Rat' film, with George Segal and James Fox. Remind yourself constantly that these are based on true stories. Not medieval fables. Recent bloody, gory massacres. This should satisfy your bloodlust.

Be vigilant. Ever vigilant.

All pigs must watch.

Not so sure about the children.

Lord of the Flies, William Golding (1954)

Is this the 'best til last'??????

Phew, readers. Where to start with this nightmare?! If you are an adult, strap yourself in for the rocky horror show. You will see your offspring in a new light. And change the house rules forthwith. And maybe leave home in an hour's time. Without them. Like, RUN.

A plane evacuating children is shot down over a deserted island (you wouldn't bother trying to save them after this story). Two of them, Ralph and Piggy (yeah, those damn pigs again…never trust a pig is the motto here, methinks)…they find a conch shell. They summon a pow-wow and make rules. Quite sensible at first (ha! ha!…don't fall asleep…the fun is about to begin). They decide to light a fire (sensible, for an alert, cooking food, warmth, security blanket), using Piggy's glasses and the sunlight trick…Now Piggy is blind without them. Who cares? (No-one.) He is also fat. Let's face it. He is an outsider. But they are about to find out that he has a brain and they need him. (We all have our uses.) Piggy is the only boy concerned that one of them is missing. The horrors of uncivilised society are already setting in. The semblance of order soon disintegrates as the boys become idle, not wanting to build shelters, nor hunt the wild pigs for food. Leadership is challenged, as the beast in the boys takes over. Leadership of what, exactly, is the question here. The boys become two tribes at war, stranded on a postage stamp of an island…(they really are aping their elders and betters on the mainland!). Any semblance of order at all is truncated when one boy drops a boulder, killing Piggy. Killing the brainy one. How's that for inanity? Hatred is ensconced by now. They are on the path to self-destruction, at an increasingly rapid rate…but are saved by a ship. Immediately, these feral boy-beasts revert to small children and start crying…like small children.

The officer who finds them berates the boys for their uncouth, uncontrolled, uncivilised behaviour…then he turns to look at the warship. Oh to be inside his head then.

Lord of the Flies is an allegory, declaring conflicting human impulses concerning living by rules, in some sort of harmony against the will to power. Group-think and individuality. Morality and immorality. All these themes are highly relevant today. The actual title, 'Lord of the Flies,' is a translation of Beelzebub (Kings 1: 2-3, 6.16).

"*Lord of the Flies* presents a view of humanity unimaginable before the horrors of Nazi Europe, and then plunges into speculations about mankind in the state of nature. Bleak and specific, but universal, fusing rage and grief, this is a novel for the 1950s and all time." (Robert McCrum)

In case you have made the wrong assumption, that I don't like children…I love them. They are the hope, the shining light, the past, and the future. But I would make them all watch "Lord of the Flies" (1990 version is the ugliest, so that one) maybe from the age of 10 or so…just so they know what happens without the bossy adults ferreting in their lives morning, noon, and night. They may even have to watch the film in a darkened room on their own.

That'll learn 'em.

MARK BEGO
Rocket Man

Mark Bego, like many of us, grew up reading *Famous Monsters of Filmland* Magazine. He became *The New York Times* bestselling author of 60 books – not on horror – on rock and roll and show business. He is best known for *Michael!* [Jackson], which sold eight million copies in 1984, at the height of the *Thriller* singer's fame. Bego has also written books on Madonna, Whitney Houston, Elton John, Aretha Franklin, Mary Wilson, Micky Dolenz, and others. His 60th book, *Murder at Motor City Records*, won a prestigious award at The Paris Book Festival.

Mark Bego's 66th published book was a fascinating and in-depth biography, *Rocket Man: The Life of Elton John*, released in 2020 by Pegasus Books. In his words: "Elton is a subject I have been following and writing about since the 1960s. I was aware of him since I first heard Three Dog Night's version of Elton's song 'Lady Samantha' on their 1969 *Suitable for Framing* album. I have followed him from his absolute career peak with 'Goodbye Yellow Brick Road' to his late-'70s slump, through 'I'm Still Standing,' 'The Lion King,' and all the way up to his 2020 zenith with the award-winning film **Rocketman**."

His newest book is a biography of Freda Payne, of "Band of Gold" fame.

Expect to see a lot more great books by Mark Bego down the line. Website: www.markbego.com.

Mark Bego's TERRORble Top 10 List

Psycho (1960): Hitchcock pulled out all of the stops for the top horror film of his career. Making the star of this movie a deranged man who dressed like his mother brilliantly let us into the twisted mind of a madman. And who would have thought that taking a shower could be so terrifying?

Alien (1979): I nearly flipped the first time I saw this classic horror film.

Those oozing pods of alien larvae and the ultimate "face hugger" scene are both terrifying and shocking.

Creature from the Black Lagoon (1954): While it looks a bit tame to see it nowadays, this was a groundbreaking '50s monster movie that I am certain ruined "hidden lagoon" travel packages for years. The creature costume is still one of the best ones in horror movie history.

Pet Sematary (1989): No one likes to lose a favorite pet; however, after seeing this film, I was convinced that, as Fred Gwynne says, "Sometimes dead is better."

Salem's Lot (1979, TV mini-series): This was a first-class production from beginning to end, and James Mason made a brilliantly chilly ghoul. The scene where the young boy vampire is scratching on the bedroom window glass to get in to kill his friend still gets me every time.

Bram Stoker's Dracula (1992): Gary Oldman made the perfect modern Count Dracula and Tom Waits was perfectly "nuts" as spider-eating Renfield. An all-star cast and great special effects helped to take this familiar story in terrifying new directions.

Van Helsing (2004): Although some of the sequences in this film are a bit cartoonish, the scenes of Hugh Jackman battling the three vampire brides are brilliantly scary. Who would have thought that monster hunting could be so much fun!?!

House on Haunted Hill (1959): Even when he was at his campiest, Vincent Price always elevated every film he was ever in. I will never forget the first time I saw the vat of acid in the basement of this haunted mansion. Sunken bathtubs have always seemed creepy to me ever since!

Wait Until Dark (1967): This Audrey Hepburn scary melodrama was brilliantly paced and edited to have moviegoers literally on the edges of their seats. I had never been in a theater where the audience actually leapt up and screamed simultaneously until I saw this movie.

Interview With the Vampire (1994): Up until this film was made, vampires were almost always creepy Transylvanian royalty. With Tom Cruise and Brad Pitt biting necks as Louis and Lestat, suddenly it became chic for vampires to be young, sexy, and just a little bit homoerotic at the same time!

CORBIN BERNSEN
The Dentist

Corbin Bernsen isn't just a great actor. He's also smart, handsome, and a truly nice guy. The masses who watch TV will know him as Arnie Becker from over 170 episodes of "L.A. Law," from "Jag," "The Young & The Restless," and "Psych," which aired for years on the USA Network.

He is a genre favorite for the films **Raptor**, **Fangs**, and **Inhumanoid**, plus appearances on "The Outer Limits," "Masters of Horror," and "Star Trek: The Next Generation." He had the role of Roger Dorn in the films **Major League**, **Major League II**, and **Major League: Back to the Minors**. He has also appeared regularly on other shows, including "The Resident," "General Hospital," and "Cuts." In 2019, we saw a different side of CB in **Life With Dog**, centering on a man who finds himself struggling after his wife's death, until he befriends a dog and forms a bond that helps him heal.

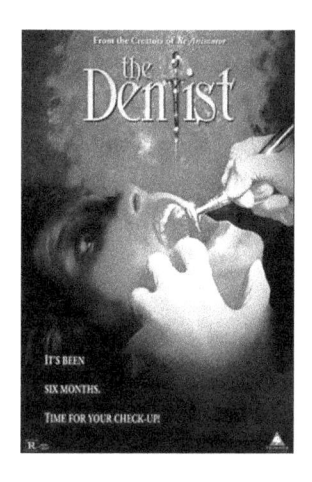

But Corbin *drilled* his name into horror history in 1996 as **The Dentist**.

Bernsen starred and also directed a movie called **Dead Air**, which was sort of the opposite of Orson Welles' "War of the Worlds." In this case, the DJ isn't giving the info – he's trying to get it – from within his locked studio while a terrorist outbreak has caused virus-crazed maniacs to run rampant in the streets. It starred Bill Moseley, who also contributed a great Top 10 List that you can read later in this book. Corbin appeared at select conventions to promote the DVD release, where fans found out what a cool guy he is.

Corbin Bernsen's TERRORble Top 10 Favorite Horror Scenes

Many are obvious and have become classics. But hey, they're on my list because they were each great and lived with me long after I saw them.

Linda Blair puking green pea soup in **The Exorcist** (1973). Never saw stuff like this before in a dark room with other people. Scary, gross, and frightening.

Jack Nicholson in almost all scenes from **The Shining** (1980). Not so scary, just all-out entertaining and weird.

Shower scene in **Psycho** (1960). Again, saw at a very young age and really set the stage for my enjoyment of being terrified.

First scene between Anthony Hopkins and Jodie Foster in **The Silence of the Lambs** (1991). The first scene ever that truly made me understand the power and sick potential of the human mind. And without any effects! All performance.

Night of the Living Dead (1968): I enjoyed all the scenes in the house where the real battle was playing out. I love how the fear of zombies drove all the characters to their wit's end. The zombies didn't really scare me, what went on in the house did.

Alien (1979): The first time we see the alien was really great, hidden among the set pieces. It made you afraid of the whole ship.

The Dentist (1996): Yes, I'm going to throw in one of my movies, but when I'm pulling teeth, watching it on the screen, it scares even me. You know when we shoot this stuff, you don't get the full effect!

Jaws (1975): OK, maybe not a horror movie, but scared the s*** out of me and millions more, to not go in the water! Classic horror actually when the kids are in the water and we see them from the shark's POV.

Whatever Happened to Baby Jane? (1962): Some won't know this film but the twisted tale between two sisters is a classic. When the "meal" is revealed, it's a classic. I've never seen hatred played so fully.

The Birds (1963): When the birds attack the house. I'm scared of birds to this day, freak out when they dive bomb for me.

PETE BEST
Beatle!

I always tried to get a Top 10 List from one of The Beatles, and finally succeeded. It's taken a few years and a bunch of e-mail requests, but we succeeded. We only got his list, and not any comments or reasons why he made the selections, but we were surprised at how many contemporary classics made his list, with a nod to the true – original – classics at the end.

No, we didn't get Ringo Starr's list or one from Paul McCartney (tricked you!), but we are honored to present one from original drummer Pete Best. Pete was The Beatles' (and the Silver Beatles') drummer alongside John Lennon, Paul McCartney, and George Harrison before Ringo Starr, in the early 1960s. He started appearing at conventions and autograph shows in the '80s and quickly became a fan favorite. He starred in a one-man multimedia college presentation, and penned the 2001 autobiography *Beatle! The Pete Best Story*. He still makes personal appearances and tours with his Pete Best Band, where he drums alongside his brother Roag, who also manages his career (and is quite the horror buff in his own right, having written a vampire novel that's yet to be published).

Best plays at the yearly "BestFest" in his family's home and legendary club, The Casbah Coffee Club, in Hayman's Green, Liverpool.

Two of the author's children, Harrison Rosenay (left) and Lauren Rosenay, with former Beatle Pete Best (right). Photos by Melissa Rosenay.

A true gentleman and a good friend for many years, Pete encourages readers to follow him on Twitter (www.twitter.com/beatlespetebest) and Facebook (www.facebook.com/petebestofficial).

Thanks to Roag for getting us the Best list!

Visit Pete Best's website: www.petebest.com.

Pete Best's Best Horror Movies List

The Omen (1976)

A Nightmare on Elm Street (1984)

Halloween (1978)

The Amityville Horror (1979)

The Shining (1980)

The Blair Witch Project (1999)

House on Haunted Hill (1959)

Poltergeist (1982)

And of course, going back to the day: **Frankenstein** (1931), **Dracula** (1931), **The Wolf Man** (1941).

BEV BEVAN

At 19, Bev Bevan was the drummer in Denny & the Diplomats. Denny (Laine) went on to be in the Moody Blues and Wings, Bev went on to be a founding member of The Move, with Roy Wood. Never breaking big in the U.S., the band was huge in his homeland, England, and other parts of Europe. The group added Jeff Lynne in 1970, and they morphed into a side project, a little band called Electric Light Orchestra. Wood departed, and ELO charted (and charted, and charted).

Bevan, as the backbeat of ELO, became a full-fledged pop/rock star, and he also sang lead, most notably on the tracks "Fire On High" and "Strange Magic." Bevan continued the band's legacy after they disbanded and Jeff Lynne went solo. In the later 1980s, Bevan toured with ELO Part ll, which was renamed The Orchestra when Bevan sold his share of the Electric Light Orchestra brand name to Lynne.

Bevan has drummed with U.S. soul singer Bobby Womack and heavy metal rockers Black Sabbath. More recent years have found him on the air as a BBC radio DJ, and respected record reviewer.

Bev Bevan's TERRORble Horror Top 10 List

1, 2, and 3 are all old '50s black and white TV shows that frightened me to death when I was a kid. I used to peep out from behind the sofa to look at the little 12-inch black and white television set:

The Quatermass Xperiment (1953, British-made)

"The Twilight Zone" (1959): Loved the presenter's voice.

"Alfred Hitchcock Presents" (1955): Thrilling and smart.

Next two are the most frightening books I've ever read – both written by the brilliant Stephen King. (In places, I could barely make myself turn the page!):

Misery (1987)

Carrie (1974)

The last five are my favourite-ever horror films – four old and one new:

Alien (1979): I have loved all of the "Alien" movies, but the first one is the best with not knowing what's to come.

The Thing (From Another World!) (1951): Truly gruesome!

The Shining (1980): Jack Nicholson's finest movie moment: "Honey I'm home!" (Great book, too.)

The Exorcist (1973): I remember all of us going to see this on an American tour with ELO. We all had nightmares!

A Quiet Place (2018): Only saw this recently and it was truly scary.

KAREN BLACK

One of the horror world's favorite and most memorable moments in cinema is when Karen Black fights the manic, toothy Zuni doll in Dan Curtis' "Trilogy of Terror" (1975), in one of her multiple roles in that beloved anthology. We wouldn't be wrong if we stated that it was the world's most favorite made-for-TV horror trilogy.

Born Karen Blanche Ziegler, the esteemed actress boasted over 100 film performances to her credit, including her role as Rayette Dipesto in **Five Easy Pieces** (1970), for which she received an Academy Award nomination for Best Supporting Actress. Some of our most memorable Karen Black genre roles include Mother Firefly in **House of 1000 Corpses** (2003), Magnificent Martha in **Soulkeeper** (2001), June in **Children of the Corn: The Gathering** (1996), Nehor in **Plan 10 from Outer Space** (1995), Karen in **Children of The Night** (1991), Ellen in **It's Alive III: Island of the Alive** (1987), Linda in the 1986 **Invaders From Mars** remake, Marian in **Burnt Offerings** (1976), Fran in Alfred Hitchcock's final feature, **Family Plot** (1976), and so many others.

Her thriller/ horror/ comedy film **Some Guy Who Kills People**, with Kevin Corrigan and Barry Bostwick, was produced by John Landis and directed by Jack Perez. Karen was very proud of it.

But it was probably her memorable role as a murderous mother in Rob Zombie's **House of 1000 Corpses** (2003) that helped cement her status as a cult horror icon.

We tried to get a list from Karen for a long time, and were very excited to finally get her to come through a few years before she passed away (in 2013). Karen shared this link: www.youtube.com/watch?v=4z0AoQTRjtA and wrote "See the 100 movies I've made in a few moments love, karen black."

Karen Black's Favorite Moments in Science Fiction, Sci-fi, Fantasy, and Horror films

Invasion of the Body Snatchers (1956): O.K. Here's my favorite moment from all science fiction, fantasy, and horror films I've seen…In this absolutely terrific movie, Kevin McCarthy knows full well that if anyone from his community – where the body snatchers are replacing humans with outer space/ unfeeling replicates of its citizens – falls asleep, during that unconscious moment, the body snatchers will take over and you will wake up, not "you" anymore and never to be you again.

McCarthy and his girl, Dana Wynter, escape the town, make a run for it. But it's late and they are getting more and more tired. McCarthy goes to search for a path for them to take. When he returns, he sees Dana asleep on the ground and tries to wake her. Here's the moment: Close up. She opens her eyes. They are unseeing, utterly passive, opaque. She's been snatched!

It's Alive (1974): One of the great science fantasy movies, this one by Larry Cohen. Sharon Farrell has given birth to a very small but deadly monster. But she's his mommy. She loves him. She hides him away. But he keeps killing people.

Finally the police are on to the little guy and with ludicrously unnecessary force, about 44 police cars surround the big building where the child is hiding. His dad is appointed to go in and get him and surrender him to the police, in whose keep his baby will surely be put to death.

John Ryan looks at his little son, knowing what he must do and what he is going to do. Great tears of love and sorrow fall from his eyes and were falling from mine, I can tell you. What a moment. It's emblazoned within me forever. But without the masterful performance by John Ryan, this moment would not have been realized and would not have become unforgettable.

Spirits of the Dead (1968) – Toby Dammit segment: This film is a collection of three shorts or segments, one by Federico Fellini, one by Louis Malle, and a third by Roger Vadim. The short by Fellini is about a tormented actor named Toby Dammit, played by Terence Stamp, and is in fact known as a great film. When it was last screened at a theater in Los Angeles, respected directors who know good film came out of the woodwork to see it.

Toby Dammit is pursued by a small, glitteringly happy little girl who represents death in the film. The great screen moment in this horror science fantasy film is as follows: Toby Dammit, a famous actor, walks through the audience toward the stage where a TV interview has been set up for him. The stage has roaring blatant white lights and looks more like a fighter's ring than a television broadcast. As he walks, he looks down upon all the faces in the audience upturned towards him. They are Fellini faces: splendid and sordid, people who are real yet seem to have arrived from a nearby circus with skin a little too white, lips a little too red.

Faces, faces, faces, and the great screen moment was there for me. I swear I got high watching them. I went into a trance of some kind. Only the genius of Fellini could transport his audience in this way.

Unearthly Stranger (1964): The only way we can tell that this beautiful woman, Julie Davidson, played so wonderfully by Gabriella Licudi, is not from our planet is that when she achieves human emotion and cries, great dark crevices appear in her face where the tears have fallen. And the other way? She experiences no heat. The moment occurs when her husband Dr. Davidson, played by John Neville, suddenly walks into the kitchen to see his wife taking a 400 degree, steaming hot casserole out of the oven with her bare hands. You've got a lot of 'splainin' to do, Lucy!

Dracula (1931): I know this is a popular favorite. That does not mean that it is not one of the best moments ever to be seen in the horror genre and really, it must be mentioned.

Count Dracula, played by Bela Lugosi, is welcoming Van Helsing, played by Edward Van Sloan, to his castle, and is standing on a vast gray, splendidly crumbling staircase. There is a noise. We all know what Dracula will say. And he says it so beautifully that many of us can remember his exact inflections: "Listen to them. Children of the night. What music they make!"

The Texas Chain Saw Massacre (1974): Would anyone but Tobe Hooper ever be masterful enough in the horror genre to think of having people be utterly casual at the moment that someone is waiting to be slaughtered?

In **Chainsaw Massacre**, the father of the ratty household and his son sit chewing on the decision, arguing in the most casual of ways, as to which one of them will slice off the girl's head and let it fall into the bucket placed in front of the chair in which she has been tied. This chair, by the way, is between the two men, each trying to impress the other with how right he is to do the task, so we can watch her enduring this contest while she waits for her horrible end. An entirely original and unforgettable moment in all of horror films.

The Terminator (1984): Here is a stunning classic moment so good I'm surprised it's never occurred before in film: Arnold Schwarzenegger holds out his hand and stops an enormous truck dead in its tracks. I think it's his right hand.

E.T. (1982): We all know and love this moment: Drew Barrymore and Henry Thomas' mom, played by Dee Wallace, looks into the closet where her children have hidden the little loveable guy from outer space! She scans the shelves. The children hold their breaths. So do we! We see a shot of what she sees: rows and rows of dolls and stuffed animals of all kinds. The moment comes when we all breathe a sigh of relief, because to their mom, E.T. looks just like every other stuffed plaything sitting to his left and to his right! Adorable.

Dawn of the Dead (1978): We are all used to that ominous knowledge, watching zombie movies, that the undead are man-eaters! But in this George A. Romero movie, a zombie simply walks toward the camera and actually takes a big bite out of someone's shoulder in a shopping mall. Pretty neat and it let me know that Mr. Romero has quite a sense of humor.

"The Twilight Zone," episode title: "Time Enough at Last" (1959): Henry Bemis, played by Burgess Meredith, absolutely loves to read, but works so assiduously at his bank that he never has enough time to do so. Outside the thick, protective walls of the bank's vault, a terrible war ensues, and at its end, there is no more work nor any world for Henry, but there is finally "time enough at last" to read and read to his heart's content. But alas, the violence of the blast has shaken him and his glasses have fallen. And now, the unforgettable moment: he steps on his own glasses and shatters them and also his own hopes for a contented future.

TONY BRAMWELL
Magical Mystery Monster Movies

Tony Bramwell was a friend of The Beatles dating back to age five. He went from being one of their mates to working by their side (and with their manager Brian Epstein) and even being the famed band's road manager. From developing the first Beatles promotional films such as "Strawberry Fields Forever," which were truly the first music videos, to heading Apple Films and partying with everyone from The Beatles to Hendrix, Ray Charles, and The Who, Tony's life truly encompasses a who's who of rock and roll. He shares credit with discovering the likes of James Taylor, Mary Hopkin, and Badfinger, all of whom were signed to The Beatles' Apple record label, and others such as Queen (who weren't signed to Apple).

In 2005, Bramwell published his memoirs, *Magical Mystery Tours: My Life With The Beatles*, one of the most respected books about the Fab Four. He has been a special guest at many fan conventions in the U.S. and overseas, and can often be seen in Liverpool during Beatleweek at the International Beatles Convention.

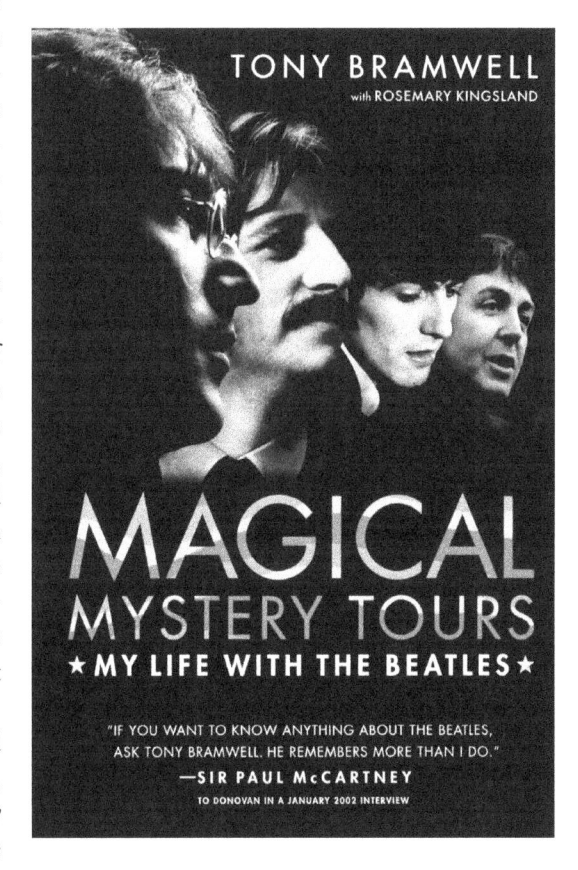

He has great memories of his years in the rock and roll world, and his monster memories lean toward the Hammer films and people he knows (or knew) personally. And how cool is it that his aunt was the Bride of Frankenstein – Elsa Lanchester?!

Tony Bramwell's Magical Mystery Monster Movies

The Bride of Frankenstein (1935): Because Elsa Lanchester was my Auntie!

Legend of the 7 Golden Vampires (1979): A crap movie but my old lady and former Miss Norway 1962 Julie Ege (1943-2008) was in it!

Next would be any of the Hammer films made by my dear friend Jimmy Sangster, a really good writer. Included in this list of Sangster's Hammer films were **The Curse of Frankenstein** (1957), **Horror of Dracula** (1958), **The Quatermass Xperiment** (1955), **Taste of Fear** (1961), **Lust For a Vampire** (1971), **Fear in the Night** (1972), and others.

The Blob (1958): One of the first I saw.

Carrie (1976): Pretty scary.

Oh yes, and anything Bette Davis was in – she was one of the most awful people I ever met!

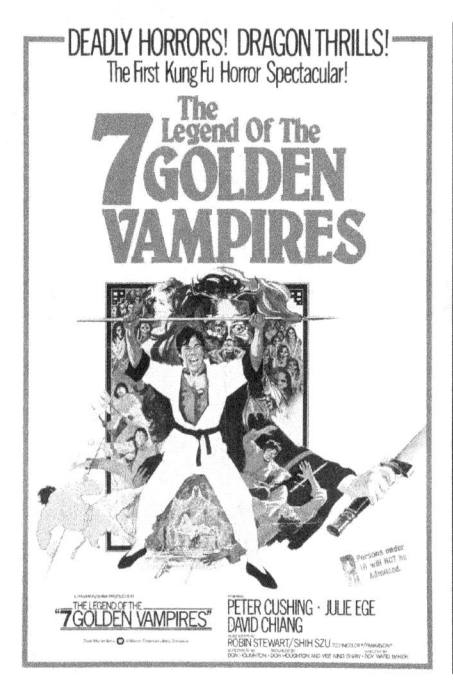

DEBE BRANNING
The Bribe of Frankenbeans?

With titles such as *Sleeping With Ghosts!: A Ghost Hunter's Guide to Arizona's Haunted Hotels & Inns*, *The Adventures of Chickolet Pigolet*, *The Bribe of Frankenbeans*, and *Murmur on the Oink Express*, who wouldn't want to read books by prolific author Debe Branning?! She is the Director of the MVD Ghostchasers of Mesa/ Bisbee in Arizona (www.mvdghostchasers.com), and has been one of the hosts on the GHOSTour to England, the GHOSTour to Scotland, and the GHOSTour to Ireland (www.GHOSTours.com).

For years, Branning was the editor for the Arizona Haunted Sites Examiner and she is currently working on future books.

Ghosthunter Debe Branning's TERRORble Top 10 List

Rosemary's Baby (1968): As an innocent Catholic sophomore girl in High School, this scared the devil out of me for a very long time.

King Kong (1976): The Jeff Bridges version...so I had a crush (and still do) on Jeff Bridges...and I always cry when King Kong is shot down.

The Last House on the Left (1972): Last time I ever wanted to sneak off on a road trip to a rock concert with my girlfriends for a while. I hated the scene where they chopped up the bodies.

The Wizard of Oz (1939): It was a long time when I couldn't decide which scared me more: the Witch flying by my bedroom window or the bellowing of the Wizard behind the curtain.

House on Haunted Hill (1959): This is the one that started it all for me...my first night of watching sci-fi movies late on Saturday night and got my first taste of ghosts!

Death of a Ghost Hunter (2007): Probably 'cause I was a paranormal consultant for the movie and trained the lead actress in the art of ghost hunting – and now I ghost hunt with the producer from time to time.

Jaws (1975): Scariest movie villain of all times. And I couldn't even put my feet in a lake after dark that year.

Invasion of the Body Snatchers (1956): Another late night watching those sci-fi movies with a babysitter and not being able to go to sleep. Made me hate eating peas out of a pod.

The Exorcist (1973): So I am on vacation and on the way home we decide to stop in Denver and see this movie...more potential scary devil therapy.

Secret Window (2004): My friends say I look like Mort (Johnny Depp) when I am home writing. They threaten to buy me a pilgrim hat. One day I was in Walmart and the movie jumped out of the $5 bin at me so I had to buy it. "Mort [staring at the computer screen]: 'This is just bad writing.'" (That's what I say on a brain dead day of writing, too!)

BEVERLY BREMERS
Don't Say You Don't Remember...
"The Crazies" Theme Song Singer

The original version of **The Crazies** (1973) was overlooked by the masses, yet many consider it George Romero's *other* classic alongside **Night of The Living Dead**. The film was remade in 2010 but one thing it didn't have was the theme song from the original film, entitled "Heaven Help Us," written by Carole Bayer Sager and Melissa Manchester and recorded by Beverly Bremers.

Beverly Bremers had a huge hit in 1972 with the wonderful single "Don't Say You Don't Remember," but that wasn't her only claim to fame. The singer was also an acclaimed theater actress, having appeared in the original Broadway productions of "Hair" and "The Rocky Horror Show." She has performed extensively in clubs and concerts, in TV films, commercials, and radio. Bremers wrote the song "Mousercise" for Disney, which went platinum and became the theme for the show "Mousercise" on the Disney Channel.

But it was her 1972 album *I'll Make You Music* that spawned three hit singles, the most popular being "Don't Say You Don't Remember," which hit #15 on the *Billboard* Hot 100 and #5 on the Adult Contemporary charts. However, it was "The Crazies" song "Heaven Help Us" that earned her a spot in our horroble hearts.

In 2014, Beverly Bremers released a CD entitled *Remembering The Sixties*, which is available on her website: www.beverlybremers.com.

My Horror Movie Top 10 by Beverly Bremers

The Exorcist (1973)

The Shining (1980)

The Amityville Horror (1979)

Jaws (1975)

The Crazies (2010)

Scream (1996)

The Birds (1963)

Rosemary's Baby (1968)

Theater of Blood (1973)

The Rocky Horror Picture Show (1975)

Admittedly Biased Choices Disclaimer:
(A) I sang the theme for **The Crazies** and…
(B) I performed in "The Rocky Horror Show" in Los Angeles, while they were shooting the iconic cult film.

T. GRAHAM BROWN
Country Time

The inimitable T. Graham Brown began his musical journey in 1973 while attending the University of Georgia in his hometown of Athens. After moving to Nashville in 1982, the Grammy-nominated, CMA Award, Diamond Addy Award for Excellence in Advertising, and back-to-back Prism Award-winning chart topper honed his skills as a songwriter after signing with EMI Music Publishing. At the same time, he began to sing songwriter's demos, and the writers and producers began to hear the power and soul in his singing and his dynamic ability to interpret words and music through a perfectly-pitched voice. The Nashville music business knew his was a talent to be reckoned with.

Within two years of arriving in Music City, Capitol Records signed him to an exclusive recording contract and what would become a long list of albums that took country music by storm. He has also recorded for Warner Brothers and Sony and now has a recording relationship with Sony Red and a retail partnership with Cracker Barrel Old Country Stores. Simultaneously, he started a long and successful career singing advertising jingles. He was the "face and voice" of Taco Bell's wildly successful "Run for the Border" TV campaign for over four years. His wide range of vocal ability could also be heard on national music ads for McDonald's, Burger King, Hardee's, Coca-Cola, Dr. Pepper, 7-Up, Almond Joy, Kentucky Fried Chicken, Ford, Dodge, Harrah's Casinos, and dozens more.

Called the "Country Otis Redding," T. Graham Brown has hit the *Billboard*, *Cash Box*, and Christian music charts 35 times with hits such as "I Tell It Like It Used To Be," the self-penned "Hell and High Water," and "Darlene." He also wrote the multiple award-winning song "Wine Into Water," which has been recorded over 100 times by artists all over the world, most recently by country superstar Loretta Lynn on her critically-acclaimed album *Full Circle*. As a recording artist, songwriter, performer, and producer, Brown has scored multiple number one songs in the country, blues, and gospel fields. Over the years, "His T-ness" has recorded with many other artists. His duet partners have included Grammy winners The Beach Boys, Tanya Tucker, Vince Gill, George Jones, Delbert McClinton, Jason Crabb, Brad Davis, The Oak Ridge Boys, and Rock and Roll Hall of Fame members Michael McDonald, Steve Cropper, and Leon Russell. Brown's first gospel album was the Grammy-nominated, critically-acclaimed *Forever Changed*. "He'll Take Care Of You," a duet with Vince Gill and the first single from that project, became an instant gospel hit.

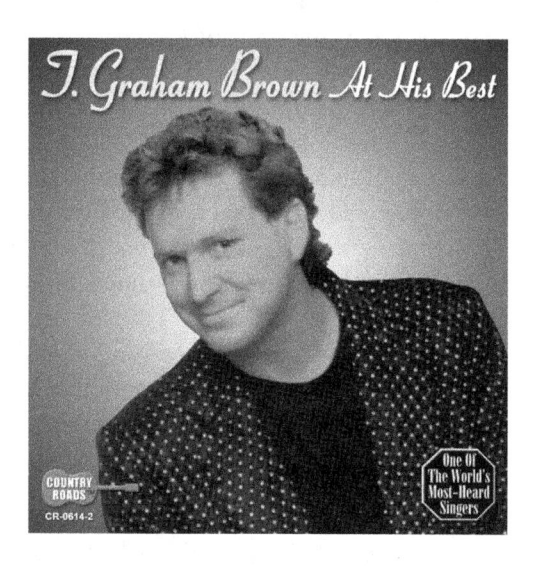

T. Graham Brown has performed on the iconic stage of the Grand Ole Opry hundreds of times, and he maintains a busy touring schedule all over the U.S. and Europe. He'll tell you with a grin, "I've got a band and a bus, and I'll keep taking the music to the people as long as God lets me. It's what I love to do!"

Thanks to PR superstars Jeremy Westby and Jason Ashcroft of 2911 Media.

Website: www.tgrahambrown.com.

T. Graham Brown's Top 10 TERRORble List of Horror Movies

The Wizard of Oz (1939): I was barely out of diapers the first of many, many, many times that I watched this classic. Firstly, the tornado scared big time. The Wicked Witch made me put my hands over my eyes. The flying monkeys terrified me. The chanting guards really creeped me out. Finally, the Wicked Witch melted, but I still hid my head under the covers that night. However, I did love Dorothy, the Tin Man, the Cowardly Lion, the Scarecrow, the Wizard, and the ruby slippers. Still, it scared the heck out of me.

Freaks (1932): I feel guilty.

House of 1000 Corpses (2003): Absolutely no redeeming value. I think I recognize the Firefly family.

Jaws (1975): I've seen this thing dozens of times because it is always there. No movie seems to be on TV more often than this one, but I still tune in. Too many scary shocks to mention. I guess I need a bigger boat.

The Birds (1963): I was a little kid when I saw this for the first time. I didn't sleep at all that night, afraid my eyes would be pecked out. Who will finally win? Man or nature?

Frankenstein (1931): It's ALIVE!!!

The Devil's Rejects (2005): Sid Haig and Bill Moseley are horror heroes. Dang! The final scene, with "Free Bird" blaring, is definitely one of my all-time favorite endings.

Psycho (1960): The shower scene alone is worth the price of admission. Dead Mama scared me out of my rocking chair. Anthony Perkins is just a plain old weirdo.

The Exorcist (1973): I remember walking out of the theater and looking over my shoulder. I'm STILL scared.

The Silence of the Lambs (1991): This is so true to life that it could be on tonight's news. I believe that's one of the reasons it is so scary. Of course, Anthony Hopkins is mesmerizing. Buffalo Bill is so creepy that I grit my teeth. This movie is ingrained in the deepest recesses of my sub-conscious id. That's why it's my number one.

RUTH BUZZI

She was Madame Gypsy in the 1989 film **My Mom's a Werewolf**, co-starred with Jim Nabors in "The Lost Saucer" television series (1975), played Dracula's mom on "The Munsters Today" TV series (1988-1990), played a witch on Rod Serling's "Night Gallery" (1971 episode "Witches' Feast"), made an appearance on "The Monkees" TV show, and was in 2008's compilation of movie trailers titled "Grindhouse Universe." But these are just a few of actress Ruth Buzzi's many film and television credits. The one she will always be remembered for – and loved the most for – is "Rowan & Martin's Laugh-In." It was on that comedy show that Ruth Buzzi became a household name, and a pop culture sensation.

Buzzi was in every single episode of NBC's "Rowan and Martin's Laugh-In" (1967-1973), where she honed her comedic role as park bench spinster Gladys Ormphby, and was among many cast members to utter the line "Sock it to me." Among her more recent acting credits was the 2009 film **City of Shoulders and Noses**, **Fallen Angels** (2006), and **Passions** (2003). She and husband Kent Perkins maintain a residence in Texas.

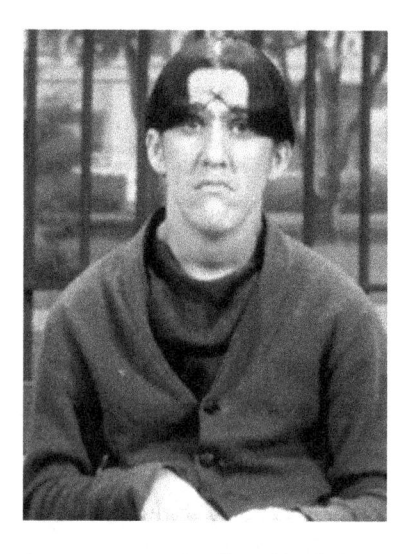

When writing her list, Ruth wrote, "I enjoyed participating, Charles...made me think about how much I've really enjoyed good horror films over the years. XOXO Ruthie. Pictured is me as I look today, at the ranch in Texas with my horse Gladys. Life is very good now, and I'm not pursuing any showbiz work at all...unless the right movie part comes along..."

Is Ruth's list any good? You bet your sweet bippy it is!

Ruth Buzzi's TERRORble Top 10 Horror Films

Diabolique (1955): The first horror movie I ever saw; I was at Pasadena Playhouse at the time. It really shook me up! Even with subtitles, it got me!

Zulu (1964): I was an adult, terrified, crouching behind my seat in fear like an idiot; that's how powerful the ending was with more Zulu warriors coming...maybe I needed therapy, I don't know.

Rosemary's Baby (1968): I remember the creepy feeling and incredible story-line merged with great acting and directing...what a film!

Sorry, Wrong Number (1948): The terror one feels when it's 2 AM and you first realize you just may not be alone in your house...

Psycho (1960): Nobody sees this without keeping a little Bates Motel in the back of their mind for the rest of their life. Anthony Perkins was great.

The Silence of the Lambs (1991): The first one, when Hannibal Lecter escapes at the end...Horribly funny thing happened the morning after we saw this. We were having breakfast with Dom DeLuise in Malibu; my husband started to get up from the table, and found himself eye to eye with Anthony Hopkins, and hubby gasped. Tony laughed so hard, hearing we had just seen the movie the night before and that he startled us by appearing at our table.

Personal photo courtesy Ruth Buzzi

The Shining (1980): Incredible special effects, camera work, directing, editing, acting...Jack Nicholson was terror personified in that.

The Exorcist (1973): For some reason, I wasn't terrified by this film like many were, but the movie held up as a great film anyway, with landmark special effects, great use of camera and lighting...and pea soup.

The Birds (1963): After a great promotion of billboards that just read "THE BIRDS IS COMING" – for weeks nobody knew it was a movie, just poor English...another brilliant move by the inimitable Alfred Hitchcock. Fear comes from the innocent and familiar and sweet turning sinister, as the birds did in this film, as the beautiful twin girls holding hands in **The Shining**... genius writing.

Fallen Angels (2007): I guess we went directly to DVD with this low budget pic; I played a psychic gypsy who foretold doom...although the movie was not among my real top 10 favorites, I'm writing it up on this list because I'm very proud of the work I did in it, and hey...it's my friggin' list.

FREDDY "BOOM BOOM" CANNON

Before Freddie "Boom Boom" Washington was a character on "Welcome Back, Kotter," many years before Gabe Kaplan gave us that TV sitcom, another "Boom Boom" was a pop sensation. With top charting hits such as "Tallahassee Lassie," "Way Down Yonder in New Orleans," and "Palisades Park," Frederick Anthony Picariello, Jr. was a rock and roll household name, but known better as Freddy "Boom Boom" Cannon.

"Palisades Park" was far and away his biggest hit, in May of 1962. Written by TV's quiz show genius and "The Gong Show" host Chuck Barris and complete with roller coaster and amusement park sound effects, the song reached No. 3 on the Hot 100, No. 15 on the R&B chart, and No. 20 in the UK. This release also sold over one million copies, gaining gold disc status.

Freddy Cannon meets Horror Host Svengoolie, courtesy Freddy Cannon

In 2016, Freddy Cannon contributed to the horror genre by releasing a tribute to the one and only Svengoolie, one of the world's greatest "horror hosts." The record was "Svengoolie Stomp" and on the flip side was "Svengoolie Stomp & Svengoolie Stomp (Sing-A-Long)."

Freddy's list is a bit succinct, but we welcome his contribution to both this book and rock and roll history.

Freddy "Boom Boom" Cannon's
TERRORble Top (almost 10) Monster List

Best Monster Films:

Frankenstein (1931)

The Wolf Man (1941)

Dracula (1931)

The Invisible Man (1933)

Creature from the Black Lagoon (1954)

The Mummy (1932)

My very favorite way of seeing monster movies is by watching Svengoolie on MeTV every Saturday night. He is the best. I wrote a song for him and did a video with him.

There may have been monster legends, but I couldn't submit a list without including the greatest, and my favorite, rock and roll legend: the great Chuck Berry. He is the only real legend.

CLAY MCLEOD CHAPMAN
Mondo Bizarro Horror Movie Closing Credits Theme Songs

Clay McLeod Chapman is the creator of the rigorous storytelling session "The Pumpkin Pie Show." He is the author of *The Remaking, Nothing Untoward, miss corpus,* and *rest area,* a collection of short stories. *Time Out New York* called Chapman "a horror-drunk storytelling virtuoso master idiot." He is also a comic book writer and author of "The Tribe," the middle grade series that includes *Homeroom Headhunters, Camp Cannibal,* and Academic Assassins. Other projects include *Whisper Down the Lane,* a psychological horror novel from Quirk Books, Origins, a graphic novel from BOOM! Studios, and *Wendell & Wild,* a middle grade novel co-authored with filmmaker Henry Selick, from Simon & Schuster.

Chapman was the host of "Fear Mongers," which *Fangoria* Magazine called "NYC's best (and only?) speaking series live talk show on horror." From 2010 to 2012, "Fear Mongers" presented public fireside chats about horror films with special guests who shared the passion. He teaches writing at The Actors Studio MFA Program at Pace University.

The '80s and '90s saw the end credits of many horror films featuring customized theme songs, serving as some sort of meta-narrative recap for the audience. Forgot what happened in the movie you just finished watching? Have no fear…there's a tune to help you remember, served up by your favorite and not-so-favorite musical artists.

Website: www.claymcleodchapman.com.

Top 10 Mondo Bizarro Horror Movie Closing Credits Theme Songs

"Ben" by Michael Jackson, from **Ben** (1972): By far the eeriest component to the titular sequel to 1971's rat-extravaganza "Willard." Most folks have long forgotten that Michael Jackson's "Ben" is actually an ode to a boy and his evil pet rat. Close your eyes. Let Jackson's dulcet tones sweep over you like Ben's hairless tail stroking your ear…

"The Monster Squad Rap" from **The Monster Squad** (1987): Before Eminem, before the Beastie Boys, even before Vanilla Ice, this song single-handedly brought hip-hop to the suburbs, turning many a Midwestern boy into a makeshift MC virtually overnight. Fred Dekker was the Rick Rubin of horror cinema.

"Dream Warriors" by Dokken, from **A Nightmare on Elm Street Part 3: Dream Warriors** (1987): Hair metal meets burnt flesh head-on, like flicking your lighter before a spritz of Aqua Net, setting those frosted tips aflame.

"Are You Ready for Freddy" by The Fat Boys, from **A Nightmare on Elm Street Part 4: The Dream Master** (1988): How much difference a year can make. The cultural shift from '87 to '88 seems best exemplified by Freddy Krueger's controversial decision to forsake his allegiance to heavy metal and embrace the ever-edgier hip-hop, bequeathing the end credits for his fourth film to those rotund hit-makers…The Fat Boys. That DJ Jazzy Jeff and the Fresh Prince would beat The Fat Boys at their own game with their far superior single "Nightmare On My Street" is beyond the point: Freddy had retired his mullet for a do-rag.

"The Blob Theme" by Burt Bacharach & The Five Blobs, from **The Blob** (1958): Highly-infectious bopper. Ahead of its time. Visions of sock hops saturated in grape jelly abound. Why-oh-why didn't Chuck Russell kick-start his 1988 remake with this classic as reimagined by Salt-N-Pepa?

"Deepest Bluest (Shark's Fin)" by LL Cool J, from **Deep Blue Sea** (1999): I always had my suspicions that LL Cool J was in fact a great white shark. Now the world knows the truth. The man who helped define hip-hop probably hopes this footnote in his long career fades fast, much like most of those people involved in Renny Harlin's ham-boned masterpiece "Deep Blue Sea," but any opportunity to see LL and Thomas Jane together is just fine by me.

"Killer Klowns from Outer Space" by The Dickies, from **Killer Klowns from Outer Space** (1988): The best Mr. Bungle song that Mr. Bungle never wrote.

"Ghostbusters Rap" by Run DMC, from **Ghostbusters 2** (1989): Watch the video for a hip-hopped Sigourney Weaver. Career highlight.

"Pet Sematary" by The Ramones, from **Pet Sematary** (1989): This always struck me as a sad song from the usually upbeat Ramones. The sludgier pace turns up the somberness, making this one of the more contemplative tomes Joey Ramone ever wrote…

"Shocker" by The Dudes of Wrath, from **Shocker** (1989): Forget The Class of '99 (featuring members of Alice in Chains, Rage Against the Machine, and Jane's Addiction) and their heroin-numbed version of "Another Brick in the Wall: Part 2" for Robert Rodriguez's "The Faculty." Wes Craven's late '80s television satire lays claim to the true super-group of all horror movie soundtracks: The Dudes of Wrath. Members of KISS, Whitesnake, Def Leppard, Motley Crue – together at last. That's more metal than one subpar slasher film can handle, even if you're Mitch Pileggi.

Honorable Mentions:

"The Ballad of Harry Warden" by John McDermott, from **My Bloody Valentine** (1981)

"He's Back (The Man Behind the Mask)" by Alice Cooper, from **Friday the 13th Part VI: Jason Lives** (1986)

"Maniac Cop Rap" by Yeshwua Barnes and "B. Dub" Woods, from **Maniac Cop 2** (1990)

"Ghostbusters" by Ray Parker Jr., from **Ghostbusters** (1984)

"Lep in the Hood" by Warwick Davis, from **Leprechaun Part 5: Leprechaun In Tha Hood** (2000)

MOTHER CHICK
Monsters & Metal

The Mother Chick is a character created by Jill Kethel after having been cast, danced in, and eventually "sacrificed" in the scandalous 1988 Danzig video "Mother." Filmed in a spooky warehouse in New York City, in Hitchcock-style black and white, this mini-horror-movie had everything a young rebellious headbanger could ask for: an altar complete with Danzig-skull headstone, a Swedish model (AKA stripper) named Sif as the sacrifice, a shiny Pentagram on the floor, a cooperative hen that spilled its blood on Sif's belly (after Glenn Danzig tore it up), heavy duty symbolism, shadows, an inverted cross, etc...

The "Mother" video featured Glenn Danzig (High Priest of some sort, I guess?) performing some sort of a ritual, with The Mother Chick (his innocent, lovely assistant). Sif, the bad girl, was placed on the altar as the sacrifice, but if you watch carefully at the end, it's the good girl, The Mother Chick, who winds up on that altar! Huh? Yes, it's a mockery of a ritual for atonement, and in that ritual a "substitute" sacrifice was required…a scapegoat.

We didn't have the internet then, so videos were released and sold in formats for VCRs. This one was up for grabs at such stores as Tower Records, along with the release of its companion album, Danzig's first record (as the band), simply called *Danzig*, in 1988. The video was played a season or two on MTV, and made heavy rotation on "Headbanger's Ball." It was short-lived, however, and pulled after careful scrutiny/ censorship, having ruffled some feathers. It is still, to this day, banned in several countries.

The Mother Chick worked for and with, hung out, and mostly got to do what she loved most: dance to some of the greatest music and artists that have ever lived! She was part of the generation where punk merged with metal. They didn't have Facebook – they went out to clubs and hung out with each other's bands.

The Mother Chick hopes her Top 10 List will bring back happy memories of such times. "Hearts & Horns to each of you who read this!!! xoxo, Jill"

The Mother Chick's Top 10 Monstrous Metal/ Headbangers Hits!

"Breakin' The Law" by Judas Priest: Man! This was a mighty metal kick-off to the '80s scene! From the 1980 release *British Steel*. He kept saying, "You don't know what it's like"...but as our beloved Beavis and Butthead would say, "Actually Judath, we DO know what ith like…huh huh." Whoever doesn't like this song...sucks! :)

"Stigmata" by Ministry: Whoa, Baby!! First time I heard this, I was at The Loop Lounge, a dance club in Clifton, New Jersey. It was 1988 and I had just gotten the part in the Danzig/ "Mother" video. Neither I nor anybody else in the room could stop dancing to this song! I asked the DJ who it was and the next day I went down to St. Mark's Sounds to buy *The Land of Rape and Honey* by Ministry. It features an aggressive punk, fast, relentless metal mix. I still love it to this day!

"Paranoid" by Black Sabbath: OK now, let's just all ponder the fact that this classic metal band released this in 1970! Yeah, 50 years ago and still a hit! I was in 3rd grade when this came out, but didn't really appreciate or understand it until much later. Ozzy and Tony Iommi, Masters of Metal!

"Crazy Train" by Ozzy Osbourne: This song was playing at a party I attended in 10th grade! It was 1980 and I'll never forget it. I watched my high school friends perform it as an "air band" (we didn't have "Guitar Hero" then). From the album *Blizzard of Ozz*. Ozzy was with Randy Rhoads at the time. Just a little interesting news about this song – when it was re-done in 2002, Robert Trujillo joined up with his bass guitar. He is now, of course, with Metallica.

"Ace Of Spades" by Motorhead: Another amazing warm-up to the '80s decade(nce)! Released in 1980, it was and will always be my first and favorite speed metal song. I like to play it very loud, throw up "the horns," and shout, "Lem-MEE! Lem-MEE!" Enuf said!

"Enter Sandman" by Metallica: Before everybody reminds me of how this song has been played too much, I will say right now that for me, too much is never enough! I LOVE IT! These Monsters of Rock, from the album simply titled *Metallica*, brought this song out with intention to do some serious business! And it worked. Check out the video to this on YouTube, from the band's show in Moscow on 9/28/91! Awesome...totally awesome!

"Thunderstruck" by AC/DC: Again, check out YouTube. It's got Angus Young up on a platform, above the drums, looking out over an enormous stadium crowd. I was a go-go dancer for 12 years and let me just say, I made piles of casheroo dancing to this song! Hell, I think I'll play it right now…

"Mother" by Danzig: Welllll alll-righty then! How can I not include this one? See my bio above for more info on this great song. I call it "Danzig's Big One"!! It surely will forever bring out the metal-monsters that reside in all of us.

"Blackened" by Metallica: Further back into the '80s we go for 1983's *…And Justice for All*. I got into this record as Danzig was about to go on their "Three Weeks In Hell" tour of the UK with Metallica! I like the apocalyptic theme and roller coaster ride I get every time I hear this. "Color my world…BLACKENED"! Kirk Hammett is amazing in this one (as usual).

"London Dungeon" by The Misfits: Anybody surprised I picked this? Let me just say that before I became involved with Glenn, I was a Misfits fan. One of my three brothers had this record on in his room one day. I went in to find out who it was. He told me, "The Misfits." The album was called *Evilive*! And I was hooked immediately!

We lived in Fort Lee, New Jersey then, and my brother also informed me that The Misfits all lived just a few towns away in Lodi, New Jersey! I immediately "decided" to go and find the man behind that amazing voice…and went to the next Misfits show at CBGB in New York City. I met Glenn and gave him my number.

It wasn't until a few years later that I auditioned for the "Mother" video, but he remembered me and called me that night. After spending some time dating the legendary singer, we eventually broke up, as he'd begun touring his new band Danzig, and I had just started a new job.

I just knew that none of this was a coincidence. "London Dungeon" changed my life and led me to the "man of my dreams." But for some reason, it was all put on hold. The following 20 years had some wild twists…and hairpin turns, for sure (including a very brief stint with another guy who played Misfits guitar, as they were training Doyle).

I still have my *Evilive* vinyl. I'll never forget the walls of my brothers' room shaking as "London Dungeon" bellowed from within…and I'll always be blonde-head-over-high-heels in love with the guy singing it!

RICHARD CHRISTY
Charred Walls of the Damned

Richard Christy is an American drummer, radio personality, and actor, best known for being the former drummer for several heavy metal, hard-rockin' bands since the early 1990s, most notably the group named Death. In 2009, Metal Blade Records released Richard Christy's album, *Charred Walls of the Damned!* His all-star metal outfit features some of the most talented musicians in the world of metal. Their collective experience is colossal and their musical pedigrees speak louder than any verbal or written praise.

At the time, band founder Richard Christy commented, "To be a part of the Metal Blade family is such an honor. I've been a fan of the label since I was an eleven year old kid ordering Metal Massacre cassettes through the mail. It's so amazing to be label mates with some of my all time favorite metal bands like Amon Amarth, King Diamond, Mercyful Fate, Cannibal Corpse, and Lizzy Borden, just to name a few. Brian Slagel is a true metal legend and I'm honored to be a part of his label. I'm beyond excited to get back into the studio and make some crushing heavy metal with my friends!" The first single from the album was "Ghost Town."

Metal Blade Records founder Brian Slagel added, "We are very happy to welcome Richard Christy and his band, Charred Walls of the Damned, to the

Metal Blade Family. In addition to his duties on 'The Howard Stern Show,' Richard has had a great career in metal. He has put together a really great new band with some of metal's most talented artists and we can't wait to have everyone hear it." The Charred Walls of the Damned returned in 2016, and you never know when they'll resurface.

Many readers of this book may already know Richard Christy from "The Howard Stern Show," where he is a regular. Aside from being a musician and satellite radio celebrity, Richard Christy is a true horror fan, and he has talked about his passion many times on Stern's SiriusXM radio show. He has expressed interest in joining the Dracula Tour to Transylvania (www.DracTours.com) but hasn't yet made the journey.

Richard Christy's TERRORble Top 10 List of Horror Actors and Actresses

Hal Havins: Stooge from **Night of the Demons** (1988) is the epitome of the 1980s rock and roll party jerk who you know is going to end up getting killed by monsters. Hal is hilarious in this movie and even though he's a jerk, he's very likable and he also turns into a really wicked looking demon!

John Saxon: John Saxon was one of the coolest movie dudes ever. He just looked like he could kick anyone's ass if he felt like it. His work in **Black Christmas** (1974) and **A Nightmare On Elm Street** (1984) is amazing!

Stephen King: Not only is Stephen King a literary genius but he's also a hilarious actor. His work in "Creepshow" (1982) makes me laugh my ass off every time. The scene where he looks down at his private parts to find that they're covered in space grass is so funny!

Joe Pilato: This was a tough decision because I also love Richard Liberty as Dr. Logan in **Day of the Dead** (1985), but Joe Pilato as Captain Rhodes is amazing. He's the ultimate heartless A*****e, and the scene where he yells at Dr. Logan and says, "I'm running this monkey farm now Frankenstein and I wanna know... what the f**k you're doing with my time?" is one of the all-time greatest horror movie lines.

Bruce Campbell: The most famous chin in Halloween, except for Jay Leno, is also one of the funniest comic horror actors ever. There are so many great quotable lines in **Army of Darkness** (1992) that I can't even begin to mention my favorite ones. Bruce rules and that's that!

Linnea Quigley: Her work in **Night of the Demons** (1988) and **Return of the Living Dead** (1985) is sexy, funny, and just plain awesome! Linnea is one of the original "Scream Queens" and her IMDb page is like an encyclopedia of horror.

Christopher Lee: The scariest Dracula and the scariest Frankenstein, in my opinion. When I saw all of the Hammer films when I was a kid, Christopher Lee was responsible for many of my nightmares and I have to thank him for that!

Donald Pleasence: Donald's work as Dr. Loomis in the **Halloween** movies is legendary. His quote in the original **Halloween** (1978), after Jamie Lee Curtis asks "Was that the Boogeyman?" and Loomis says, "As a matter of fact, it was," is probably my favorite movie line ever!

Kurt Russell: Kurt Russell is so freaking badass in **The Thing** (1982) and **Escape From New York** (1981) that I think he could kick any monster, bad guy, or alien's ass in the universe! His line at the end of **The Thing** where he yells, "Ya F**K You Too!" at the creature is indescribably awesome!

Tom Atkins: Hands down the coolest dude in horror movies, in my opinion! His characters in **The Fog** (1980) and **Halloween 3** (1982) always get the chicks and always like a cold beer. Tom's line "Thrill me" from **Night of the Creeps** (1986) is one of the most memorable and cool horror quotes ever. I had the pleasure of meeting Tom this past Halloween and even got to share a cold beer with him! It was a dream come true to meet one of my heroes, he was so freaking cool and nice in real life too!

KEVIN CLEMENT

Chiller Theatre – The First List Ever Obtained

Back when the author of this book was editing the Horror Happenings newsletter for examiner.com, the spark to get Top 10 Lists, TERRORble as they may be, started here.

This is what "Cryptmaster Chucky" wrote to introduce the very first of these Top 10 Lists:

"Ah, a Top 10 List. Either you love them or feel that they're a waste of time. In any case, they're a quick read, so you usually scan over them. Not in this case! When they're a TERRORble Top 10 List of Horror Films, you just can't resist seeing if your favorites are on the list. We are compiling some of these dreaded Top 10 Lists of Horror Films from celebrities, actors, sports stars, people in the news, and people in the horror field. It will be interesting to see what films have scared famous and not-so-famous notables, and what films have left their mark.

"For the first TERRORble Top 10 List of Favorite Horror Films, we went to Kevin Clement of Chiller Theatre Expo fame, and a member of the band The Dead Elvi. We didn't pick him because he was a musician or because he played in a band with one of the funniest names in band-naming history.

"We picked Kevin to inaugurate this regular feature because he is the producer/ promoter/ main man of the Chiller Theatre conventions, one of the best-known and best-attended events of its kind in the world. The Chiller Theatre Expo that Kevin puts on draws thousands of fans and an amazing array of special guests twice a year.

What started as a modest horror convention has morphed into one of the greatest pop culture celebrity shows in existence for over 30 years.

"New York area readers of a certain age will know where the name 'Chiller Theatre' came from. The Saturday night television show started on WPIX Channel 11 in 1961 and in 1963 included DJ/ MC/ host Zacherley ("The Cool Ghoul") as the on-air host. Viewers were either greeted by the unforgettable six-fingered hand that ascended from the bloody swamp or the montage of clips from various 1950s sci-fi films beginning with the classic scene from 'Plan 9 From Outer Space' of Vampira coming out of the woods.

"Kevin didn't give his reasons for selecting the films. He simply stated, 'Here's a list of my Top 10 favorite horror films. Really hard to do because I like so many.' Too true. Are any of these on your list too? By the way, we also asked Kevin for his list of Top 10 Horror Convention Guests, but we haven't gotten the results of that one yet."

The Very First TERRORble Top 10 List of Favorite Horror Films by Kevin Clement

The Exorcist (1973)
Psycho (1960)
Night of the Living Dead (1968)
Dawn of the Dead (1978)
The Innocents (1961)
The Haunting (1963)
Suspiria (1977)
House on Haunted Hill (1959)
The Devil's Rejects (2005)
Dead of Night (1945)

CLAY COLE
Zacherley is His #1 Cool Ghoul

If you grew up in New York in the late '50s or '60s, you had a number of childhood television heroes: Zacherley for monsters, Officer/ Chief Joe Bolton for The Three Stooges, Sonny Fox for "Wonderama" (before Bob McAllister), Bozo (yes, he was big, before clowns were scary!), and Clay Cole for rock and roll. It may have been Lloyd Thaxton or Dick Clark in other areas, but in the New York Metro area, "The Clay Cole Show" (or "Clay Cole's Discotek") was the coolest and grooviest of them all. Cole's television show aired in New York City on WNTA-TV and on WPIX-TV Channel 11 from 1959 to 1968. Historical fact: he's the only rock and roll host to ever have The Beatles and The Rolling Stones on the same show (albeit one of the two acts was via videotape)!

In 2009, Clay Cole released his book, *Sh-Boom: The Explosion of Rock 'n' Roll (1953-1968)*, brimming with gossip, heartbreak, and truth in a behind-the-scenes look at "live" television, mom and pop record companies, mob-run Manhattan, and the infancy and innocence of the rock music biz before it exploded. The book is out of print and very collectible.

Clay was a Special Guest of Honor at BEATexpo 2009 in Stamford, Connecticut. It was his first fan event, and he loved every second of it so much that he was also an Honored Guest at "Rock Con: Weekend of 100 Rock Stars" in the New Jersey Meadowlands the following year. He loved meeting fans, signing autographs, and reminiscing.

At that "Rock Con," Clay Cole was presented with the distinguished "Rock Con" Icon "Fame" Award. He and Sid Bernstein, the famed promoter who brought The Beatles to America and presented their concerts at Carnegie Hall and Shea Stadium, are among the few music business legends to receive the "Rock Con" Icon "Fame" Award. Sadly, Clay Cole passed away in 2010.

TERRORble Top 10 List: The 10 Things Clay Cole Associates with Scary Stuff

Zacherley: After working with and knowing the "Cool Ghoul" for so many years, I found John to be a kind and gentle man. I was no longer fearful of "monsters."

Elvira, Mistress of the Dark: The beast is a beauty. The truly scary thing is she's still so beautiful!

Eddie Munster (Butch Patrick): The kid's a monster, haunted by his childhood success.

Vincent Price: A refined gentleman and a gourmet chef, but hardly as scary as the Iron Chef, Gordon Ramsay. Now that's scary.

House of Wax in 3-D (1953): Nothing is more frightening than a paddle ball in the wrong hands.

Billy Mays was frightful. Sadly, he's gone, only to be replaced by the insufferable Sham-Wow monster.

Greta Van Susteren, **Nancy Grace**, and **Suze Orman** scare the pants off me. They are the Patty, Maxene, and LaVerne of revulsion.

Ellen DeGeneres: Only when she dances. Stop that dreadful dancing…

Spencer Tracy in **Dr. Jekyll and Mr. Hyde** (1941): This is a true fear-provoking monster movie; Tracy is truly frightening as Mr. Hyde.

Walt Disney's **Bambi** (1942): This is the scariest movie ever made. A child's worst fear is abandonment by a parent. Disney dishes it out in a hellish forest fire. Don't take the kids.

STEVE CUDEN
Broadway's "Jekyll & Hyde" Musical Co-Creator's Top 10 Horror Stories

Writer-director-producer Steve Cuden is best known for co-creating the international hit Broadway musical "Jekyll & Hyde." He also directed and co-produced the multi-award winning horror-comedy feature film **Lucky** (2004). Steve has written nearly 90 episodes of TV animation for such well-known series as "X-Men," "Iron Man," "Mummies Alive," "Xiaolin Showdown," "Skeleton Warriors," "Extreme Ghostbusters," "RoboCop," "Savage Dragon," "Gargoyles," "Creepy Crawlers," "Beetlejuice," and many others.

He is an alumnus of the 2003 Dracula Tour vampire vacation to Transylvania (www.DracTours.com), which he describes as simply the best trip he's ever taken, and by far the most fun he's ever had on a bus (and we can add that he was a great Wolfman at the Halloween costume gala).

Photo of Cuden as a Werewolf, courtesy of Steve Cuden

"I like being scared. A lot. But only in the controlled environs of a movie theater or in my own living room where I know with some certainty that I'll get out alive. Or at least I hope I will. I truly hate being scared by my real life. Gives me heartburn. Agita I don't need. Sleepless nights. I've certainly had days that were far scarier than anything the great fiction horrormeisters could ever dream up. Losing myself in a good piece of scary fiction helps. It allows me to work through my fears on a different level, helps me blow off some of the steam from the real fears that inevitably come pre-packaged with every life. If you're breathing, you will inevitably be scared by something – if not by many somethings – as you work through your day-to-days. For me, the best of the worst (or would that be the worst of the best?) are those stories that feature as their main ingredient a heaping helping of dread; those tales in which the hero must undergo the most skin-crawlingly heinous, disgusting, and vile of circumstances in order to just stay alive. I find these flights of fiction satisfyingly troubling. Here are a few of my absolute favorites."

Steve Cuden's **Lucky** is a film worth finding.

Steve Cuden's TERRORble Top 10 Favorite Horror Stories

Jaws (1975): Does it get any better than this? Superior filmmaking by a true master. Fear of the known, dread in the Atlantic (the biggest, bleakest bucket imaginable), puny humans cast adrift to fight an inescapable feeding/killing machine. What more can you ask for? It's Moby Dick on a scale that we can all relate to. It taps into the oldest of man's fears – being swallowed by the beast. Any time it is on TV and there's nothing better to watch (how sad it is that this is so often), I can jump on this sucker at any point of the story and be instantly dragged in. There are, to this day, people who will not go near the ocean because of **Jaws**. It has not aged one bit. A magnificent monster movie.

The Exorcist (1973): I saw this as a young man on its opening weekend. I did not know what the word exorcism meant and knew absolutely nothing about the movie. I was dragged by a friend to see it. It stripped my senses bare and left me gasping for air. Upon returning home that night at 1 AM, it took every ounce of courage to cross the yard from the car to the house.

Aliens (1986): Another movie I can watch starting at any point and get sucked right in every time. The relentless intensity of that bit of nastiness is a modern marvel. A true thrill ride deluxe. "They can bill me." I laugh every time. The crab alien jumping on Ripley in the med lab. I jump every time.

Psycho (1960): It's only the granddaddy of all the sicko killer movies. And it still holds up. Mostly (it does get a little creaky – not in a good way – in some places). Most of the slasher movies we know of today would likely not exist if it weren't for Hitchcock's twistedly ingenious storytelling. Many have tried to copy that shower scene. No one has ever done it better. Watch for the nearly imperceptible overlay of Mother's skull on dear Norman's face at the very end. I hope Norman isn't what they have in mind when they say the meek shall inherit the earth.

Halloween (1978): Simply great storytelling on a small budget. The Michael Myers POV shots make it work so well. It's the mask, the mask, the mask. Shatner at his scariest. The music gets under your skin, too. Did Donald Pleasence ever give a bad performance in anything? Candy anyone?

The Omen (1976): That nasty little boy with the evil eyes. I saw this movie when it was released in the Egyptian Theatre (a cavernous place) during a mostly empty performance. Some bum (literally a smelly bum) came in and sat in the row behind me and fell asleep. I did not notice that he had put his foot up on the back of the seat next to me. As the movie became more intense, and the scene evolved in which David Warner was about to be decapitated by a sheet of glass, and the music was Wa-Wa-Waaaing, the bum's foot slipped and smacked me on the shoulder. I nearly leaped out of my skin straight through the roof. My heart didn't stop pounding for three days. Gregory Peck is simply amazing. And Jerry Goldsmith's score is eerily memorable from top to bottom.

The Terminator (1984): A futuristic chimera that can't be stopped. Don't think too hard about the machinations of the future-into-the-past-into-the-future plot because you will wind up in a straitjacket – its improbable probability will worm its way into your brain and absolutely, positively not let go. Ever. There's barely enough time in this one to come up for air. And here's how to end a movie – four or five times – and make you still want more. I wish James Cameron would go back to producing this kind of movie again. No one spins horrific mayhem better.

Jekyll & Hyde: The Musical (2001): Not really very scary to watch, but since I spent nine years of my life writing the original book and lyrics, I had to include it here. After almost four years on Broadway, it has been produced hundreds of times in the U.S. It's also been translated into more than 20 languages and has had many more hundreds of productions worldwide. Pretty good for a musical adaptation of a 120-year-old novella containing no women upon which a writer can build a romance – and no real plot on which to hang your hat. *The Strange Case of Dr. Jekyll and Mr. Hyde* has probably been interpreted in more ways, more times than any other single story in the history of fiction. "The Hulk" is Jekyll and Hyde. "Spiderman" is Jekyll and Hyde. "The Mask" is Jekyll and Hyde. You get the point – lots of stuff is actually "Jekyll and Hyde." Robert Louis Stevenson was the first person to figure out this good/ evil, light/ dark character dilemma – even before Freud started mucking around in our psyches. The world has had a field day with it ever since. Thanks R.L. I owe ya.

Lucky (2004): This nasty puppy of a movie was made for next to nothing in little more than nine days. It won Best Feature awards at the first-ever New York City Horror Film Festival, AKA Shriekfest, in Los Angeles and at MicroCineFest in Baltimore. It's one of the sickest, yet funniest, stories you'll ever see. Totally off the wall nuts. Very unHollywood. Not for the faint of heart – and absolutely not suited to all tastes. No one I've ever spoken to who has seen **Lucky** is indifferent; they either looooove it or haaaaate it – not much in between. Unfortunately, not too many have seen it – even though it's available for rent on Netflix, for sale on Amazon.com (and lots of other sites) online. I still can't believe it's a part of who I am, but how can it not be? If you haven't seen **Lucky**, and can tolerate a truly twisted low budget horror story mixed with some totally sick humor, then check it out. I dare you.

Stephen King: Just about anything he's written. Books only, please. Though **Misery** (1990) is a pretty damned good movie. So are **The Shawshank Redemption** (1994) and **Stand By Me** (1986) (actually both are superb, though neither really falls in the horror genre). My favorite King book: *The Stand* (1978). That is true dread. End of the world stuff that curled my hair.

Bonus. Speaking of apocalyptic visions, read *The Road* (2006) by Cormac McCarthy. That is maybe the bleakest, darkest, most endlessly dread-filled book I've ever laid eyes on. I don't know how good or bad the movie is, but the book is one of the most masterfully told tales I've had the pleasure (if that's the right word) to peruse. Well worth your time, even if you can't sleep for a week or two after reading it.

Let the trembling begin. Enjoy!

DEBBI D
The Ultimate Fantasy Queen

Debbie D is known as the Ultimate Fantasy Queen, but she could just as easily have been titled the Ultimate Scream Queen, having worked in over 200 movies and still counting.

She started her career as a singer and landed a record contract, but it wasn't until she acted in her first low budget film that she found her home. Her first roles were in **Burglar From Hell** (1993) and **Naked Horror** (1995). In 2019 alone, she was in six indie films including **Horror Odyssey, Earth Girls Are Sleazy, Giftwrapped & Gutted,** and **Deep Undead.** In between, she appeared in such titles as **Requiem for a Vampire, Vampyre Tales, Kill The Scream Queen,** and **Cannibal Hillbillies.**

Debbie D has been in hundreds of magazines for her modeling, acting, and singing. Horror magazine fanatics will know her best for her alter ego, Destiny the Vampire Mermaid. Her comic book character was featured every month in *Scary Monsters* Magazine. Destiny the Super Heroine came to life straight off the pages of the magazine and onto video, portraying the comics and stories that were published in the magazine.

Website: www.DebbieD.com.

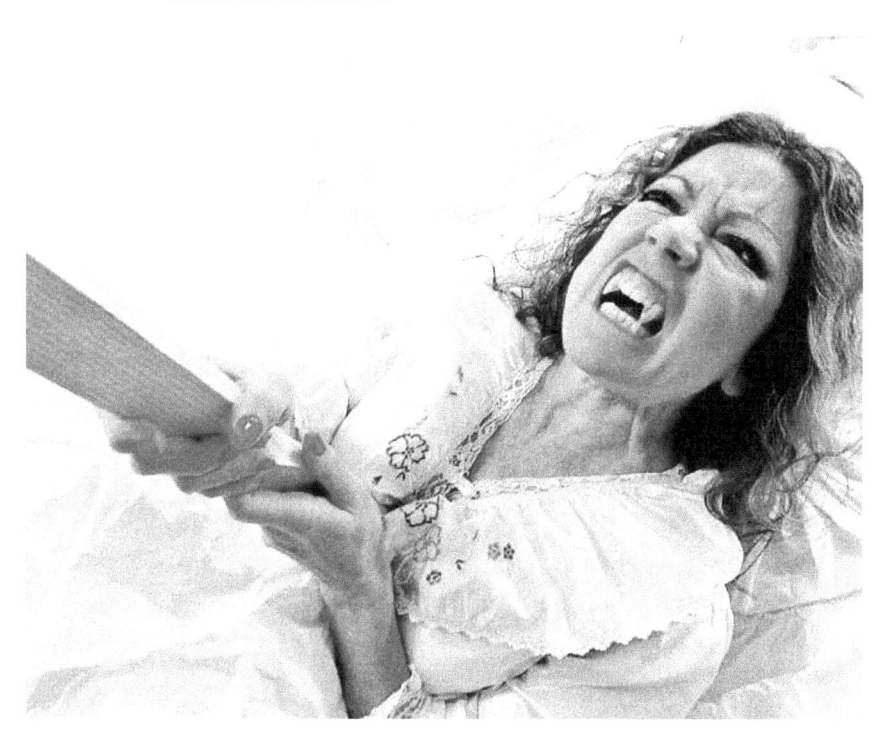

Debbie D's TERRORble Top 10 Horror List

After.Life (2009): This 2009 movie, starring Liam Neeson, Christina Ricci, and Justin Long, affected me for a long time after it was over and not too many current movies have that capability, mainly because I'm also in the movie-making business. It's very well-acted and believable. Maybe this could really actually happen if it went the direction you saw unfolding. I don't want to give away too much. It's my number one, so this one comes highly recommended.

Lost In Space (1965, television series): Was my favorite TV show, still a classic. In black and white, it was scary when the unknown space creatures would upset the life they made for the group who were all lost in space. All characters were original and creative. Add that to the good writing, gives us a show much appreciated for years.

Lost Horizon (1937): A world where people do not grow old. A mystical land that will keep you happy and young forever. I watched the original movie as a young child where it went from black and white to color for the effect of altered vision, an effect similar to **The Wizard of Oz** but two years earlier.

The story is about a plane crash in the Himalaya Mountains, in which all passengers survived. They walked on foot, and found themselves in another world on the other side of the mountain. One of the passengers falls in love with a woman there in this wonderful place and he wants to take her back to his world.

The scary part is watching a young woman age as she slowly leaves her place of origin on foot following the man she loves, until she slowly becomes so old she simply dies – for she would have been dead a long time ago had she ventured out sooner.

So many questions to ponder:

* Did she have a soul that stayed on earth forever?

* Who really were these people who lived on this mountain, so happy and full of life?

* What was their true purpose there?

This movie stayed with me through life. I sought out the DVD decades later.

Logan's Run (1976): The original movie came out in 1976. I watched it as a child and was horrified that they would kill you when you became a certain age as a way to control the population. The "logans" tried to run but usually never made it. One set made it out, but soon realized how good they had it inside the dome of their existence, where there was plenty of everything they needed to survive. Once on the outside, they had to fend for their lives and it was not very glamorous, to say the least. With earthly uncontrolled elements and animals and no food simply handed to them, the alternative was death.

Quite a story.

Ultra Man (1972): This 1972 TV show had the typical scary monsters who could crush your home with one gigantic foot, and your world could end at any given time. That was very scary, as my mind would escape in panic during those 30 minutes. Ultra Man could save the day and kill them with his body made of steel. I do think this was my first childhood crush. I couldn't completely relate the feeling at such a young age but it was felt. Super heroes can affect a person like this.

The Hand (1981): I remember my mother giving me the A-OK to watch this one, but for a good year I slept in a ball thinking The Hand was touching me. If I kept my extremities close I'd be OK. The mind of a child.

A hand staying alive after being cut away from the body and actually killing is something you don't easily forget.

The underdeveloped mind of how the world actually works to a growing, learning child is much different than adults can really comprehend. I survived...

Dark Shadows (1966, television series): Jonathan Frid as Barnabas Collins was simply magnificent and could never be forgotten. He is truly marked in stone as this character, and he played it so perfectly. I remember not wanting the vampire to hurt the women. Little did I know I would grow up to be a "Scream Queen," who would portray a vampire in comic form, as well as in many movies. I found out the vampire bite is not that bad.

Frankenstein (1931): This story was portrayed many times over. The original concept was that a scientist could piece together body parts to form one human being and make him come to life using electricity. I was raised as a Catholic and I remember feeling sorry for this man-made creature who had no soul and no reason to be alive – and he knew it.

In one of my many "Destiny the Vampire Mermaid" comic stories in *Scary Monsters* Magazine (where I was published for 22 years), my character of Destiny came across Dr. Frankenstein. I decided to film a live comic story based on this writer's version of his Frankenstein story. I still sell copies of that video to this day.

The Wolf Man (1941): The werewolf was another creature that was to be feared because when a full moon came, he was out to kill with no control. This story was told many times and still we are fascinated. I wrote a few short stories based on the werewolf creature. In one story I decided to write it so that neither the victim nor the beast knew their true being or their fate.

Mother's Day (1980): This 1980 film screened in select theaters, and I never realized it wasn't a major movie until much later in life. Little did I know I would end up working with this movie producer's brother so many years later: Lloyd Kaufman of Troma films. In the film **Mother's Day**, Hicks is living in the sticks and possibly interbreeding. That in itself was always a scary thought, but this movie had its own story and its own take on crazies living in the sticks. It was creepy and horrifying. I felt bad that other people were tortured and killed pleading for their lives and ultimately losing them due to this family's sheer craziness and lack of caring. It worked and it became a classic. It's where nightmares and scary thoughts take over.

SYBIL DANNING

Sybil Danning is one of the genre's all-time favorite screen scream queens. Can you believe that she's been in over 50 films now? From **The Swap** in 1979 through more recent appearances such as the Rob Zombie **Halloween** remake and Quentin Tarantino and Robert Rodriguez' **Grindhouse**, her presence is always a welcome addition to any film, whether it's a major Hollywood release or an independent grind-out. Who can forget any film where the beautiful and alluring cult star was behind or in front of prison bars?

Nicknamed "Queen of the Action Flicks" for her cover story in *Playboy*, some of Sybil's most famous roles are in titillating R-rated lesser-known delights, but readers may be most familiar with these Sybil-filled films: **Amazon Women on the Moon** (1987), **The Tomb** (1986), and **Howling II: Your Sister Is a Werewolf** (1985).

From 2002 to 2003, Danning was a shareholder of the German ice hockey team SC Riessersee. As the first-ever female co-owner of a German hockey team, Danning brought three American players to the team, and saw SC Riessersee return to the Vice Championship.

Photo of Sybil Danning with Rob Zombie, courtesy of Sybil Danning

Sybil was a Special Guest at the world-famous Chiller Theatre Expo back in 2003, and has made numerous return appearances. She was also a booked Guest for the 2020 Chiller show.

In 2008, Danning returned to her homeland, Austria, to play Patrick Swayze's witness Anna Gruber in the film **Jump!** She also appeared in five episodes of the vampire television series **The Lair** as a sinister vampire out for revenge. In 2010, Danning was cast in the horror film **Virus X**. In 2011, she starred in and produced a horror/ music video for heavy metal/ rock band The Last Vegas.

We look forward to seeing more of Sybil Danning on the big screen. Meanwhile, check her out on the little (computer) screen and visit her website here: www.sybildanning.net.

Thanks to author Marshall Terrill for arranging this article.

Sybil Danning's TERRORble Top 10 Horror Film Favorites

The Howling II (1986): My movie with Christopher Lee (whom I did five films with).

The Wolf Man (1941): Lon Chaney Jr. and Bela Lugosi: a classic.

The Howling (1981): Directed by my dear friend Joe Dante.

I Was A Teenage Werewolf (1957): Michael Landon, classic Sam Arkoff movie.

An American Werewolf in London (1981): Directed by my dear friend, John Landis.

Werewolf Women of the SS (2007): Writer/director Rob Zombie, a trailer but a full feature soon.

Drag Me to Hell (2009): Sam Raimi's masterpiece.

Halloween (2007): Remake by Rob Zombie (I played the nurse).

The Shining (1980): Stanley Kubrick, with Jack Nicholson.

I Drink Your Blood (1970): Classic, directed by David Durston.

JOE DANTE
Gremlins and Trailers from Hell

Joe Dante is a lifelong film buff who turned his obsession into a career. He got his start cutting trailers for Roger Corman and later directed the hit movie **Gremlins**, as well as **Gremlins 2: The New Batch**, **Innerspace**, and **Small Soldiers** for producer Steven Spielberg. His feature films include **The Howling**, **Piranha**, **Matinee**, **The 'burbs**, **Looney Tunes Back in Action**, **The Hole** (first winner of the 3D Persol Award at the Venice Film Festival), and the zom-com **Burying the Ex**. His TV directing work includes "Police Squad!," "Amazing Stories," the HBO film **The Second Civil War**, the Masters of Horror titles "Homecoming" and "The Screwfly Solution," and episodes of "Eerie, Indiana," "CSI: NY," "Hawaii 5-0," "Witches of East End," "Legends of Tomorrow," and "Salem."

"Trailers from Hell" was released on DVD in separate volumes, showcasing rare vintage trailers that were exclusive to the sets. Now, the focus is on the well-trafficked website www.trailersfromhell.com, a brainchild of Dante, with some of the best-known names in the horror/ sci-fi genre providing amusing commentary on rare vintage cult film trailers. Joe is also the frequent co-host of the official podcast for "Trailers from Hell," titled "The Movies That Made Me" and available everywhere podcasts are streamed and downloaded!

Enjoy this TERRORble Top 11 List from the man who gave us **Gremlins** and so many more cinematic treats (thanks to Mark Alan from Renfield Productions).

Joe Dante's Favorite "Trailers From Hell"
(well, *some* of them anyway – and not including any of his own)

Corruption (1968): Edgar Wright joined "Trailers From Hell" early on and this is one of his most fun commentaries, highlighting the many absurdities of one of Peter Cushing's seedier outings.

Dead and Buried (1981): Guillermo del Toro invokes his angst-ridden teenage trip to view this small-town-with-a-deadly-secret cult favorite.

Forbidden Planet (1956): Eli Roth shares his love for the '50s sci-fi classic starring Robby the Robot. "Welcome to Altair 4, gentlemen."

Hell Up in Harlem (1973): Larry Cohen spills on the various ruses he employed to shoot this sequel to his hit **Black Caesar** simultaneously with another picture, **It's Alive**.

Horrors of the Black Museum (1959): Mick Garris demystifies Hypno-Vista, the audacious promo gimmick that turned this British horror pic into a stateside hit. The late Michael Gough turns in one of his most, um, *vigorous* performances.

The Human Tornado (1976): Larry Karaszewski gives black comedian/ director/ R&B singer Rudy Ray Moore his due. This is one of those "Trailers from Hell" that introduces, we hope, audiences to films and personalities they may not have encountered elsewhere.

Masters of the Universe (1987): Josh Olson was on the set and spills the beans behind this beloved misfire from Cannon Films.

Mr. Billion (1977): You can't win 'em all, and Jonathan Kaplan lets us in on some of the reasons that his attempt to make Euro western star Terence Hill into a US household name didn't work out.

Queen of Outer Space (1958): Allan Arkush tries to make sense of this cheerfully chauvinistic space opera starring Zsa Zsa Gabor as a Hungarian-accented Venusian on yet another planet ruled by women.

The 7th Voyage of Sinbad (1958): Brian Trenchard-Smith takes us behind the scenes of the baby boomer classic that set the stage for a decade of Arabian Nights extravaganzas from FX maestro Ray Harryhausen.

Taxi Driver (1976): Rod Lurie fills in some details on one of the key films of the '70s. We here at "Trailers From Hell" still haven't gotten over the fact that this lost Best Picture Oscar to **Rocky**!

MICHAEL DANTE

There are four Dantes in this book: filmmakers Joe Dante and Dante Tomaselli, rock and roll's Ron Dante, and also Michael Dante.

Award-winning actor/ award-winning author/ radio show host Michael Dante appeared in 30 films, including **Kid Galahad** with Elvis Presley, and the famous rat attack movie **Willard**. He was also in over 150 television shows including "Bonanza," "Star Trek," "Maverick," "The Six Million Dollar Man," "General Hospital," "Perry Mason," "Cheyenne," "Colt 45," "Lawman," "Tales of the Texas Rangers," "Cagney & Lacey," "Get Smart," "Custer" (as Crazy Horse), and many more.

Dante has won countless awards including The Golden Boot Award (Oscar of Westerns), The Silver Spur Award, The Southern California Motion Picture Council Award for the 'Best of the Best' in the Entertainment Industry & Performing Arts, Honoree of the Year by the Order of Sons of Italy of America, Honorary Arizona Ranger (only two in the State of Arizona), and the 2018 Ella Dickey Literacy Award for his autobiography, just to name a few. But he was almost a major league baseball player; he signed with the Boston Braves and went to spring training with the Washington Senators.

*Michael Dante as "Del Giorgio" in **Beyond Evil** (1980), courtesy Michael Dante.*

As a celebrity radio talk show host, millions know "The Michael Dante Classic Celebrity Talk Show" (one-hour show) and "Michael Dante: On Deck" (three-minute show) with 265 of the top names in entertainment and sports. He was heard on broadcast radio for 12 years in Palm Springs and surrounding areas of California.

Dante has had several books published: his autobiography in 2014, *Michael Dante: From Hollywood to Michael Dante Way* (recipient of the Ella Dickey Literacy Award), *Winterhawk's Land*, a novella, in 2017 (the sequel, in book form, to the film that Michael Dante played the title role and starred in, **Winterhawk**), and *Six Rode Home*, a novella in 2019 (about six post-Civil War horsemen coming home from the war…to what?).

Michael Dante Way is a city street named after Michael in his hometown of Stamford, Connecticut, dedicated in 2011.

Website: www.michaeldanteway.com.

Thanks to Marshall Terrill and MaryJane Sante.

Before offering his list, Dante wanted to talk about his horror film roles:

Michael Dante as "Brandt" in **Willard** (1971): "All my life I've had an eerie feeling about rats, but when I met with the animal trainer on the set of **Willard**, he introduced me to the rats he had trained for the film. He used the Pavlov method, in that he used a beeper associated with food. He would use it to control the rats from wandering off and they stopped immediately and returned to the group, when he used that beeper. Another thing that amazed me was when the trainer put peanut butter, which the rats love, behind the ear of Bruce Davison; when he gave them the signal to go get the 'food,' it made it look like the rat was kissing his ear, but it was the peanut butter the rat was licking. When the rats were together, I saw how they cuddled and were very affectionate with each other. The trainer was outstanding, making all the scenes with the rats look so authentic, based on what they were needed to do in each scene they were in. The great character actress Elsa Lanchester and my friend and wonderful actor Ernest Borgnine found it easier than they thought to work with the rats, too. I didn't have as much of an eerie feeling about rats after I appeared in **Willard**."

Michael Dante as "Del Giorgio" in **Beyond Evil** (1980): "I co-starred in **Beyond Evil** with John Saxon and Lynda Day George, in this horror film with a spooky story and lots of good special effects. The house that was used on location in the film, located high up in the Hollywood Hills of southern California, lent to the haunting presence of the story. Personally, I had a feeling that probably tragic, evil things took place there. It was the perfect setting, although I never felt comfortable in the dark, cold atmosphere that was continuous throughout the house. The special effects in the film, and the makeup used for Lynda Day George, plus the weird way she portrayed her character, made it very frightening and truly, beyond evil."

Michael Dante's TERRORble
Top 7 List of Favorite Horror Films

Frankenstein (1931, original version): Excellent portrayal by Boris Karloff, so believable and scary. His monstrous and invincible presence was so frightening to me and all my siblings when we were growing up and first saw **Frankenstein** and then later on, when we saw it again. His wardrobe and overall physical makeup were outstanding.

The Wolf Man (1941, original version): Lon Chaney Jr.'s performance as The Wolf Man was superb. So convincing! The transition from his character to werewolf was so evil, deadly creature he had become. It was scary! My siblings and I were watching Lon Chaney Jr. transform into something we had never seen before. Again, the wardrobe and makeup complimented the scary aspect of the character. It looked so real.

Abbott & Costello Meet Frankenstein (1948): It was a great comedic piece of work added to the threat of Frankenstein. The timing and the life-threatening near-misses were extraordinary. The drama between Abbott and Costello and Frankenstein held me on edge throughout the movie. I thoroughly loved watching Abbott and Costello's timing and comedic genius. It was a departure from all of the other types of scary movies, another dimension of the Frankenstein films.

Alfred Hitchcock's **The Birds** (1963): Tippi Hedren, starring in this film, was a strange, visual, phobic experience for me. After I saw the movie, I was aware of flocks of birds that flew overhead, from time to time. It brought back my memories of Tippi Hedren running from the attacking birds. The great director Alfred Hitchcock made those scenes so believable, along with all the technical talent associated with making it look so real. Tippi and Rod Taylor, my friend for many years, did an excellent job.

Rosemary's Baby (1968): I watched **Rosemary's Baby**, starring John Cassavetes and Mia Farrow, and their performances were quite good and very convincing. I had a very intense feeling watching the film because it kept me in suspense throughout. I waited pensively to see what that baby would look like, thinking it would be a freaky, demonic creature lying in that crib. It scared the heck out of me!

Motel Hell (1980): This film starred my friend Rory Calhoun, who played the deranged character Farmer Vincent. I co-starred in five television shows with Rory Calhoun: "Desilu Playhouse" in "The Killer Instinct" episode and four segments of his television series "The Texan." Rory was young, handsome, and rugged in those days, so when I saw him in **Motel Hell**, he was much older and portrayed a character very different from anything he had ever done. It was such a departure for him to play this sleazy, creepy character. He did a great job and showed another dimension of his versatility as an actor.

The Silence of the Lambs (1991): Anthony Hopkins' portrayal of Dr. Hannibal Lecter was superb. His overall countenance was extraordinary. His performance was one of the most evil characterizations I've ever seen on film. He was so frightening and maintained that threatening, demonic quality throughout. That's probably why he's one of the scariest characters in a movie, ever.

RON DANTE
Dante's Inferno: More Than "Sugar, Sugar"

He wasn't scary as the singing voice of The Archies, but he has great taste in both music and horror films. Ron Dante was the lead singer for The Archies, as well as The Cuff Links. The Archies' single "Sugar, Sugar" was the Number One selling record of 1969 in the United States. That same year, Dante hit the U.S. Top 10 with the single "Tracy," fronting The Cuff Links at the very same time that "Sugar, Sugar" occupied the top of the chart. Another Archies single, "Jingle Jangle," was thought to be sung by either the character of Betty or Veronica, but it was none other than Dante using his falsetto vocal. From 1973 to 1981, Dante was the record producer for singer Barry Manilow, and often sang backup on Manilow's recordings, including the 1974 #1 hit single "Mandy."

Andy Kim (left), songwriter of the bubblegum classic "Sugar, Sugar," with Ron Dante, lead singer (right). Photo credit: Bobby Bank

Dante was one of the very special Guests of Honor at the 2010 "Rock Con: Weekend of 100 Rock Stars," at the Meadowlands Sheraton Hotel & Conference Center in East Rutherford, New Jersey. More recently, he has toured with "Happy Together" and is currently one of the lead singers of The Turtles.

"...You are my Candy Girl, Candy Girl, Candy Girl"

Visit Ron's website: www.rondante.com.

Dante's Inferno: TERRORble Top 10 List of Monster Movies by Ron Dante

House of Wax (1953): Great in 3D. Vincent Price is really scary and it even had Charles Bronson in one of his first roles as the evil assistant.

The Bride Of Frankenstein (1935): Best of the Frankenstein series. Great Karloff line: "You live!"

Alien (1979): Spent the 'key scene' under my seat.

The Exorcist (1973): Went to church right after seeing it.

Repulsion (1965): Catherine Deneuve going nuts. Made me swear off blondes for a year.

Psycho (1960): Still shower with the door locked.

Freaks (1932): Creepy with a moral.

The Curse of the Werewolf (1961): With great actor Oliver Reed. Loved the Hammer films of the '60s.

The Howling (1981): Unbelievable makeup and transformation.

The Universal Monsters trio: **The Wolf Man** (1941), **Dracula** (1931), and **Frankenstein** (1931) still rock.

DINKY DAWSON

It's not often that a horror book contains a submission from a person named "Dinky." Innovator and visionary in the field of sound, Dinky Dawson's genius has contributed to the success of many of the most prominent artists in the music industry.

Dawson worked on design and operation of WEM equipment, which was used by all British groups of the '60s era (e.g., The Beatles, Led Zeppelin, Rolling Stones, Pink Floyd, Rod Stewart, Eric Clapton, Jimi Hendrix).

Another claim to fame was that he was on the Apple rooftop when The Beatles played their last live concert together.

Born in Worksop, Nottinghamshire, England, Dawson's life has been dedicated to music, and his accomplishments in the field of live rock and roll are legendary.

Realizing the importance of technical production in this new music, he modified the band's equipment and became Fleetwood Mac's tour manager and sound engineer for their European and American tours, concerts, radio, and TV shows.

Dinky confesses that he's not the biggest horror fan, but the original **Haunting** "scared the crap" out of him.

Dinky's website is www.dinkysworld.com.

Dinky Dawson's TERRORble Top 10 List of Fright Flicks

Gremlins (1984): Simple rules and they still can't follow them...

Leprechaun 1-6 (1993-2003): So bad it is good. What I don't understand about horror movies: why do they start out with Roman numerals and then switch to Arabic numerals after V (5)?

Poltergeist (1982): Creepy little girl...Creepy little woman...

The Thing (1982): Purists will say the original, but I like special effects.

A Nightmare on Elm Street (1984): The first one was the scariest. Everyone has to sleep!!!

Willy Wonka & the Chocolate Factory (1971): The scene where they cut off the chicken's head...Scary because it comes out of nowhere!!! (La la la...Oh, a nice little boat ride...What the heck?!?!?!?!)

The Shining (1980): So many classic lines. Also again, creepy little girls...

The Sentinel (1977): Not sure why, but this one scared the bejesus out of me (whatever a bejesus is...).

Prince of Darkness (1987): Has a little of everything: Zombie street people, hints at time travel, religion, science...and Satan in a jar...(or was it God in the jar?).

The Evil Dead (1981): Campy fun. It is just so all over the map...

EDDIE DEEZEN
Eugene from "Grease"

Eddie Deezen is one of the zaniest comedic character actors ever, and although you surely know his voice (and probably his face), you may not know him by name. Perhaps best known as Eugene in **Grease** and **Grease 2** or from his lovable role in **1941** or the vastly-underrated **I Wanna Hold Your Hand**, Deezen has made acting as a nerd an art form. Any Beatles fan who saw Eddie create the character of the ultimate Fab Four fan alongside the late Wendie Jo Sperber will forever remember and love him and that under-appreciated 1978 Gale/Zemeckis motion picture.

His horror or genre films (some of which are obviously spoofs) include **Teenage Exorcist, Critters 2: The Main Course**, and **Polish Vampire in Burbank**. He was also in **WarGames, Laserblast**, and **Zapped**. With over 30 films to his credit, Deezen may best be known (albeit unseen) for his voice-over work on such projects as Disney's "Kim Possible" (as Ned), the voice and most of the motion capture for Know-It-All in the film and video game **The Polar Express**, The Mouth on "Darkwing Duck," and Gibby on "What's New, Scooby-Doo?" Look (or listen) for Eddie in several SpongeBob movies and episodes.

Why hasn't Eddie Deezen ever portrayed Jerry Lewis in a bio? Oh, that's right, because Eddie is actually a nice guy! Deezen is a strong Facebook presence and a fan as much as he is a celebrity. He's a true mensch.

Website: www.EddieDeezen.com.

Eddie Deezen's Top 10 or 11 TERRORble Favorite Monster Movies

Scared Stiff (1953): With Dean Martin & Jerry Lewis – My all-time favorite "horror film" just because I worship Martin & Lewis.

Young Frankenstein (1974): One of the funniest movies ever made – a Mel Brooks masterpiece.

Frankenstein (1931): The film that made Boris Karloff a major star.

A Hard Day's Night (1965): Not the Beatles film, but the Beatles cartoon where the Fab Four visit a haunted house. It is also my all-time favorite Beatles song.

King Kong (1933): Adolf Hitler's favorite film and a great monster classic.

Godzilla (1954): A great '50s monster flick.

Beverly Hills Vamp (1989): I had such a ball filming this one (circa 1988). I love Fred Olen Ray as a comedy/ horror director.

Teenage Exorcist (1991): Another fun comedy/ horror film I did with Fred Olen Ray.

Abbott & Costello Meet Frankenstein (1948): Maybe Bud and Lou's most popular film besides **Buck Privates**.

The Hunchback of Notre Dame (1939): The finest version of the classic story. This Charles Laughton version is one of my all-time favorite films. Just awesome.

Bela Lugosi Meets a Brooklyn Gorilla (1952): Duke Mitchell and Sammy Petrillo, the bargain basement version Martin & Lewis, are hilarious. This might be my all-time number one horror genre movie! Definitely. Move it to #1.

DEANA DEMKO
Psycho Sister

Deana Demko is both an actress and writer, and also a sculptress. She has over 50 film credits, most of which are independent horror straight-to-video releases. Titles include **Psycho Sisters**, **Zombie Holocaust**, **Sorority Slaughter**, **Chronicles of the Beyond, A.K.A. Jersey**, **Attack of the Killer Chickens: The Movie**, and **Theta States**. How many of these have you seen or heard of?

Equally impressive is DD's amazing line of hand-crafted clay creations of movie monsters, called "Little Replicants." They can be found at many horror conventions on the East Coast, where their creator is a regular, and where you can often hear her blood-curdling screams fill the ballroom.

When not playing with these creatures, Deana volunteers for an exotic animal education facility known as The Wildlife Conservation and Education Center in Ridgefield Park, New Jersey. It's the only zoological facility specializing in bats and bat conservation in the tri-state area. People can find out more at her web page: www.njbatman.com. Stop by and say hello!

Follow on Facebook: https://www.facebook.com/deana.demko and check out her sculptures and artwork at www.facebook.com/LittleReplicants/.

Deana Demko's TERRORble Top 10 Creatures

The Bride of Frankenstein (1935): The first absolutely wonderful female monster to me! I would love to play her in a remake!!!

Pumpkinhead (1988): I have just always loved the art that went into designing this creature. Awesome!

Julie from **Return of the Living Dead 3** (1993): Sexy, fun, and a strange take on a female zombie.

Bride of Re-Animator (1990): Love Frankenstein stuff...but this particular character has always been what I thought a human sewn back together would look like.

The Kothagao from **The Relic** (1997): ...what a piece of sculpture and art that went into that!

Wishmaster (1997): Same reason...love the details of the art as an artist myself.

Chucky from **Child's Play** (1988): Killer dolls...uh, yea, I have a whole evil doll collection (wink).

Michael Myers from **Halloween** (1978): Scary...without all of the fancy effects or scary makeup.

Jeepers Creepers creature (2001): Again, we go back to artwork.

Tie: Darkness from **Legend** (1985) and Pan from **Pan's Labyrinth** (2006): Yes, I combined them so I didn't go over my 10. They have to be two of the most beautifully-designed creatures ever. I love sculpting both of them.

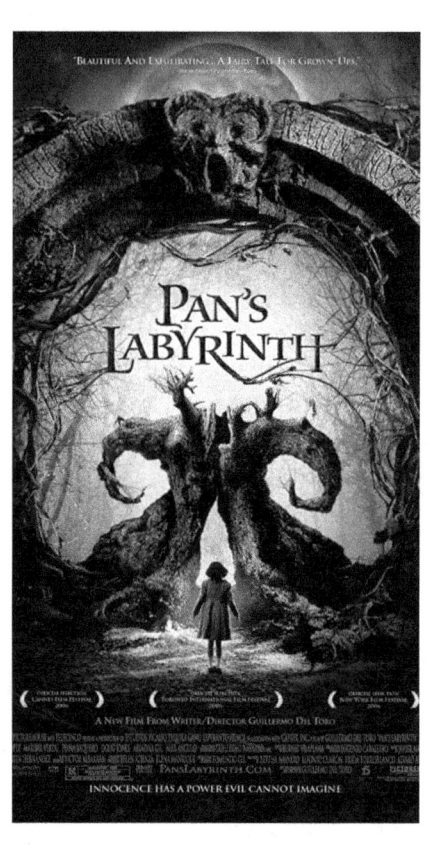

MICKY DOLENZ

The world knows Micky Dolenz as one of The Monkees, but horror fans may recall that he appeared in Rob Zombie's **Halloween** (2007) as gun shop owner Derek Allen, and as himself in Syfy Channel's 2011 film **Mega Python vs. Gatoroid**.

We contend that Micky is still one of the most underrated voices in music history and we're continually amazed at the notes he still hits. There's no doubt that he belongs in the Rock and Roll Hall of Fame.

Having already starred in live stage productions of the musicals "Grease," "Pippin," "Aida," "Hairspray," and others, in 2015 Micky took a comical/dramatic role opposite veteran actress Joyce DeWitt ("Three's Company") in the play "Comedy is Hard," by Emmy award-winning "Simpsons" writer Mike Reiss. The play was staged at the prestigious Ivoryton Playhouse in Connecticut.

Along with his autobiography, Micky released a children's book with illustrator David H. Clark, *Gakky Two-Feet* (Putnam/ Penguin), as well as the Buzztime Trivia-associated game book *Micky Dolenz' Rock 'n Rollin' Trivia* (Square One Publishers).

Photo of Micky Dolenz onstage being interviewed by the author, Charles F. Rosenay!!! ("Cryptmaster Chucky"), at the 2013 David T. Jones Memorial Monkees Convention in the Meadowlands, New Jersey

A true star of screen, stage, film, TV, concerts, radio, and every aspect of pop culture media, Micky still tours and records. His most recent album was a live collection from The Monkees' last tour featuring himself and Mike Nesmith. The pair continue the tour that was delayed when the COVID-19 virus hit in 2020, and their tour dates were rescheduled to 2021. They'll be coming to your town! In May of 2021, the 7A record label released the album *Dolenz Sings Nesmith*, with Micky covering some of band-mate Mike Nesmith's compositions.

Looking over his list, Micky's cinema tastes clearly leans towards '50s sci-fi, and he's too modest to include his own genre film appearances.

With special thanks to Micky's wife Donna, author Mark Bego, and one of the world's greatest entertainment publicists, David Salidor.

Website: www.MickyDolenz.com.

Micky Dolenz' TERRORble Top 10 List

The Day the Earth Stood Still (1951 version): The robot, Gort, made a big impression on me. Years later, I produced a show about a robot for the BBC called "Metal Mickey."

The War of the Worlds (1953): The invaders are wiped out by Earth's bacteria…Cool!

This Island Earth (1955)

Forbidden Planet (1956): Another movie starring a robot…

The Sixth Sense (1999): I had to watch this one twice!

Alien (1979): Ripley was Hot!

The Exorcist (1973): I couldn't eat split pea soup for years.

Invaders from Mars (1953)

Star Wars (1977)

Back to the Future (1985)

DENNIS DUNAWAY
Billion Dollar Baby

In 2011, Dennis Dunaway was inducted into the Rock and Roll Hall of Fame as a founding member of the band named Alice Cooper.

The original Alice Cooper group sold millions of singles and albums and was on the cover of *Forbes* for having the largest-grossing tour in 1973 – over Led Zeppelin and the Rolling Stones. The original Alice Cooper group was in the Guinness Book of World Records for largest indoor audience up until that point, with some 120,000 to 148,000 fans in Sao Paulo, Brazil in 1974. The group is recognized as the innovators of theatrical rock shows, which included giant balloons, hangings, snakes, and makeup. Dennis is in the Grammy Hall of Fame for co-writing "School's Out."

The bassist/ songwriter/ singer occasionally records and tours with Blue Coupe, featuring brothers Joe and Albert Bouchard of Blue Öyster Cult fame, and singers Tish and Snooky of Manic Panic. He also does select shows under the name Billion Dollar Babies with Michael Bruce and Neal Smith from the original Alice Cooper band.

Dennis Dunaway and author Charles F. Rosenay!!! ("Cryptmaster Chucky") meet at Ives Concert Park in Danbury, Connecticut at 2019's "Fore N Aft Benefit Concert."

Dunaway's book *Snakes! Guillotines! Electric Chairs!: My Adventures In The Alice Cooper Group* was released in 2015, and the self-narrated audiobook is available at Audible.com. A newer paperback version features an introduction by Alice Cooper.

Dennis wrote, "Whenever I see a list, I look for what I think could be replaced by something that I think is better. I can't even look at my own lists without doing that. Anyway, here's my list of 10 scary musical compositions."

Website: www.dennisdunaway.com.

Dennis Dunaway's TERRORble Top 10 List of 10 Scary Songs

"Gesang der Jünglinge" (literally "Song of the Youths") is a 1955-56 composition by Karlheinz Stockhausen combining electronic music and vocal parts supplied by 12-year-old boy soprano Josef Protschka. I find it to be haunting and disturbing.

"I Walk on Gilded Splinters" by Dr. John. The Night Tripper explores the subject of voodoo. Another musician, Papa Mali, covered the song with his own edgy impact, which was magnified by a vivid hallucination-filled video.

"Long Black Veil" is a country song that Danny Dill and Marijohn Wilkin co-wrote for Lefty Frizzell. Since then, many other artists have covered the song including Johnny Cash and Mick Jagger with the Chieftains.

"Where The Wild Roses Grow" is an uncharacteristically gentle Nick Cave song with a dark story of murder. Nick recorded the song as a duet with Kylie Minogue, which was a perfect choice. The song is beautifully reenacted in a video that seems to borrow from a painting titled "Ophelia" by Sir John Everett Millais (1851).

"Signed D.C." is a ballad by the rock group Love. It's about their former drummer's addiction. The song has no drums.

"Night on Bald Mountain" by Mussorgsky is so majestically eerie that even Disney's "Fantasia," featuring Mickey Mouse, had a hard time taming it down.

"Theme from 'Jaws'" is universally scary. The musical message is very clear – Danger! There's a very big shark coming. The melody resembles a section of "Night on Bald Mountain."

"Nosferatu" is a sprawling song by Blue Öyster Cult, the first group to do a vampire song.

"A Hard Rain's A-Gonna Fall" by Bob Dylan sent shivers up my spine in the '60s era of bomb shelters and covering your head while hiding under your school desk. The abstract lyrical images are as accurate as any scientist could conjure up.

"Fire" was co-written by Liam Paul Paris Howlett/ Peter Ker/ Michael Ivor Finesilver/ Vincent Crane/ Arthur Wilton Brown and was a devilish single produced by Pete Townshend and delivered in stage shows by Arthur Brown while wearing a flaming headpiece.

Notice that I haven't listed any of my songs. Well, here is a separate list of my Top 10 Alice Cooper songs:

"Fields of Regret"
"Levity Ball"
"Ballad of Dwight Fry"
"Killer"
"Dead Babies"
"Sick Things"
"I Love The Dead"
"Fireball"
"Sound of A"
"Cold Cold Coffin"

ELLIOT EASTON
Just What We Needed: A List from One of The Cars

As lead guitarist for the legendary rock band The Cars, Elliot has sold over 30 million records worldwide. Well respected in the guitar community, Elliot's reputation is that of a tasteful musician with a knack for coming up with memorable solos, great tones, and an uncanny ear for creating unforgettable "hooks" on pop records.

Over the years, Elliot has recorded and performed with many respected artists including Hall and Oates, Squeeze, Linda Ronstadt, Peter Asher, Yoko Ono, Sean Lennon, Jerry Lee Lewis, The Lovin' Spoonful, and many others.

Elliot has done much recording with the legendary Brian Wilson, playing on his first solo album as well as many others of his recordings. He has also performed in concert with the famed Beach Boy. Also, for over a decade, Elliot was lead guitarist for Creedence Clearwater.

In 2006, Elliot and Greg Hawkes, original members of The Cars, teamed up with Todd Rundgren, Prairie Prince, and Kasim Sulton as The New Cars, toured successfully, and recorded a great live CD, playing classic Cars and Rundgren favorites.

2011 proved to be a landmark year for Cars fans: the band released its first new album in 23 years, *Move Like This*, with all the surviving original members. Elliot has also played in the band The Empty Hearts, with members of The Cars, Blondie, and The Romantics.

Elliot Easton is a well-known first generation Beatles fan and scholar, and he has been performing a great deal of Beatles music recently. It appears that he may know his horror as well as his Fab Four.

Elliot writes: "Being a '60s Saturday double feature kinda kid, Castle, AIP, Zugsmith, Papa Laemmle, Hammer, etc. are very near and dear to my heart. Also, growing up on Long Island on a steady diet of Zacherley! Soooooo… limiting the list to 10 may be the most challenging part, but here goes":

Elliot Easton's TERRORble Top 10 List

House on Haunted Hill (1959): Best moment: Nora tapping on the wall while Mrs. Slydes, the blind caretaker, goes by on rollers, making that grotesque face, scaring the daylights out of Nora!

13 Ghosts (1960): William Castle was a great showman, and all his films had cool gimmicks that had audiences interacting with the movie! For **13 Ghosts**, we were given special cardboard viewers with two cellophane strips to look through: red if you didn't want to see the ghosts, blue if you did!

The Haunting (1963): All the more terrifying for the fact that you never actually "see" any of the evil forces that are terrorizing the guests. Julie Harris: "The House wants me!" Also some very "sophisticated" (for its time) sexual tension between Claire Bloom and Julie Harris!

The Bride of Frankenstein (1935): It's impossible to be a fan of the genre without acknowledging contributions of Carl Laemmle and his series of horror films made for Universal. **Bride** is just one of those perfect films, like **Psycho** or **Lolita**, where there's not a wasted frame in the entire movie. For me, **Bride** is superior to **Frankenstein** in pretty much every way – plot, production value, and the fact that you can drop pretty much any scene from this film into **Young Frankenstein** (or vice versa) without losing one iota of continuity! THIS is the film that Mel Brooks used as his template, not the first one!

Nosferatu (1922, silent): Ground zero. This is where it all begins, and if there's a creepier, scarier horror film, I'm not sure I've seen it! Max Schreck, in the title role, makes Lugosi seem almost comical: "I never drink…wine." Plus Bram Stoker co-wrote the screenplay, so this is the real deal.

The Pit and the Pendulum (1961): Vincent Price and Edgar Allan Poe – a match made in hell!

Abbott & Costello Meet Frankenstein (1948): Another Saturday Matinee fave! Hilarious AND scary – what's not to love? Also, any film that has Lon Chaney Jr. as the Wolf Man, begging "Please! Lock me in my room!" is a winner with me!

A twofer! **Attack of the 50 Foot Woman** (1958) and **The Incredible Shrinking Man** (1957): The Yin and Yang of special effects in classic Horror. Who could forget the sight of a 50 foot Allison Hayes knocking down telephone poles, shouting "Harry! Harry!"

Mark of the Devil (1970): In which Herbert Lom is an 18th century witch hunter. The torture scene, in which he puts this large apparatus over the suspected witch's head, which has a device that holds her mouth open and attaches to the seat so that he can pull her tongue out with a pair of tongs – I almost passed out!

The Last House on the Left (1972): Not the greatest film, or even the scariest, but the finale is every man's worst nightmare! The trailer said, "Just keep telling yourself, 'It's only a movie, it's only a movie.'" Arggggghhhhhh!!!!!!!!

WALTER EGAN

In his vast catalogue, Walter Egan has released songs about such monsters as werewolves and vampires. He is a musician, singer, composer, writer, artist, sculptor, and general Renaissance man who is most widely known for his 1978 million-selling smash record "Magnet and Steel" (from his second album, *Not Shy*).

"Magnet and Steel" was featured in the 1997 film **Boogie Nights**, the 1998 film **Overnight Delivery**, and the 1999 film **Deuce Bigalow: Male Gigolo**. The main track from the film **Boogie Nights** saw the unexpected usage of Walter's song "Hot Summer Nights" as the inspiration for Eminem's comeback Top 10 single "We Made You" (talk about out of the blue). Also, noted sci-fi/ horror genre writer and creator of the PunkTown series, Jeffrey Thomas, has made Walter Egan a fictional character in his story "Waltered States," a segment of his collection *Nocturnal Emissions*.

It is very appropriate for Walter to be part of this collection due to his last charted single, "Fool Moon Fire." The song explores an encounter with the werewolf in his soul and charted on *Billboard*'s Top 100 in 1983. Check out the video on YouTube and see Walter transform into a werewolf in the flesh. It should be noted that his song and accompanying video predated Michael Jackson's "Thriller" by eight or nine months (not that MJ or any of the producers stole the video idea, but well, you be the judge). Egan also has a vampire song on the *Apocalypso Now* CD called "My Love is in Your Veins."

Website: www.walteregan.com.

Walter Egan's TERRORble Top 10 Films of a Scary Nature

The Creature from the Black Lagoon (1954): This flick haunted my young dreams for months.

Dracula (1931): Bela Lugosi's iconic portrayal set the standard for creepy. "Children of the night, they make such sweet music."

I Was a Teenage Werewolf (1957): Starring Michael Landon from my hometown of Forest Hills, New York. Also the inspiration for my "Fool Moon Fire" video.

The Horror of Dracula (1958): Peter Cushing and Christopher Lee's masterpiece. When I saw this at age 11, it scared the hell out of me.

Invasion of the Body Snatchers (1956): The 1956 classic of cerebral terror.

Night of the Living Dead (1968): Those Zombies are relentless!

Plan 9 from Outer Space (1959): None better for sheer zaniness.

Red Planet Mars (1952): When he sees the red "X" on his parents' necks, it's paranoia at its best.

The Exorcist (1973): Its creepiness is only enhanced by the familiar scenes around Georgetown University, my alma mater (although I guess in many ways **Exorcist III** could be the most frightening film ever, made all the more unbelievable with Richard Burton's performance).

The Dead Zone (1983): I really love Christopher Walken in this deceptively eerie movie.

SHARON FARRELL
The Actress Who Gave Birth to a Killer Monster Baby

If the villagers blame Frankenstein for creating the Frankenstein monster, would they blame a mother for giving birth to a killing monster baby? The ads warned us... "There's only one thing wrong with the Davis baby...It's Alive." Actress Sharon Farrell played the mom (alongside John Ryan as the husband) in **It's Alive**.

Sharon was one very busy actress until her career was tragically interrupted when her heart stopped beating for four and a half minutes, and she incurred brain damage. Sharon was virtually unable to read, write, or memorize. Amazingly, her tremendous courage and love of acting propelled her back into a pursuit of her childhood dream. Her complete recovery, after extensive sessions of therapy during the re-learning process, was hailed as a medical miracle.

When Farrell returned to acting, her workload increased as her recovery progressed. In 1991, she joined the cast of the long-running soap opera "The Young and the Restless," where she acted until 1999. But for horror fans, Farrell is better known from her genre roles as "Mrs. Wax" in "Freddy's Nightmares" AKA "Freddy's Nightmares: A Nightmare on Elm Street: The Series" (1 episode, 1989), as Lila Morton in "Kolchak: The Night Stalker" (1 episode, 1975), in a few episodes of "The Alfred Hitchcock Hour" (1962), from the film **The Premonition** (1976), where she won Best Actress, from the Film Fantastique Award, and from the aforementioned greatest baby monster movie ever, **It's Alive**.

Top 10 List from Sharon Farrell, thanks to author Marshall Terrill.

Sharon Farrell's official website is: www.SharonFarrell.com.

Sharon Farrell's TERRORble Top 10 Horror Movies

The Bride of Frankenstein (1935): It is actually better than the original, which is pretty good. Elsa Lanchester's dual performance as the Monster's Bride and Mary Shelley is beyond superlatives. She was my first very favorite actress.

The Shining (1980): It's a true-blue horror film. It is often said that the human mind is the most powerful force on earth. When the human mind has gone demonic, what could be more horrible? Even now when I remember it, I start getting scared!

Frankenstein (1931): A horribly thrilling film. British Director James Whale was able to marry German film craft and Hollywood storytelling into a "well-stitched" final result.

Invasion of the Body Snatchers (1956): Small town in America during the postwar boom of the '50s looked too dull and boring to provide the

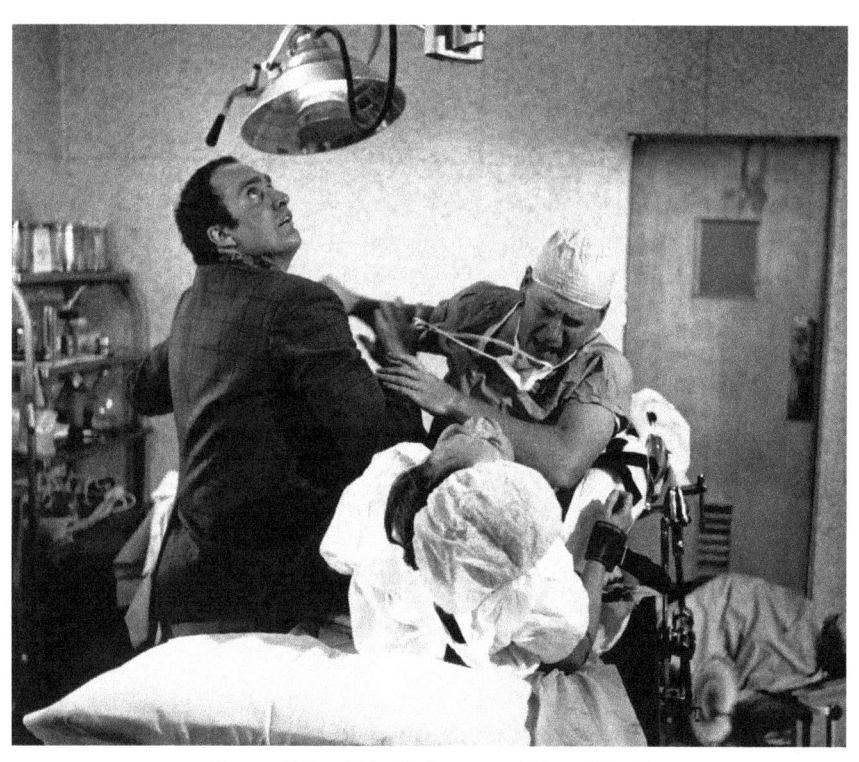

Promo still from "It's Alive" courtesy of Sharon Farrell

source for a scary film. But that is the genius of the film. The contrast between the backwater local and the chilling story matter makes it all the more believable.

Night of the Living Dead (1968): The low budget, grainy documentary look of the film made all the difference. It has the feel of a terrible real live event happening right in front of us, yet beyond our ability to control.

Psycho (1960): The multi-dimensional performance of Anthony Perkins makes the film more than horrible, but truly dramatic. No who has seen it could ever think about taking a shower again without a tinge of fear.

Aliens (1986): Another sequel that was better than the original, with Sigourney Weaver's character, Ripley, given some real dimensions, and the monster as well.

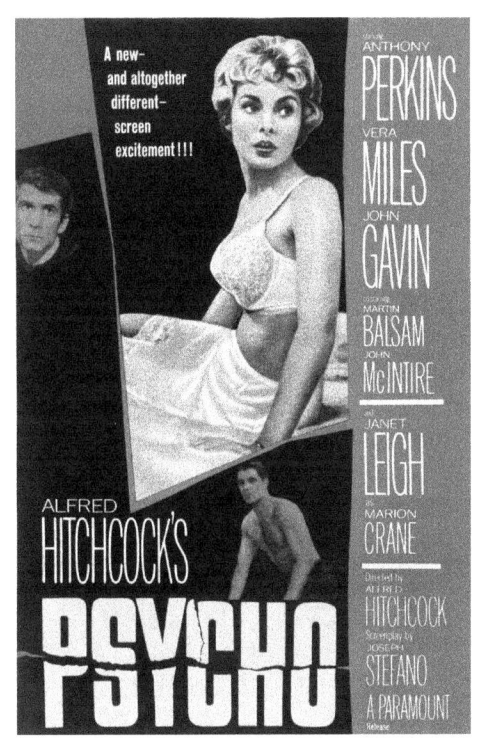

The Thing (1982): This remake is better than the original. The original was campy before campy became a pop culture expression. This one is a straightforward, nuts and bolts horror tale with the special effects of the day put to good use.

The Exorcist (1973): Stronger for the most religious. Actually, it was just an excuse to create some scary special effects. It's nice when you're swindled and you don't mind too much. The film managed to convince a large part of the audience that it was a fairly accurate retelling of a thousand-year-old tale.

The Blob (1958): I had to include **The Blob**. Steve played it straight in the film and we all followed him. Steve's performance made us want to believe. I worked with Steve McQueen in **The Reivers** and am going back to his hometown to dedicate the new highway named in his honor. What fun!

BRUTE FORCE
The King of Fuh (think about it)

Brute Force's claim to fame is a song that barely saw a release: "The King of Fuh." "The King of Fuh" needs to be said out loud, and then you realize the dirty pun. It's a song including at least two intentionally obscene double entendres, referring repeatedly to a "Fuh King" and telling everyone to "all hail" with a pronunciation that makes it sound suspiciously like "aw, hell."

This was wildly amusing to The Beatles, especially George Harrison and John Lennon. Harrison found it entertaining enough to press and distribute 2,000 copies on the Beatles' label in 1969 (look it up if you don't believe us: Apple Records Catalogue Release 8).

Brute Force was born Stephen Friedland and started out as both a singer and songwriter. He wrote and performed with The Tokens in the '60s and wrote songs that were recorded and released by Peggy March, Del Shannon, The Chiffons, The Cyrkle, and others.

In June 2006, "The King of Fuh," a musical comedy written by Friedland, was produced at the Players Club, New York City, with Brute Force himself as the King.

In 2010, "The King of Fuh" was released by Apple Records on their first "best of" compilation album, *Come and Get It: The Best of Apple Records*.

Brute Force continues to perform at venues in the 21st century. In 2015, he appeared briefly in the film "Birdman," and he plays The Director in the English version of the Enrique Iglesias/ Nicky Jam music video "Forgiveness." He entertains both in the music and comedy fields.

Brute Force may have been responsible for one of the most notorious records ever, but you've got admit he writes a fuh-king good list; after all, Bela Lugosi appears twice.

Website: www.brutesforce.com.

Brute Force's TERRORble
Top 10 Mostly Monster Movie Lines

Bela Lugosi as **Dracula** (1931): "I never drink…wine."

George Hamilton at the opening of **Love At First Bite** (1979), to the howling wolves: "Children of the night, shut up."

Sir Charles Laughton in **Island of Lost Souls** (1932) as Dr. Moreau: "No! Not the House of Pain!"

Also in **Island of Lost Souls**: "What is the law?" and Bela Lugosi, as the Sayer of the Law, responds, "Not to eat meat."

Sir Charles Laughton as The Hunchback in **The Hunchback of Notre Dame** (1939): "Why was I not made of stone, like Thee?"

The Hulk (2003): "Hulk bash!...Hulk smash!" And especially: "Puny human!"

Sigourney Weaver in the ending scene of **Aliens** (1986): The upshot of her getting into the spacesuit, and for the camouflaged body of the Alien, to look like machinery, in the escape pod.

James Cagney in **White Heat** (1949) as he's about to shoot into the trunk of a car in which a person is imprisoned: "Oh, stuffy, huh? I'll give ya a little air."

Buster Crabbe's **Flash Gordon** (1936) as the beginning of sci-fi for me.

Pitch Black (2000): Vin Diesel.

Dune (1984) for its beautiful spaceships, weaponry, and the worms.

The Thing (From Another World!) (1951), when the door opened and the Thing (James Arness) appeared, my first theater-seat-armrest-clutching moment.

Night of The Living Dead (1968), the original black and white.

Planet of the Apes (1968): Charlton Heston pounding the sand at the end...

The Hare Krishna adherent dancing on a car at the end of **Ghostbusters** (1984): Why?...Because it's me, Brute Force!

The Jean Cocteau **Beauty and The Beast** (1946)

The Elephant Man (1980): "I am not an animal! I am a human being! I...am...a...man!"

Anthony Hopkins, just because.

OK. It's more than 10, but who gives a fuh.

DEAN FRIEDMAN
I Bought a Vampire Motorcycle – She Runs on Blood

Dean Friedman composes and produces music soundtracks for TV and film, including the soundtrack to the underground cult horror film classic **I Bought A Vampire Motorcycle** (Hobo Films/ U.K.), in which he performs the unforgettable track "She Runs on Blood, Not Gasoline." Friedman also served as presenter/producer of the acclaimed radio series "Real American Folk," featured on BBC Radio Scotland. He tours extensively in the UK and select dates in the U.S.

But fans growing up on AM radio will best remember Dean Friedman from his chart-topping infectious hit single "Ariel," that quirky, lovable, irresistible, and uncategorizable pop song about a free-spirited, music-loving, vegetarian, Jewish girl in a peasant blouse who lived (as the lyric goes) "...way on the other side of the Hudson." 2019 marked the 40th anniversary of his classic hit and over that period of time, Friedman's consummate songwriting and performing have earned him a loyal international following, devoted to the sophisticated, funny, and profound work of a master songsmith.

Much more on Dean Friedman: www.deanfriedman.com.

Dean Friedman writes his Top 10 Lists as well as he writes his musical compositions, as we see in...

Dean's TERRORble Top 10
(plus sequels) Horror Films

I Bought a Vampire Motorcycle (1990): A horror cult classic from the UK, which included many of the same cast and crew of the hit British TV series "Boon" – folks like Michael Elphick, Neil Morrissey, and David Daker (Elphick is hilarious as a garlic-chewing police detective). I'd been doing music for the TV series and the film's writer/producer, Mycal Miller, asked me to compose and produce the soundtrack for **Vampire Motorcycle**. A Norton motorcycle becomes possessed and hilarious carnage ensues. It was great fun and a true professional challenge. Scoring the scene with the talking turd remains one of my all-time proudest musical achievements: www.youtube.com/watch?v=HalD12wJ2_s (WARNING: GROSS!). Well, that and the part where the nurse gets cut in half! Don't miss it!

Monkeyshines (1988): This unusual horror film was based on a book of fiction, based in turn on an actual program for the handicapped called Helping Hands, which trained capuchin monkeys as aids to quadriplegics. It was directed by one of modern horror's founding fathers, the great George Romero, whose classic **Night of the Living Dead** remains the standard of the genre. Sadly, due in large part to the maddeningly bad acting of its leading actor, **Monkeyshines** is, hands-down, the single *worst* film the honored director ever made. Yet this film is still worth seeing for its inane premise (a killer monkey, telepathically connected to the paralyzed human she assists) and the brilliant performance of the monkey, played by Amelia. Actually, five monkeys, in total, play the role of the film's leading monkey. And as it happens, the monkeys were all trained for the film by my lovely wife, Alison, who had previously trained the very same monkeys for the actual Helping Hands program.

Amelia, the leading monkey, still lives with us, and has for almost 30 years! (Note: Although Amelia performed all of the most difficult stunts, she was replaced, in some of the close-ups, by a younger, "prettier" monkey! ;-) Typical Hollywood! www.youtube.com/watch?v=rpG4R3Sjf4Y)

Basket Case (1982): First in this classic series of low-budget, ridiculously grotesque, brilliantly-costumed, and hilariously funny horror films. A tragi-comic tale of two brothers, Duane and Belial (whom Duane carries around in a basket), separated (surgically) at birth, and their quest for revenge. Poignantly horrific!

Basket Case 2 (1990): An apt sequel to a classic, continuing the adventures of Duane and his deformed brother Belial, as they seek sanctuary in a haven for even more of nature's anomalies. Bigger budget and even better cheesy mutant costumes and makeup. Contains episodes of gushing violence, but done good-naturedly!

Basket Case 3 (1991): This may actually be my favorite of the three films. This second sequel provides even *more* dramatic twists and turns in the heartfelt saga of two brothers who can't seem to escape each other's lives and destructive impulses. Filled with horror, romance, mutant sex, and violence PLUS, to *my* mind, the single FUNNIEST musical scene in any horror film *ever!* This sublimely inane cinematic moment includes a bus-load of freaks in a group sing-along and is guaranteed to bust your stitches!

Motel Hell (1980): Deliriously horrible and disturbingly plausible while retaining an inanely macabre sense of humor. Ghastly tale of a sausage-making farmer and the unusual garden he so lovingly tends. Strange, and true to its twisted self, the film is a genuine horror delight. I can't tell you anything more because…it would be *horrible* of me!

Night of the Living Dead (1968): I actually saw this film, my very first time, on late-night terrestrial television, when I was around 17, living in the Bronx. It was mind-blowing! I remember thinking to myself, "Is she actually chewing a severed arm on broadcast TV?!" I remained transfixed by director George Romero's naturalistic style; its verisimilitude made the flesh-eating zombies seem that much more terrifying. I don't think any of the film's zillions of zombie successors capture, as intensely, the pure fear aroused by Romero's realistic treatment of his flesh-hungry hordes.

The Crawling Eye (AKA **The Trollenberg Terror**) (1958): This was my very first horror movie, I remember seeing it as a kid on Chiller Theatre in New York. It was played very straight and to a 7 year old, the location – a ski resort, high up in the frozen Swiss mountains – provided an appropriately spooky setting for the terrible events to come. The strange radioactive fog and the looming horror it foreshadowed, delivered a perfectly chilling dose of teeth-chattering fear to my young self.

The Stuff (1985): Both this and my following choice, **Q**, were written and directed by Larry Cohen and star the terrifically idiosyncratic actor Michael Moriarty. This film's wonderfully goofy plot involves an oddly delicious, yogurt-dessert-like substance that's discovered oozing out of the ground. Its sinister purpose is gradually revealed as it begins to exhibit subtly insidious, sentient group-mind-control properties. Decidedly delicious viewing!

Q (1982): As with the above, a perfect balance of ludicrous plausibility combined with Larry Cohen's skewed vision and Michael Moriarty's compelling acting make this a fun evening's horror flick. A supposedly mythological giant flying beast may be nesting in the skyscrapers of New York. Entertaining and sometimes goofy, with occasional limbs falling out of the sky.

From Beyond (1986): Here's another cinematic pair, both directed by Stuart Gordon, both based on H.P. Lovecraft stories, and both starring Jeffrey Combs. They're very different in terms of plot but similar in style, both sharing a bizarre sense of lethal humor and similarly skewed take on reality. **From Beyond** envisions a frightening parallel universe inhabited by fantastic, lethal creatures who swim among us in a higher dimension and only become visible when a person's pineal gland is stimulated by a resonating device. Beautifully conceived and depicted, and viscerally frightening.

Re-Animator (1985): Following the discovery of a liquid agent capable of re-animating dead flesh, a medical student conducts secret experiments. Gory and hilarious hi-jinks ensue. Equally entertaining sequels: **Bride of Re-Animator** (1990) and **Beyond Re-Animator** (2003).

Fido (2006): This recent Canadian export is the sweet culmination of the slew of zombie movies wrought by **Night of the Living Dead**, except by contrast with the dark, gritty, realistic tone of **NOTLD**, **Fido** is a gentle, warmhearted, and side-splittingly funny romp through post-zombie-war suburbia. In a world where zombies are now domesticated by means of a subduing collar device, we discover empathy, even affection, for those we fear the most, and are forced to ask that most awkward question: which of us is the *real* monster? Truly brilliant and original film-making!

Hellraiser (1987): Written and directed by the inimitable master of horror Clive Barker, this mind-blowing film is genuinely *scary!* No over-the-top, play-it-for-yuks comedy here, just sheer, sophisticated, stylish, relentlessly hopeless horror. If you're looking for guaranteed terror and long for a waking nightmare, this is your ticket. Hauntingly beautiful and disturbingly grotesque, the inspired art direction and creature design combine with a complex, sometimes puzzling, adult storyline to yield a truly laudable cinematic lament on life, death, sin, and punishment.

GLORIA GAYNOR
First I Was Afraid…I Was Petrified

"I Will Survive" could be the mantra of the cast of "The Walking Dead" or for survivors of a vampire attack. The opening line, "First I was afraid…I was petrified," could sum up most kids' first monster-movie viewing experiences! In any case, it's a song that will never die!

DJs have played it for decades. It's a staple at karaoke clubs and parties worldwide. It's literally an anthem. Yet many people have no idea who the singer is. Some people think it was sung by Donna Summer and some guess Diana Ross, but it is the signature song of another queen of disco – Gloria Gaynor.

Gloria Gaynor was only 19 when she signed her first record contract. In 1973, she made history as *Billboard* gave birth to the Disco Action Charts and "Never Can Say Goodbye" hit #1 on the charts, becoming the first dance song to reach #1 status in that category. But it is "I Will Survive" that will always be her trademark song. Although we don't recall the karaoke favorite ever being used as the theme for survivors of zombie attacks, the film industry continues to feature "I Will Survive" on soundtracks of more than half a dozen motion picture releases. VH-1 honored Gloria Gaynor with the #1 spot during their countdown of the Top 100 Dance Records of All Time for

"I Will Survive," and on September 19, 2005, Gloria was inducted into the Dance Music Hall of Fame.

Her autobiography, appropriately entitled *I Will Survive*, is a revealing trip through her journey in life. Her signature song was inducted into the Library of Congress' National Recording Registry in March of 2016, preserving sound recordings with great cultural and historical importance to the U.S.

Thanks go to Gloria Gaynor for the fine list, though we wish we also got some comments or descriptions of the choices, and very special thanks to her manager extraordinaire, Stephanie Gold.

Website: www.gloriagaynor.com.

Gloria Gaynor's TERRORble Top 10 List of Scary Films

Invasion of the Body Snatchers (1956)

Friday the 13th (1980)

Rosemary's Baby (1968)

The Amityville Horror (1979)

The Shining (1980)

Jaws (1975)

A Nightmare on Elm Street (1984)

Se7en (1995)

Darkness Falls (2003)

Alien (1979)

LITTLE ANTHONY GOURDINE
Rock and Roll Hall of Famer

Well I think I'm going out of my head. That could be a line from the film "Scanners" or any monster movie with an exploding head. Here, though, we're referring to the classic song "Goin' Out of My Head" by Little Anthony & The Imperials, which was a Top 10 song in 1965. "Goin' Out of My Head" was an AM radio staple, but the group's first hit was the 1958 classic doo-wop ballad "Tears On My Pillow," co-written by Al Lewis (no, not the Al Lewis who played Grandpa Munster, but the guy who wrote "Blueberry Hill").

Little Anthony & The Imperials' other best-known hits were "Shimmy, Shimmy, Ko-Ko-Bop," "Two Kinds of People," "I'm On the Outside (Looking In)," and "Hurt So Bad." After celebrating their 50th anniversary, the vocal group was announced as inductees to the Rock and Roll Hall of Fame on January 14 of 2009, and they were inducted by Motown legend Smokey Robinson on April 4 of that year. Previously, Little Anthony & the Imperials were inducted into the Long Island Music Hall of Fame in 2006, the Vocal Group Hall of Fame in 1999, and they received The Rhythm and Blues

Photo of Little Anthony (left) and two of the Imperials, along with author Charles F. Rosenay!!! ("Cryptmaster Chucky") and his older son Harrison at the 2010 "Rock Con: Weekend of 100 Stars" in the Meadowlands, New Jersey

Foundation's Pioneer Award in 1993. At 2009's "Rock Con: Weekend of 100 Rock Stars" in the New Jersey Meadowlands, founding members Clarence Collins and Little Anthony Gourdine were presented with the "Rock Con" Icon "Living Legends" Award, and they were inducted into Mohegan Sun's Wolf Den Hall of Fame on January 8, 2011 (which was Anthony's 70th birthday).

Little Anthony & The Imperials' album *You'll Never Know* features 12 original songs including four remakes of the group's million-selling hit songs. Little Anthony is still touring the world, and his voice sounds as great as ever.

A while back, Little Anthony turned his memories into a screenplay that has yet to be made into a film or stage musical. Hopefully, it will be produced someday. We didn't get explanations for his choices, but we appreciated the list from one of the all-time rock and roll/ doo wop greats. Thanks to Little Anthony for his list and for singing so beautifully for over 60 years. Nothing scary about that.

Thanks to super PR man George W. Dassinger of Dassinger Creative, a public relations/ marketing/ media management agency.

Website: www.littleanthonyandtheimperials.net.

Little Anthony Gourdine's TERRORble Top 10 Horror Films

Invasion of the Body Snatchers (1956)

Abbott & Costello Meet Frankenstein (1948)

Dracula (1931)

Frankenstein (1931)

The Wolf Man (1941)

Alien (1979)

The Thing (From Another World!) (1951)

Predator (1987)

The Fly (1958)

Psycho (1960)

DON GRADY
One of My Three Sons

Is it possible that the kid who played Robbie Douglas on "My Three Sons" was in show biz over 50 years? He sure didn't look it. Before he passed, Don Grady still had the looks of a matinee idol, and he also very much looked like a contemporary recording artist, which he was.

Born Don Louis Agrati, Grady was an American actor, composer, and musician. He was known foremost as one of the three sons on the network series "My Three Sons," but before that he was one of the Mickey Mouse Mouseketeers. After his tenure on "My Three Sons" ended in 1971, Grady set a course for a musical career. His works included music for the Blake Edwards movie **Switch**, the theme song for "The Phil Donahue Show," and for "EFX," a Las Vegas multimedia stage show starring David Cassidy, Tommy Tune, Rick Springfield, and (from the original "Phantom of the Opera" musical) Michael Crawford. As a stage performer, he starred in a national touring production of "Pippin" and also had roles in "Godspell" and "Damn Yankees."

A wearer of many hats in the entertainment field, he scored high points for being a fine connoisseur of genre films (and although he never had a horror role, the only genre movie he appeared in may have been 1960's **Ma Barker's Killer Brood**). Don Grady passed away in 2012.

Don Grady's TERRORble Top 10 List (+1)

Diabolique (1955): Not the '96 re-make but the original, French version in 1955 with Simone Signoret. I saw it when I was 1...had nightmares about it 'till I was 15. So real, with such a great twist. Loved it! Watched it again when I was older...it was even better.

The Fly (1958): Again, the 1958 original with Vincent Price. I mean, what kid didn't see this and end up squeaking out the famous quote, "Help me! Help me!" for the next five years of his life!? The re-make with Jeff Goldblum was not too bad, either.

Outbreak (1995): With Dustin Hoffman. What's more scary than a virus? Who can avoid a cold? It's what you can't see that undoes you the most.

The Blob (1958): The original, starring Steve McQueen. "It crawls...It creeps...It eats you alive!" Ha ha! Great stuff.

Misery (1990): I don't care how nice of a role she takes on, I can't look at Kathy Bates without seeing that knife in her hands. I've had a few nutsy fans myself...maybe that's why this flick gets to me.

The Shining (1980): Again, a movie with a quote that lasted forever. All together now: "Heeeeere's Johnny!" Nicholson at his deliciously scary best.

It Came from Outer Space (1953 classic): This was before Lucasfilm figured out how to create anything the filmmaker could think of and put it on film. This was when you had to overlook the jerky movements of the alien ship as it landed and fill in the blanks with your imagination. And the truth is, there's nothing more scary than your imagination! Granted, I probably would laugh out loud at this one today, but when I was a kid, this was underwear-changing time.

Creature from the Black Lagoon (1954): OK, I keep dating myself. Problem is, as you get more experience with films (another way of saying "older"), it starts taking better special effects and more interesting stories to get the goose bumps up. Back then, all it took was a guy in a bad wetsuit.

The Man with the Golden Arm (1955): Since I'm on a roll with the '50s, you must check this one out. I fell in love with Kim Novak in this film, and since I was only 11, that's scary enough! The film is not in the thriller genre at all. But it's about straight-vein drug addiction and at 11, it scared the hell out of me. So did Kim Novak. How was I ever going to get to her?

The Sixth Sense (1999): I know, I know. Not an original pick. But who can deny the sweetness of this thriller? It's been under my skin since the first time I saw it. And that was at least four views ago.

Bonus: **Ma Barker's Killer Brood** (1960): Shameless plug. I played Herman, the sensitive one. Not a horror film...a bad B-film. But Ma (Lurene Tuttle) scared the bejeezus out of me as her method-acting reality slaps-to-my-face practically cold-cocked me on the set! At 16, it was an introduction to the brutality of the acting profession. I've been scared ever since. (Editor's note: Lurene Tuttle played Mrs. Chambers in **Psycho**.)

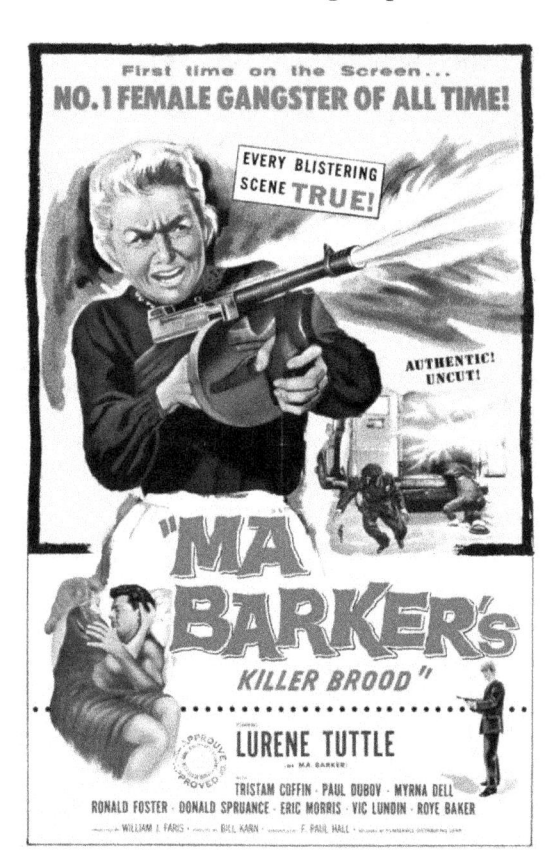

DONNA HAMBLIN

Scream Queen of Las Vegas

Known as the "Scream Queen of Las Vegas," actress Donna Hamblin has created quite a stir in the horror industry. She is best known to monster movie buffs for her roles in such films as Ted V. Mikels' **Astro-Zombies M3: Cloned**, **Killer Biker Chicks**, **Clawed**, **Hellcat's Revenge**, **In The House of Madness**, **Sinister**, **Catacomb of Creepshows**, and others. Hamblin has also done theater in Las Vegas casinos and even took to the stage portraying the Kathy Bates role in the play "Misery."

Donna grew up with the entertainment industry in her blood, with a grandmother who worked on many of John Wayne's films and a father who was a musician.

You can find her interviews in the book *Queens of Scream* (available on Amazon.com). In her own words, "I have been described as an 'old world with exotic flair' as an actress."

Donna loves life and has a huge compassion for helping the less fortunate. You can look her up on IMDb, find her on Facebook, or her website donnahamblin.weebly.com/.

Donna Hamblin's TERRORble Top 10 List of Horror Films

Sinister (2011) by Steve Sessions: "IT'S NOT THE HOUSE THAT'S HAUNTED, IT'S YOU!" Of course this is my number one. IT ROCKS...!!! (Had to get my promo in there!)

The War of the Gargantuas (1966): This movie used to scare the hell out of me when I was a kid.

Jaws (1975) by Steven Spielberg: I could not even take a bath after watching this movie! Didn't want to be anywhere near water PERIOD!

It by Stephen King (2017): Who is not scared of Pennywise? What a creepy, creepy, movie.

The Entity (1982): With Barbara Hershey – this movie really freaked me out. Any movie that is based on a true story and as horrifying as this one? Eek.

Halloween (1978) by John Carpenter: Love the Michael Myers character. To this day, I am on the edge of my seat every time I watch this. I really believe this started a new genre for the '80s as far as horror goes.

A Nightmare on Elm Street (1984) by Wes Craven: What a wonderful original movie. Couldn't sleep for days after watching this movie. One Two Freddy's coming for you...

Pet Sematary (1989) by Stephen King: Well, because who doesn't love Stephen King???!!!

War of the Worlds (2005) by Steven Spielberg: For some reason this movie really freaked me out. Great sound effects!

Willy Wonka and the Chocolate Factory (1971): Now I know a lot of people are probably saying, "WHAT??" Let me tell you, those Oompa Loompas are crazy, creepy little kidnappers. And when they go through that scary tunnel!!?? Wow, this is supposed to be a nice little pretty candy factory. Well, you don't get out of there! Do you really know what happened to all the little children that the Oompa Looompas took? I HAVE ALWAYS WANTED TO KNOW!!! It would give me peace of mind.

BOBBY HART
Worst Horror Movies

Here is the rare exception to a Top 10 List, from someone who we wanted to include in this book, who wanted to be included, but who simply isn't a horror movie fan.

Composer/ musician/ performer/ author Bobby Hart, as a solo and collaborative composer, has produced record sales of over 85 million! He has been nominated for an Academy Award, a Golden Globe, and a Grammy.

With partner Tommy Boyce, Hart wrote the theme to "Days of Our Lives" (1965) as well as hits for such artists as Dean Martin, Andy Williams, Del Shannon, Little Anthony & the Imperials, and The Monkees, to name but a few. Coincidentally, this book features Top 10 Lists from both The Monkees' Micky Dolenz and Little Anthony. "Hurt So Bad," the follow-up hit for Little Anthony after "Going Out of My Head," climbed the charts three separate times in three separate decades: 1965 for Little Anthony & the Imperials, in 1970 (The Lettermen), and in 1980 (Linda Ronstadt).

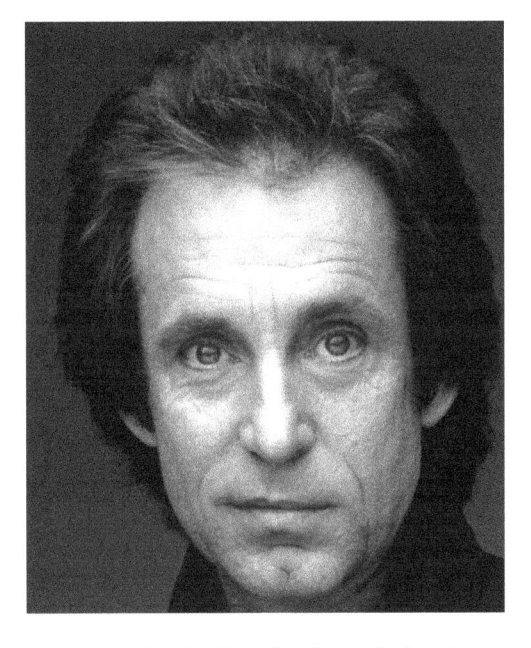

Boyce & Hart wrote 30 (!) songs for The Monkees, and the duo even recorded and toured on their own before teaming with Dolenz and Davy Jones to tour and record. Dolenz, Jones, Boyce & Hart, also known as "The Guys Who Sang 'Em with The Guys That Wrote 'Em," recorded two albums for Capitol Records in 1976 and embarked on a highly successful world tour to commemorate the 10th anniversary of The Monkees.

In 1968, Boyce & Hart campaigned to support Senator Robert F. Kennedy in his run for Presidency, and they spearheaded the "Let Us Vote," or "L.U.V.," campaign, which ultimately helped to lower the voting age to 18 in the U.S.

Bobby Hart, Tommy Boyce, Davy Jones, Micky Dolenz, and Peter Tork were Special Guests at the National Monkees Convention in 1987, which was co-produced by the author of this book. Hart continues to make select guest appearances at celebrity shows and special events.

He published his first book, *Psychedelic Bubble Gum*, in 2015 and a new book is due out soon.

Website: www.BobbyHart.com and www.officialboyceandhart.com.

Bobby Hart's Top 3 Worst Horror Movies

Since I generally make it a habit to stay away from this genre, I'm hard-pressed to come up with a list of my 10 favorite horror movies. Instead, I'll list my three *worst* horror movies, and I'll tell you why.

The Thing (From Another World!) (1951): It's hard to comprehend why my conservative parents would allow me to attend this science-fiction thriller when I was only 12 years old. But it's completely mind-blowing that they actually let me take my five-year-old sister along! Only a few scenes in, my baby sister could not contain her horrified screams. And it wasn't just Rebecca. For most of the movie, the two of us stayed hunkered down, hiding our heads behind the seat-backs in front of us.

Decades later, my wife and I became friends with James Arness ("Gunsmoke"). **The Thing** may have been the first major role for "Big Jim," whose imposing 6' 7" frame was perfect for the title role, although he was undetectable behind his costume and makeup.

King Kong (1933): I guess I'm not so shocked by my parents' behavior when I remember that they had taken me along with them when I was only five to see **King Kong**. It had been released in 1933 but brought back into theaters for re-runs. I don't remember being as scared at that young age but Rotten Tomatoes lists **King Kong** as the #4 horror film of all time. I'll stick with #2.

The Exorcist (1973): By 1973, I should have known better. I had heard the reports of heart attacks, miscarriages, and movie-goers fainting in the aisles. Director William Friedkin, who lived two blocks down the street from me at the time, took horror to another level and scared me away forever from darkening the door of any horror movie theater.

By the '80s, my wife and I had become more discriminative about what we subjected our minds and senses to, as we became more serious about our spiritual path. But following this path also never allows room to entertain any judgmental thoughts toward my parents and others who enjoy horror films.

GREG HAWKES
Let's Go: A List from Another One of The Cars

Greg Hawkes, famed keyboardist and co-founder of The Cars (1977-1987), helped define the sounds of the '80s with his signature keyboard style heard on The Cars' "Let's Go" and "Just What I Needed," as well as his syncopated synth lines on "Shake it Up" and "Heartbeat City."

Greg's music took an exciting new direction in 2001 when his wife gave him a "Fluke" as a gift. He has been hooked on Ukulele ever since. "It made playing music fun again," he says. Greg started collecting Ukuleles and getting involved in the 'Uke' scene in and around Boston. Greg's experimental nature led him to try duplicating Beatles string parts on Ukulele. Longtime friend Elliot Easton of the Cars heard his Uke recording of "Eleanor Rigby" and suggested doing a whole CD of Beatles songs. The release of *The Beatles UKE* CD (Solid Air Records) – covers of Greg's favorite Beatles classics – is timeless testimony to the inspiration and influence Paul McCartney and The Beatles have had on Greg's music and career. "They got me interested in music," Greg says. A Beatles concert in 1964 was the first concert he ever experienced, and everything came full circle when Greg was a musician on one of Paul's albums.

Hawkes has toured with The Turtles and in reunion versions of The Cars. He continues to tour and record, and this is one of two Top 10 Lists from a member of The Cars (the other being Elliot Easton).

Follow him: www.facebook.com/Greg-Hawkes-173756902645898/.

Greg Hawkes' TERRORble Top 10 Favorite Fright Flicks

The Bride of Frankenstein (1935): For me, this is the classic Universal horror film. It's more stylish than the original, plus there's Doctor Pretorius!

Frankenstein (1931): The original. Karloff and Colin Clive are both superb! I love the machinery. "It's alive!!!!"

Son of Frankenstein (1939): With Karloff, Basil Rathbone, Bela Lugosi, and Lionel Atwill. "What strange looking country…" Cool art direction.

Young Frankenstein (1974): I know, this isn't supposed to be here, but it's such a loving tribute to the above films that I just couldn't resist. Plus, Frau Blucher is pretty scary…

The Shining (1980): "Redrum, redrum." Boy, this movie scared me when it came out. Shelley Duvall and Jack Nicholson were both great. "Here's Johnny!…"

Dracula (1931): The Bela Lugosi original. Very surreal and stilted. "The children of the night, what beautiful music they make…"

House on Haunted Hill (1959): I wanted to include one with Vincent Price, this is probably my favorite (though **The Tingler** would be up there as well, complete with electrical shocks…).

Creature from the Black Lagoon (1954): This one seems oddly erotic. I always felt sorry for the Creature.

The Horror of Party Beach (1964): Totally ridiculous. This is the one where all the teenagers got together to defeat the monster by turning on their headlights. Sheesh…

Plan 9 from Outer Space (1959): Is it a horror film or a science fiction film? Who cares? Aliens plan to take over the earth by using the living dead. Sounds like a good plan to me. What could go wrong? With Vampira, Tor Johnson, and the last footage of Bela Lugosi (his stunt double looks just like him!…) – totally crazy!

MICHAEL J. HEIN
Top 10 Overlooked Horror Films

Usually held around Halloween when it began, the New York City Horror Film Festival would traditionally take place at the Tribeca Cinemas in Manhattan. Independent horror features, shorts, and scripts were accepted for the festival, which was the brainchild of MooDude Films CEO/ Producer/ Director Michael J. Hein in 2001. Sadly, Hein passed away in 2011.

In a short time, the NYCHFF turned into a week-long event that took place at venues throughout New York City, and grew to be a world-recognized event, with industry, filmmakers, and press attention from around the globe. The festival was quite competitive, screening approximately 50-60 films each year. In the past, the winners have been awarded prizes including the Dracula Tour vampire vacation to Transylvania (www.DracTours.com).

Filmmaker Michael J. Hein, CEO of MooDude Films and founder of The New York City Horror Film Festival, was one of the leading proponents of independent film in New York City and highly respected in genre films. Michael had done it all, from Special Effects Makeup Artist to Screenwriter, Director, and Producer. Hein produced and directed various feature film projects including **The Word**, **Blood Rails**, **Red Hook**, **Dead Serious**, **Biohazardous**, **Cyclone**, **This is How My Brother Died**, and **Killer Shorts Parts 1 & 2**, to name just a few. He was featured in the documentary "Even More Scarier Moments," broadcast nationally on Bravo, and was one of the subjects of the book *Splatter Flicks: How to Make Low-Budget Horror Films*. Michael J. Hein is very much missed. He left a huge black hole when he passed.

Top 10 Overlooked Horror Films by Michael Hein

Children Shouldn't Play With Dead Things (1972, Bob Clark, USA) – Zombies.

Den (2001, Greg Arce, USA) – Serial killer.

Audition (1999, Takashi Miike, Japan) – Serial killer.

Night of the Creeps (1986, Fred Dekker, USA) – Zombies.

The Serpent and the Rainbow (1988, Wes Craven, USA) – Voodoo.

Strange Things Happen at Sundown (2003, Marc Fratto, USA) – Vampire.

The Great American Snuff Film (2003, Sean Tretta, USA) – Serial killer.

Burnt Offerings (1976, Dan Curtis, USA) – Haunted house.

Galaxy of Terror (1981, Bruce Clark, USA) – Aliens.

Don't Look in the Basement (1973, S.F. Brownrigg) – Nut House Serial Killers

LAURIE JACOBSON
Haunted Hollywood

Laurie Jacobson is a celebrated Hollywood author, who gave the world *Haunted Hollywood*. A reformed stand-up comic, she worked out in Harvey Lembeck's Comedy Improv Workshop for years with classmates Robin Williams, John Ritter, and John Larroquette. The stories she uncovered became the basis for her debut, archetype book *Hollywood Heartbreak* (Simon & Schuster), a 75-year history of Hollywood told through the lives and deaths of 31 people. Following its publication, Laurie emerged as a leading Hollywood historian.

Since then, she has written and produced documentaries, television series, and specials, including: "Mary Tyler Moore: The 20th Anniversary Show," "The Museum of Television and Radio's Salute to Funny Women of Television," "The WarnerBros. Studio Rededication Party," "The Suzanne Somers Show," "Photoplay," and "Hollywood Chronicles." For nine years, she served as head of development for legendary producer Jack Haley, Jr.

Her fourth book, *Timmy's in the Well: The Jon Provost Story* (Cumberland House), is a memoir she co-wrote with Provost, her husband, who starred as Timmy in the iconic TV series "Lassie." She and Jon Provost make their home in northern California. You can find Jon's list elsewhere in this book.

In 2016, she hosted and co-wrote a new documentary, "Haunted Sonoma County," and in 2017, she did the same for the sequel, "Haunted Wine Country." That same year, the Southern California Motion Picture Council presented Laurie with their Lifetime Achievement Award for her outstanding literary contributions in the entertainment industry. She is currently at work on a book about The Beatles' 1965 Shea Stadium concert.

Website: www.lauriejacobson.com.

Laurie Jacobson's TERRORble Top 10 Scary Movies

Night of the Living Dead (1968): I was in trouble the minute it started…grainy black and white, driving up some creepy road, I just knew no good would come of it. Something told me to leave while I had the chance, but that wasn't possible. I stayed, hiding behind my fingers most of the time. This was 1971, before the zombie craze; I knew there weren't any zombies, but it was still so scary and really gross. And the whole "last man standing" thing, fighting the good fight, making it until dawn and being taken out in a cruel twist of fate. I was completely wrung out by the end. I went back to the dorm and cleaned my room until the sun came up.

The Shining (1980): **The Shining** is like a box of chocolates. Open any door, go down any hallway – you never know what you're gonna get. And when I finally saw the manuscript Jack Nicholson had been typing all winter long…punch in the gut time. Did not see that coming. Great moment right before everyone runs for their lives.

The Exorcist (1973): The way that chest of drawers hurtles toward the door of Linda Blair's bedroom to keep her mother out is the strongest image that I have. That scared the hell out of me. Of course, the head-spinning, the green stuff, the voice did, too. Even the words! When a possessed Blair says, "Your mother sucks cock in Hell" while using a cross as a marital aid – I mean, that was just about the most shocking shit we'd ever seen. It was just a complete assault. It takes you to the edge and then pushes you over.

Us (2019): Doppelgängers show up and fight to eliminate their look-alikes. The trailer led me to believe it was going to be stupid. It was not stupid. Not only was it very scary, it was also deeply disturbing.

It's where those doppelgängers come from, who and what they are. The more you learn, the more you understand what's going on. It is brilliantly layered and asks some pretty deep psychological and sociopolitical questions. It completely freaked me out, and stimulated much conversation. In some horror movies, things pop out and scare you for a moment and then it's over. **Us** scared me to my very core and it was days before it finally released its grip.

The Bad Seed (1956): I'm about nine. It's Saturday night, parents are out. Big brother is watching **The Bad Seed**. I see a cute blonde girl with braids and I join him. "It's a movie about a little girl?" I asked. "Yes," he answered. A few minutes later, the cute blonde kills the old lady upstairs. Whoa! What's this? A murderous child without a shred of remorse? I was fascinated, couldn't look away. My parents came home before the end. Mom was horrified that I was watching it and immediately sent me to bed. Years passed before I was able to see the dock scene. Patty McCormack is perfect, and Henry Jones is so great. But Eileen Heckart as Claude Daigle's mother gives one of the greatest performances I have ever seen.

M (1931): Only thing worse than a killer child is a child killer. What a taboo subject that was in 1931. Took the Germans to make it. Intense, suspenseful, they did so much with light and shadow. Playing a part like that could ruin a career, but it made Peter Lorre, who could play sinister like nobody's business. Unspeakable crimes committed by an unseen monster. And a blind man is his downfall. Brilliant.

The Haunting (1963): All our friends were going to see **The Fly**, so my brother and I asked to go to a scary movie. Our parents took us the see **The Haunting** (1963). At first, I felt cheated…no scientist, no laboratory, no part-man/ part-fly. But that was quickly forgotten as the story unfolded. Four wildly different people cooped up together in a spooky, rotting mansion that has a tragic and lurid history. I believed in ghosts even back then, so I was hooked right away. Whatever was in that house quickly learned the name of the weakest in the group and targeted her. (My theory has always been: if they know your name, run like hell.) The deafening pounding through the hallway is beyond terrifying. I could not move. And when it stops at her bedroom door and unleashes on it, I couldn't breathe. You never see it, never learn exactly what is happening – which is worse than seeing someone else's vision. Your own imagination is enough. In a scream-inducing finale, the house claims her, leaving me completely unnerved for weeks. My brother pounding on my bedroom wall every night did not help.

What Ever Happened to Baby Jane? (1962): Not your typical monster movie, but horrifying nonetheless. A helpless paraplegic is tortured and starved by her mentally unstable sister, who exists in the past when she was a Shirley Temple-like child star. Bette Davis is the monster in ringlets and a child's dress with thick pancake on her face. Then we discover that Joan Crawford is the real monster who set the entire scenario in motion, causing her own paralysis, her sister's mental deterioration, and eventual mayhem and murder. It has everything I love: old Hollywood, cool classic cars, grand old home, suspense, palpable fear, and Davis and Crawford, two of Filmland's grand dames battling it out. It's absolutely fabulous.

Rosemary's Baby (1968): The really scary thing for me is watching wonderful Ruth Gordon turn into such a twisted character. The whole devil thing is dark and effective. Sidney Blackmer is wonderful. But what really gets me is the elaborate conspiracy, the constant surveillance, the number of people involved in Mia Farrow's manipulation. It is utterly suffocating, like drowning. And I was manipulated right along with her, carried from a happy space to the epicenter of evil...utterly surrounded with no escape and worse – no hope.

King Kong (1933): The 1933 version, of course. New York in the '30s...beautiful dame down on her luck goes with fast-talking show biz folk to a prehistoric island. Kong's entrance is phenomenal. A panicked islander runs across the screen, grabbing the arm of a crying child without ever slowing down. I laughed when I first saw it, but only to relieve the fear and tension. Fay Wray is spectacular. Kong's devotion to her, displaying tremendous bravery and machismo to keep her safe...well, it's what almost every girl wants in a guy. He's a great boyfriend. His capture and enslavement are heart-breaking. When he rebels, they send the planes. By then, I'm sobbing. "T'was Beauty killed the beast." Epic romance with the worst kind of break-up.

FRANK JECKELL
Dr. Jeckell and The Hydes

Originally named Dr. Jeckell and The Hydes, The 1910 Fruitgum Company is an American bubblegum pop band of the 1960s, and they're damn proud of it. At a time when the Top 40 charts had unforgettable, hook-filled, two-minute classics by groups such as The Ohio Express and The Lemon Pipers, The 1910 Fruitgum Company recorded hit after hit. Their *Billboard* Hot 100 hits were "Simon Says," "May I Take a Giant Step," "1, 2, 3, Red Light," "Goody Goody Gumdrops," "Indian Giver," "Special Delivery," and "The Train." Their first single, "Simon Says," was released in 1968, became a #2 record on the U.S. charts, and reached the top of the charts in the UK. The group toured, released records, appeared on Dick Clark's "American Bandstand," and played alongside many of the musical greats of the past 50 years. They haven't stopped!

Managed by original founding member Frank Jeckell – no relation to Dr. Jekyll – the band continues to play concerts for audiences guaranteed to sing along with the hits.

Website: www.1910FruitgumCompany.com.

Image used with permission of Frank Jeckell

Frank Jeckell's TERRORble Top 10 List of Scary Memories

The War of the Worlds (1953): I was 6-1/2 years old when I saw this movie. I can distinctly remember lying in my bed scared out of my wits that the Martian probe on the end of a long fat cable that came in through a window in the movie was going to come in through my bedroom window. It took me over a month to get over it.

20,000 Leagues Under the Sea (1954): I was 7-1/2 years old when I saw this movie. I remember trying to crawl under my seat when the giant squid attacked the *Nautilus* submarine.

Gog (1954): Gog was a robot who goes rogue and kills people. Turns out he was being controlled by a plane flying overhead but he was scary nonetheless. One of my favorite B movies.

The Blob (1958): This movie came out right around my 12th birthday. I was still quite impressionable at that age, so when the monster (which looked like a big glob of red translucent Jell-O with the consistency of Silly Putty) dragged the mechanic under the car, I was transfixed. I remember having nightmares about this one, too.

Alien (1979): I recall jumping a good six inches off my seat in the movie theater when the alien monster sprouted out of the guy's chest. I just wasn't expecting it, and it was quite the shocker.

'Salem's Lot (book by Stephen King, 1975): This book had me spellbound and I could not put it down. I can still picture Danny Glick the vampire floating outside the second story window. One of the scariest books I ever read.

Carrie (book by Stephen King, 1974, and movie, 1976): I especially liked the scene where she threw all the knives at her mother. I read the book first and then saw the movie. As usual, the book rules since no movie, no matter how well it's done, can possibly compete with your imagination. But there was a shocker in store for me with the very last scene in the movie, where Carrie's hand comes up through the ground at her gravesite and grabs her friend's arm. Again, I jumped off my seat because I certainly was not expecting that.

The Shining (book by Stephen King, 1977, and the Jack Nicholson movie, 1980): Excellent story that I really enjoyed reading and excellent movie with Nicholson and Scatman Crothers. Here again, the book trumped the movie for me. I was especially disappointed in the scene where they are fleeing the hotel in the snowmobiles. In the book, the topiary animals come to life and make an almost-successful attempt to stop them. The movie did not include this bit of action.

Frankenstein (1931, with Boris Karloff): Boris created a very scary monster who gave me nightmares. Early horror movie that was very well done.

Psycho (1960): The shower scene is amazing. You would swear you see more than you actually see. Such is the genius of Alfred Hitchcock and the awesome power of the human imagination. And when Norman's mother is slowly turned around in a chair under a naked light bulb so you can see her face...it just doesn't get any better.

SARAH KARLOFF

Sara Karloff was born on her famous father's 51st birthday, November 23, 1938. Boris Karloff was filming **Son of Frankenstein** at the time.

Now in her 80s, Ms. Karloff has two grown sons and grandchildren. In 1993, following the death of her stepmother, Evelyn Karloff, Sara assumed the responsibility for the persona and licensing rights relating to her famous father, and formed Karloff Enterprises. The company's goal is to maintain a standard of excellence and appropriateness when the name or likeness of her father is used. Through the licensing process, she has been able to make merchandise and collectibles available to her father's fans.

In 1993, Sara met Ron Chaney (great-grandson of Lon Chaney Sr. and grandson of Lon Chaney Jr.) and Bela Lugosi Jr. (son of Bela Lugosi) for the first time at a Famous Monsters of Filmland convention. As a result of that meeting, a very special alliance was formed.

Although initiated by Ron Chaney, Ms. Karloff spearheaded a three-year effort to have their respective famous relatives immortalized in a series of commemorative USPS stamps, which were issued on September 30, 1997.

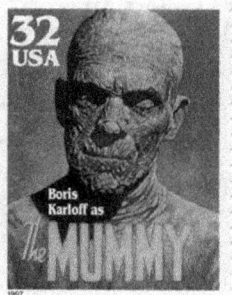

In 2003, Boris was honored once again on a third U.S. commemorative stamp, an honor which heretofore had been reserved only for U.S. Presidents.

One of the worst-kept secrets is that Sara Karloff does not like scary movies. She has been known to leave the room during "Murder, She Wrote." So her exclusive Top 10 List for us is quite eclectic and made up from life experiences (with a touch of humor). Sara continues to attend conventions around the world speaking about her iconic father and his remarkable legacy. It's no surprise that Boris Karloff and his beautiful monsters are in so many lists in this book.

Sara Karloff's TERRORble Top 10 Scariest Life Experiences

1. Being a parent.

2. **The Wizard of Oz** (age 5) (1939)

3. **Psycho** (1960)

4. **The Black Cat** (1934)

5. Speaking at MENSA.

6. The Eiffel Tower – 3rd floor elevator ride.

7. High spanned swinging rope bridge in Africa.

8. Madison Square Garden Haunted House special guest.

9. Head-on car crash.

10. Making this list!

JACK KETCHUM

Jack Ketchum was one of the greatest horror writers ever. Period.

He never played it safe, and his work is always frightening, unnerving, and often shocking. We are huge fans of his books, some of which were turned into films, including **Red**, **Offspring**, **The Lost**, and **The Girl Next Door**. The latter is one of the most disturbing films in the history of cinema.

Jack, or "Dallas" as his friends called him, wrote both the book and screenplay for **Offspring**. His story "The Visitor" is contained in John Skipp's massive anthology called *Zombies: Encounters With The Hungry Dead*. He won multiple Stoker Awards, and in total wrote over 20 novels and novellas. His novella *The Crossings* was cited by Stephen King in his speech at the 2003 National Book Awards. In case you missed Stephen King's famous quote, here it is: "Who's the scariest guy in America? Probably Jack Ketchum."

Jack Ketchum – real name Dallas Mayr – passed away on January 24, 2018.

He was a great guest at conventions, and you could clearly count on him to come up with an original TERRORble Top 10 List (even if it may be rated "M" for mature audiences): the Top 10 Most Memorable Nude Scenes in a Horror Movie!

Website: www.JackKetchum.net.

Jack Ketchum's Top 10 Most Memorable Nude Scenes in a Horror Movie

Halloween (1978): P.J. Soles gets the anti-boyfriend of her dreams.

The Howling (1981): Elisabeth Brooks. Nice doggie.

Rosemary's Baby (1968): I don't give a sh*t if it might be a body double with Mia's voice-over – it's hot!

The Hunger (1983): Oh for god sakes, does anyone have to ask? Sarandon and Deneuve, soft focus or not. Good grief!

Repulsion (1965): Deneuve again, both in and out of her see-thru nightie.

Innocent Blood (1992): Anne Parillaud in her handcuffs scene. Does it seem I have this thing for French women? I do.

Ghostbusters (1984): Yeah, I know it's a comedy and yeah, I know Sigourney's not exactly naked crawling around Bill on that bed. So what. Sue me.

Ghost Story (1981): Alice Krige more than makes up for all those terrible male performances. The most gorgeous ghost who ever floated through a movie.

Jaws (1975): Susan Backlinie from the shark's perspective. Yum…

Species (1995): Natasha Henstridge sliding out of that vagina-shaped cocoon. Human babies never look that good!

IRWIN KEYES
"Joe Rockhead"

Actor Irwin Keyes passed away in 2015, but before he left us, he logged in his share of horror films, and he was kind enough to provide us with his Top 10 List.

Raised in Amityville (oh, the horrors), New York, he moved to Los Angeles and accumulated nearly 100 film and TV credits. Although his famous face may be best known by some for his role as Joe Rockhead in **The Flintstones** or his appearances as Hugo in "The Jeffersons" from 1981 to 1984, Irwin's genre credits include 1979's **Nocturna: Granddaughter of Dracula**, an uncredited cameo in the first **Friday the 13th** in 1980, the monster in **Frankenstein General Hospital** (1988), 1995's **Here Come The Munsters**, Ravelli in 2003's **House of 1000 Corpses**, 2005's **Horror High**, 2006's **Wrestlemaniac (AKA El Mascarado Massacre)**, 2011's **Evil Bong 3-D: The Wrath of Bong**, and others. His IMDb bio says that he "was considered for the role of Freddy Krueger in **A Nightmare on Elm Street** (1984)."

Photo inscribed by Irwin Keyes to the author's daughter Lauren Rosenay in 2004, at Chiller Theatre convention

When we got him to provide his list, he wrote that his list came "from my padded cell...No more electricity please!"

Irwin Keyes' TERRORble Top 10 List of Favorite Horror Films

Frankenstein (1931): Great.

The Exorcist (1973): Swiveling head!

House of 1000 Corpses (2003): I like the guy in the mask!

Night of the Living Dead (1968): Drama of story.

Dawn of the Dead (1978): I hate shopping malls.

The Hunchback of Notre Dame (1939): I got a thing for All Fool's Day.

Nosferatu (1922, silent with Lon Chaney Sr.): I love the golden age of film.

The Thing (From Another World!) (1951)

The Bride of Frankenstein (1935): Great female acting at its best.

Wrestlemaniac (AKA El Mascarado Massacre) (2008)

THE AMAZING KRESKIN

The Amazing Kreskin, one of the foremost mentalists, refers to himself as an "entertainer" first, never as a psychic, who operates on the basis of suggestion, not the paranormal or supernatural.

Now in his mid-80s, Kreskin has authored over 20 books, had his own television show, appeared on "The Tonight Show" with Johnny Carson numerous times, was the subject of his own ESP board game by Milton Bradley, was the inspiration for a major motion picture, and has made thousands of personal appearances. He also has one of the strongest handshake grips ever.

When Kreskin received the request to participate in this book, he wrote: "I'm delighted that you're doing such a unique project. I can't imagine a more delightful topic for me to be able to contribute to, as horror movies and horror writings have been one of my great intrigues through the years – from the days I would spend hours in the public library that was only five minutes from my house. By the time I was in high school I read every single solitary book in the children's department of the library and started to move upstairs. It's fascinating that I know you personally, Charles, and I did not know you had written a daily newsletter series called 'Horror Happenings.' What an interesting theme. The people you got to communicate with you about their favorite horror themes made it all the more appealing and unique to your readers. I'd be pleased to join your list of celebrities who have added their thoughts to your book."

Photos of Charles F. Rosenay!!! ("Cryptmaster Chucky") with The Amazing Kreskin at the "NYC FAB 50" Beatles' 50th Anniversary Celebration at Town Hall in New York, February, 2014

Kreskin probably predicted he would be in this book even before he was invited!

Website: www.amazingkreskin.com.

Kreskin's ESPecially TERRORble Top 9 List

The Lodger (1944): One of my all-time favorite Top 10 movies from my own personal enjoyment, and I just looked at it literally a few weeks ago. This was a movie that came out in 1944. It was based on an earlier Jack the Ripper movie by Alfred Hitchcock, but this is generally considered the finest of all the "Lodger" presentations, done by 20th Century Fox. What made it so extraordinarily special is the setting, the actors, and of course, the writing. 20th Century had a lot that was designed to reflect earlier periods of England, and since the original serial killings were around the 1880s, it was just a perfect scenario. The murders in the movie were of women and it was a cautious decision on the part of the production people, because of course the real Jack the Ripper scenario was that he was killing prostitutes, which would not have been allowed. It would have been censored at that period of movie-making, but the murder of women worked out perfectly. The stars of the movie were Laird Cregar, Merle Oberon, who played a singer, and George Sanders, the British actor who was perfect as a part of Scotland Yard. The supporting cast (because 20th Century had a fine group of British supporting actors and actresses) included Cedric Hardwicke, Sara Allgood, and Queenie Leonard, amongst others.

Laird Cregar played Jack the Ripper and it was a masterpiece role, his finest acting role, although he was in a number of other movies. Sinister, quiet in his speaking, heavy in his weight – and you knew in the remarkable introductory scene of the black and white movie – after the men on the streets were selling a newspaper special because of another Ripper murder – and then you saw at night, in the fog of London, a figure walk down the street and stop and look up at a gas lamp. You knew right then and there that he was the Ripper. I've heard movie critics point out in television interviews that there is no question that he was the finest. What is also brilliant about this movie is there is no blood. It is more frightening because of the mood that it creates, with the darkness and shadowy scenes, and the behavior of Laird Cregar. He is one of the finest maniacal murder characters I've ever seen represented in movies.

When the movie opened in New York, Cregar attended the showing and was stunned to find the audience cheering, almost approaching a standing ovation at the end. He didn't leave other nights either – he stayed most of the movie's run at that theater. He was overwhelmed with the reception that his acting received. He did a movie after that about a mad pianist, which did not receive the tremendous success of **The Lodger**, but he wanted to become a romantic actor and tried to lose weight rapidly. He ended up going into the hospital for some type of surgery and died on the operating table, early in his career. A tragic disaster. Additionally, Merle Oberon was brilliant as a singer who he stalked but also communicated with in ominous ways, and George Sanders as the member of Scotland Yard remains one of my favorite actors in all movie history. His support in the story made it all the more intriguing, but then when you have the other supporting actors and actresses that I mentioned, just brilliant. The British performers made the movie a masterpiece.

Psycho (1960): In the same breath, here you have what has been voted, in a number of surveys, the greatest horror movie: Alfred Hitchcock's **Psycho**. I often mention to college groups I am speaking to (when the subject comes up in my Q & A or in other interviews) that I had the blessing of going to see this movie with a group of friends. There were two other gals and a male friend, and we loved great horror movies, but we went to see **Psycho** knowing nothing about it. At the end of the movie, you hear Alfred Hitchcock's voice asking his audience – admonishing them – not to tell others what the movie is about. I had read no reviews and that is the way to see this movie the way it was meant to be seen, not knowing anything about it. It was a frightening, menacing story. The brilliance of Hitchcock was how he threw a curve at his audience early on; no one would have dreamt that the main star of the movie, Janet Leigh, would be murdered so early. I was in shock just to realize what had happened. Hitchcock was one of the greatest directors of all time, and to this day there are people who remember seeing the red blood in the shower murder scene, and of course the truth of the matter is that the movie was in black and white. There was no color! There was not blood all over the place; it was the way he captured our minds.

Dracula (1931): Another favorite movie of mine is **Dracula**, starring Bela Lugosi. While it does not have the chilling fright of the previous horror movies I just listed, it is the mood and atmosphere and of course, the involvement of the main character Dracula, who is a vampire. When one studies Bram Stoker's fabulous 400-page novel, we realize the research that he made in putting together and creating a vampire while he was a road manager for a famous actor in England. During the time he was often off-stage, he was writing *Dracula*. What made the movie so spellbinding is Bela Lugosi. He fled Hungary with the onset of the Nazi invasion and the Second World War, came to this country, and was traveling the United States on the stage doing Dracula. His way of speaking was unique as he hadn't mastered the English language by any means, so a lot of it was phonetic, but it was such a way of pacing the dialogue that was so mesmerizing. You couldn't imagine anyone else as Dracula. Lugosi captured and highlighted the power of the Vampire with his use of hypnotism. Even years later, when Lugosi was no longer in movies, he would re-enact the hypnotizing of the housekeeper in the hallway when he appeared as a Special Guest for shows.

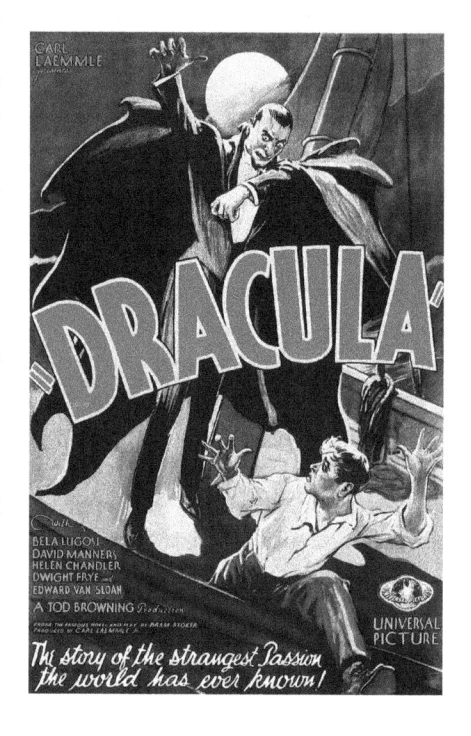

Frankenstein (1931): The tragedy of Lugosi's life was in the movie **Frankenstein**. While **Frankenstein** was not one of my favorite horror movies, Boris Karloff was brilliant in the role. He was actually friends with Lugosi. Because of the gigantic success of **Dracula**, the movie company came to Lugosi and said that they had another feature for him. They would have historically become the two biggest classic horror movies made with the same actor – but he decided not to do **Frankenstein** because he said that his public was aware of his face and enamored with his face – and that he would've destroyed his image to do such. Of course, he made the gigantic mistake of not appearing in what turned out to be a second major success of a talking horror movie, and that is **Frankenstein**. Lugosi's career was never the same, and they found another actor to do the role and of course it was Boris Karloff. Bela finally played the role later on in 1943 in **Frankenstein Meets The Wolf Man** (alongside Lon Chaney Jr., who also played Frankenstein's monster).

The Picture of Dorian Gray (1945): I have enjoyed another classic movie, 1945's **The Picture of Dorian Gray**, starring Hurd Hatfield. It's a beautiful story with the music and the dramatic acting. It has always been a favorite. What makes it incredibly dramatic and unexpected is the scene when Gray goes up to the attic and uncovers the painting that he did early in the story, and we suddenly see it in color. To me that is one of the most dramatic moments I have ever witnessed in movie-making. The other memorable dramatic scene, of course, is the ending with the stabbing of the portrait, and him dying in front of it.

Diabolique (1955): I am not a fan of movies with subtitles, but one of my most intriguing experiences was seeing the very successful horror movie **Diabolique**. It was meant to be in subtitles, not in voice-overs and filling in for moving lips, because this is one time when doing it in that way seemed to capture a special quality about the movie.

The Invisible Man (1933): An early highly successful black and white movie was **The Invisible Man**. They could not have picked a better actor than Claude Rains, whose voice is mesmerizing, especially when we become aware of the fact that aside from earlier in the movie, we don't see Claude Rains again until the end. Yet it is his voice that seems to haunt and make more powerful the entire story.

Play Misty for Me (1971) and **Fatal Attraction** (1987): I have found that the most frightening villains in movie stories are maniacal deranged individuals, whether man or woman. The perfect example is **Fatal Attraction**, starring Glenn Close and Michael Douglas, from 1987. The other is 1971's **Play Misty for Me**, starring Clint Eastwood and Jessica Walters. In both cases, the women are the maniacal potential killers. In the case of **Play Misty**, Clint Eastwood is a radio personality being stalked, with unexpected confrontations taking place. Of course, the unforgettable scene from **Fatal Attraction** is when Douglas returns home to find a pot boiling on the stove and when he removes the lid, he finds his daughter's pet rabbit boiling in the pot. I find both movies frightening because of the unpredictable quality of stalking maniacs. The fact that they were woman did not ease the terror.

There have not been horror movies in recent years that I've seen that have been memorable. I don't get to see that many motion pictures with the heavy schedule my career has kept. What has happened in so many movies today is they have become more violent and bloody, but there is something to be said for the reason Hitchcock didn't allow the movie **Psycho** to be made in color. He recounted it to me personally that this was not meant to be a bloody movie. The terror he created was best in a black and white scenario where you had shading and shadows and a mood that was maintained. What is detracting so much from movies today is not only the attempt for blatant visual real violence with very little left to the imagination – which, of course, is the key to great horror, the stimulation of the imagination – as well as the tremendous noise. Noise seems to be a powerful factor, whether music is used or the special effect of explosions and weapons and what have you, but the noise has become more of an irritation than a stimuli.

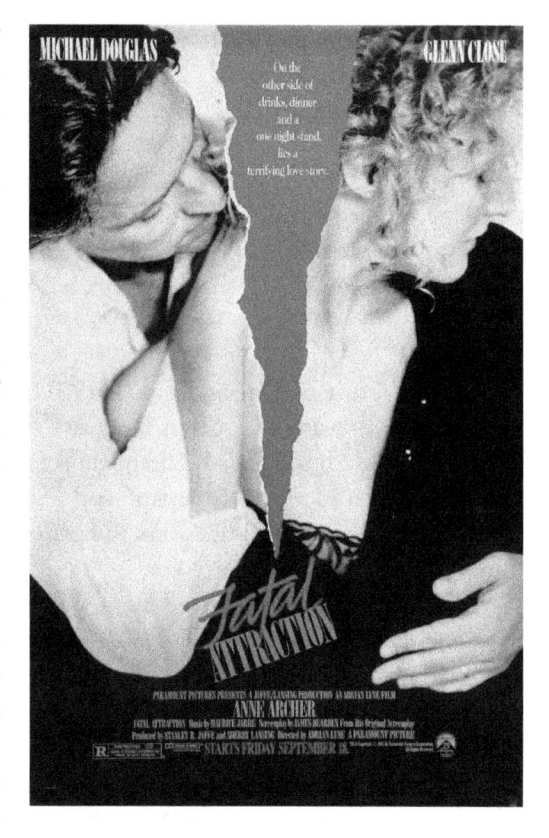

I could devote an entire program introducing my favorite classic horror movies with the background information I could present at the end of the movies. It was a joy, though, recounting this for your coming readers.

Much success with your project, all my best thoughts,
ESPecially, Kreskin

MURRAY LANGSTON
The Unknown Comic

Serial killers in slasher films aren't the only characters on-screen with bags on their head! "The Unknown Comic" is the stage name of actor/comedian Murray Langston, best known for his comedy on "The Gong Show," where he actually appeared regularly with a paper bag over his head.

Langston began his show business career in 1970 on "Rowan & Martin's Laugh-In," and he later became a regular performer on "The Sonny & Cher Comedy Hour." After more than 100 appearances with Sonny and Cher, Langston began to make appearances on other prime-time television shows, including "The Hudson Brothers Razzle Dazzle Show," "The Wolfman Jack Show," and "The Bobby Vinton Show."

Initially, he accepted an offer to appear on "The Gong Show." However, he was reportedly embarrassed about appearing on the show, so with permission from the director, he put a paper bag over his head, fitted it with holes for his eyes and mouth, memorized a few old jokes, and burst onto the show as "The Unknown Comic." The character, a frenetic speed-jokester in smarmy attire, was a hit, and soon developed a cult following. Langston's "Unknown Comic" appeared on more than 150 "Gong Show" episodes. Who can forget his "Chucky Chucky Chucky!?" By the way, we tried, unsuccessfully, to get a Top 10 List from the late Chuck Barris.

Langston later produced "The Unknown Comedy Hour" for Playboy TV, followed by "The Sex and Violence Family Hour," starring a very young Jim Carrey. He also wrote the screenplays for the films **Night Patrol** (1984), **Up Your Alley** (1988), and **Wishful Thinking** (1997), and was co-host of "The NEW Truth or Consequences" (1987). He also had a role in the 1989 children's TV series "E.M.U.-TV" as Murray the Technical Director.

Langston went into semi-retirement from show business to concentrate on raising his daughters. His elder daughter, Myah Marie, is a singer-songwriter who wrote and published more than 50 songs by the age of 19! She has recorded with notable pop stars including Britney Spears. His younger daughter Mary lived with Langston on their hillside ranch near the mountain town of Tehachapi, California, about 70 miles from Los Angeles.

He reappeared as "The Unknown Comic" in the film "Confessions of a Dangerous Mind," and occasionally does stand-up in Las Vegas. In what sounds more like a horror or sci-fi film, *Journey Thru The Unknown*… is Langston's 2014 memoir. It's a detailed account of each year of his life starting from 1944, a "bags to riches" account of how one poor kid from Montreal, influenced by Jerry Lewis, longed to follow in his funny steps and somehow leave Canada and make it to Hollywood.

He has been very active in charity work, particularly for children's advocacy causes. Rumor has it that Murray Langston was Linda ("The Exorcist") Blair's roommate for a while, and – judging by his list – he still has quite a sense of humor!

Check out footage of Murray Langston as his alter ego on YouTube: "The Real 'Unknown Comic' – Murray Langston – Exclusive – Circa 1991."

TERRORble Top 10 List of Scary Films With a Funny Twist

Pretty Woman (1990): Did you say Horror or Whore movies…???

I Was a Teenage Werewolf (1957): Starring Michael Landon – Scary part was when they shaved his face to find it covered with zits…

Son of the Invisible Man (2009): Sad story of a young boy who wants to follow in his father's footsteps…but he can't find them.

Bambi (1942)

King Kong Plays Ping Pong with His Ding Dong in Hong Kong (Porn Film, no date available)

Brokeback Mountain (2005): Guys hitting on each other always scares me…

Jaws (1975): When I saw **Jaws** in a theater it was so scary…not only did I wet my pants but I also wet the guy's pants in front of me…

Any movie with Mel Gibson in it…

The Fly (1958): When the guy turns into a fly and gets attacked by a giant turd.

Halloween (1978): When the guy shows up at homes with a paper bag over his head…

JOE R. LANSDALE
Top 10 Horror Books by A Top Horror Author

Joe R. Lansdale is the author of 45 novels and 400 shorter works, including stories, essays, reviews, film and TV scripts, introductions, and magazine articles.

His work has been made into films, **Bubba Ho-Tep** and **Cold in July**, as well as the acclaimed TV show "Hap and Leonard." He has also had works adapted to "Masters of Horror" on Showtime, and has written scripts for "Batman: The Animated Series" and "Superman: The Animated Series." He scripted a special Jonah Hex animated short, as well as the animated Batman film **Son of Batman**. He has also written scripts for John Irvin, John Wells, and Ridley Scott, as well as the Sundance TV show based on his work, "Hap and Leonard."

His novel *The Thicket* is set to film in the near future, and will star Peter Dinklage. Many of his works have been optioned for film multiple times, and many continue to be under option at the moment.

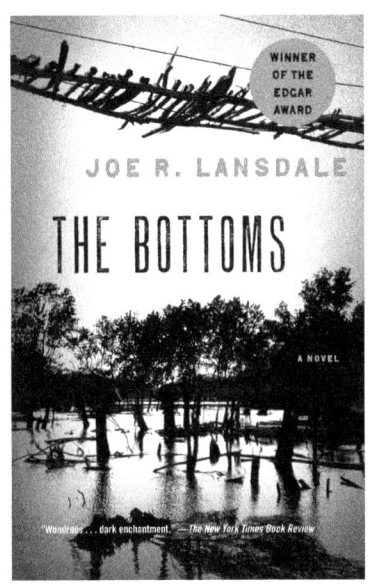

He has received extensive recognition for his work. Among the recognition is The Edgar Award for his crime novel *The Bottoms*, and The Spur for his historical western *Paradise Sky*. He garnered 10 Bram Stokers for his horror works. He has also received The Grandmaster Award and the Lifetime Achievement Award from The Horror Writers Association. He has been recognized for his contributions to comics with the Inkpot Life Achievement Award, and has received the British Fantasy Award along with two *New York Times* Notable Books. He has been honored with the Italian Grinzane Cavour Prize, the Sugar Pulp Prize for Fiction, and the Raymond Chandler Lifetime Achievement Award. *Edge of Dark Water* was listed by *Booklist* as an Editor's Choice, and the American Library Association chose *The Thicket* for its Adult Books for Young Adults list. *Library Journal* voted *The Thicket* as one of the Best Historical Novels of the Year.

Lansdale has also received an American Mystery Award, the Horror Critics Award, and the Shot in the Dark International Crime Writer's Award. He was recognized for his contributions to the legacy of Edgar Rice Burroughs with The Golden Lion Award. He is a member of The Texas Institute of Literature, has been inducted into the Texas Literary Hall of Fame, and is Writer in Residence at Stephen F. Austin State University.

His work has also been nominated multiple times for The World Fantasy Award and numerous Bram Stoker Awards, and the Macavity Awards, as well as The Dashiell Hammett Award, and others.

His books and stories have been translated into a number of languages.

He is also part of the "DracPack," having taken the Dracula Tour vampire vacation to Transylvania with his family (www.DracTours.com).

Lansdale lives in Nacogdoches, Texas with his wife Karen, a pit bull, and a cranky cat.

Website: www.joerlansdale.com.

Top Horror Books According to Joe R. Lansdale

Dracula, Bram Stoker (1897): Still the king of vampire books and the source for all the ones to follow, good or bad. Bram Stoker deserves both praise and blame for that fad.

I Am Legend, Richard Matheson (1954): Films have never captured the claustrophobic terror of the novel. Best modern vampire novel written.

The Haunting of Hill House, Shirley Jackson (1959): Still the king of haunted house novels. Spooky and smart and with an echo that remains long after the reading.

'Salem's Lot, Stephen King (1975): Wonderful take on modern Dracula meets Peyton Place. King was smokin' in those early days, and this one is raw and creepy.

The Shining, Stephen King (1977): Second best haunted house novel. Wonderful stuff. The film didn't get it.

Psycho, Robert Bloch (1959): Lean and fast and suspenseful with an underlying factor of disturbia. Bloch opened the doors for all kinds of new suspense tales. Readers forget he was the source of the film. Good as it is, his short stories are far better. If you can find his collections, that's the stuff to read.

The Silence of the Lambs, Thomas Harris (1988): Best serial killer novel where the focus is on the serial killer. Been just as good in other ways, but for its approach, unique and well written and really frightening. A page turner.

The Day of the Triffids, John Wyndham (1951): Wow. Scary plants, but really well done. One of my favorites, period.

Something Wicked This Way Comes, Ray Bradbury (1962): Best read late at night and more creepy than horror, but really good.

The Stand, Stephen King (1978): Maybe the greatest end-of-the-world novel ever.

BARBARA LEIGH
Vampirella

Actress Barbara Leigh may be more famous for a film that never came out than for her fine body of work in the '60s and '70s. "Vampirella," based on the Warren comic magazine, would have been Barbara Leigh's star-making role, and was also expected to be a huge hit for Hammer studios. After two long years of pre-production and work, the ill-fated film project, also starring legendary Hammer actor Peter Cushing, never materialized. Many believed the film would have brought Hammer back to the forefront of successful film studios; instead it signaled the end of an era.

And Barbara Leigh's career stalled because of it. Some of Barbara's notable genre roles included Gene Roddenberry's **Pretty Maids All in a Row** (1971), **Mistress of the Apes** (1979), **Seven** (1979, which originated the "shooting the swordsman" gag that was popularized in **Raiders of the Lost Ark**), **Terminal Island** (1973), **Smile Jenny, You're Dead** (1974), "The Incredible Hulk" episode titled "Killer Instinct" (1978), and "The Most Deadly Game" episode titled "Witches' Sabbath" (1970).

The actress's fine body of work may be overshadowed by her fine body, and the story of "what might have been." Leigh was romantically connected to both Steve McQueen and Elvis Presley, and she recounted some of her life stories in a book called *The King, McQueen and the Love Machine*, which chronicles her decade in Hollywood.

Thanks to author Marshall Terrill.
Website: www.barbaraleigh.com.

Barbara Leigh's TERRORble Top 10 List of Favorite Films

The Uninvited (1944): Starring Ray Milland and Ruth Hussey and directed by Lewis Allen. It is a story of betrayal, love, and heartbreak and has all the elements for a great ghost movie.

House on Haunted Hill (1958): Starring Vincent Price and directed by William Castle. This was my first glimpse of Vincent Price and from then on, I was a huge fan. The haunted house is a famous Frank Lloyd Wright design and one I shot in with photographer Helmut Newton. You can imagine how I felt driving around the bend up to meet Helmut and realizing it was the haunted house I saw so long ago and NEVER forgot. I was thrilled.

The Wolf Man (1941): Starring Lon Chaney Jr. and directed by Roy William Neill. I love ALL of Lon Chaney Jr.'s movies. There are too many to mention but his version of the Wolf Man is still the best to date. I also loved **Wolf** (1994) starring Jack Nicholson and Michelle Pfeiffer. It had a GREAT ending.

The Student Nurses (1970): Starring Elaine Giftos and me, and directed by Stephanie Rothman. This was my first big movie. The plot involves four student nurses and what they go through, their ups and downs, their loves, and their personal problems. I had a nude scene that turned out quite beautifully because it was shot on the beach with Richard Rust. For a low budget film, it still stands the test of time. Amazon gives it 4 stars out of 5.

Wuthering Heights (1939): Starring Merle Oberon and Sir Laurence Olivier and directed by William Wyler. One of the greatest love stories ever told, with a sad ending. This movie pulls on my heart; it is also a ghost story.

Van Helsing (2004): Starring Hugh Jackman and Kate Beckinsale, and directed by Stephen Sommers. I love this movie because it has vampires and werewolves, AKA Lycans. And I am a huge fan of Stephen Sommers, who directed **The Mummy**. The special effects are spectacular.

Junior Bonner (1972): Starring Steve McQueen and me (along with a very talented cast) and directed by Sam Peckinpah. I love this movie and feel quite lucky to have been a part of the picture. Of all my films, it has the best cast. Steve plays a washed-up rodeo star who wants to ride Sunshine, a bull, one last time. It is also the story of a dysfunctional family struggling to change and survive with the times: an interesting father and a son relationship and a love interest that comes and goes. In the end, Junior walks away from it all – to where, no one really knows.

Horror of Dracula (1958): Starring the GREAT Christopher Lee and Peter Cushing, and directed by Terence Fisher. I saw this movie when I was nine and it scared me to death. However, I became a HUGE fan of Dracula and BOTH Christopher Lee and Peter Cushing. Years later, I was under contract to Hammer Films to play Vampirella (which never got made) based in London. Hammer made this film and so many more wonderful and scary horror movies. This picture has it all: the lavish costumes, castles, romance, and murder. I love this film even though special effects today are so much better than in the '50s.

The Fountainhead (1949): Starring Gary Cooper and Patricia O'Neal, and directed by King Vidor. It is about Howard Roark, a man's man who wouldn't give in to society's rules and stuck to his principles. It is a real love story, a story of one man's honor. Howard Roark is my personal hero.

Pretty Maids All in a Row (1971): Starring Rock Hudson, Angie Dickinson, and me, and directed by Roger Vadim. This is a story of lust, murder, and innocence. Rock Hudson conducts affairs with several high school cheerleaders, then murders them to keep his wife (me) from finding out. The cast also included Telly Savalas and Roddy McDowall. This picture was a lot of fun and I fell in love with Rock Hudson because he was a kind man and a good actor. He is surely missed.

ELIZABETH LEIKNES

Never Babysit. Ever

When an author submits their TERRORble Top 10 List, you know it's got to be interesting, because – clearly – they're writers! When the topic is "life lessons learned from horror films," it fits right into a book with better-known celebrities.

Elizabeth Leiknes' debut novel, *The Sinful Life of Lucy Burns*, was described as a cross between Buffy the Vampire Slayer and Bridget Jones. In a review of the author's first published novel, the author of the book you're reading right now wrote: "There's no doubt about it, Leiknes has a likeness about her. You may have heard the saying, 'The devil made me do it,' well, you don't need that kind of influence to buy this book – it's worth getting all on your own. Let's hope this is the first of many original, fun books from this author."

Her subsequent books have been *The Understudy*, *Black-Eyed Susan*, and *The Lost Queen of Crocker County*.

Website: www.elizabethleiknes.com

"Life Lessons Learned from My Top 10 Horror Films"

Jaws (1975): Okay. This is my ALL-TIME favorite movie, in or out of the horror genre. Great story, great script.
<u>What I learned</u>: The monster that we can't see (for over three-quarters of the movie) is always the scariest. Oh, and "I'll never wear a life-jacket again."

The Silence of the Lambs (1991): Smart, scary, and best use of a Tom Petty song in a movie.
<u>What I learned</u>: Just because the bad guy is really smart and really engaging, it doesn't mean he won't kill you and eat your face.

Halloween (1978): Truly stopped breathing for a couple of minutes when Jamie Lee Curtis ran in terror from door to door.
<u>What I learned</u>: Never babysit. Ever.

Carrie (1976): This is what happens when school bullies don't get detention.
<u>What I learned</u>: The Bible is often misinterpreted.

The Shining (1980): Favorite Kubrick film by far.
<u>What I learned</u>: (1) Twins are doubly scary; (2) Writers need sunlight.

Se7en (1995): You might not label this one horror, but you should.
<u>What I learned</u>: The true definition of scary is not what someone can do to you, but what they can do to someone you love.

Saw (2004): I don't care what the critics said, I think they enjoyed this and lied about it.
<u>What I learned</u>: Evil is often closer than you think.

A Nightmare on Elm Street (1984): The movie that dared to make the '80s even scarier!
<u>What I learned</u>: Don't trust Where's Waldo – that sweater is evil.

28 Days Later (2002): This film put the smart back in zombie movies.
<u>What I learned</u>: Zombies can run!

The Ring (2002): This movie was so scary, it lived in your head even when you shut your eyes.
<u>What I learned</u>: Throw all your VHS tapes away. It's just not worth it.

BUZZY LINHART
Jimi Hendrix Musician

Who was Buzzy Linhart? William Charles "Buzzy" Linhart may have been best known as the vibraphonist/ keyboard player/ vocalist/ drummer with Jimi Hendrix (Buzzy can be heard on Jimi's *First Rays Of The New Rising Sun* CD), but he was also songwriter/ guitarist on Carly Simon's debut album and had incredible street cred. Linhart was producer of Labelle featuring legendary vocalist Patti LaBelle, and was co-writer on Bette Midler's signature tune "(You Got to Have) Friends." He performed his own music at Carnegie Hall, and two of his albums, *Buzzy's Studio* and *Buzzy's Buzzy*, are still in release.

Linhart passed away on February 13, 2020. We are pleased to present his Top 10 Horror Films (including three to avoid) courtesy of super PR impresario Joe Viglione.

Website: www.buzzylinhart.com.

Buzzy Linhart's TERRORble Top 10 List of Horror Films

The Tenant (1976): Starring Roman Polanski. Truly horrifying mindscape if there ever was one.

It Came From Outer Space (1953): My actual first horror film viewed at a theater at about the age of 11. I wasn't really scared, but it was interesting to think that some adults were making a movie about things coming from outer space. I was just about as frightened of this movie as I was happy to be viewing it with my mother sitting next to me as a chaperone.

Creature from the Black Lagoon (1954)/ **Revenge of the Creature** (1955): Mom's still sitting beside me, you know how dangerous it can be to go to a Saturday afternoon matinee alone in Cleveland Heights, Ohio in 1954/ 55. At least the production values seemed to be improving as far as I could see.

Forbidden Planet (1956, with Leslie Nielsen): I'm finally alone, mom is home making fudge or something like that. I'm working as an usher in the theater. The films are in color now, but either they are getting sappier than ever or I am getting a bit older.

The Wolf Man (1941, Lon Chaney Jr., **Phantom of the Opera**): Although I had not yet seen **Frankenstein**, I caught this around Halloween on local TV and couldn't help but notice the low production values amidst some excellent time lapse photography. By the way, when I finally saw **Phantom of the Opera** in an "art" theater, it was with subtitles and an organ soundtrack that repeated over and over. (Not scary.)

Frankenstein (1931): Even though this is one of the oldest of these films, **Frankenstein** was one of the very best of them. At this point I would like to mention that, because back then there was a need to have films that were viewed by adults and children together, it was important to not be too scary for the children, and this added a kind of campy experience for the adults.

Strait-Jacket (starring Joan Crawford, 1964): An over-the-top black and white axe murderess film, this offering went all the way from being scary to being ridiculous. Heads rolling towards the camera like grotesque melons and it doesn't get funnier than this.

The Shining (1980): Finally delivers the goods in color and convinces me that the great horror/ monster movies have to be too scary for the kids to entertain the adults.

The Servant (1963): Although not commonly thought of as a monster film, I was as terrified by this movie as I hoped I would be when I saw my first.

Honorable Mention: **I Was A Teenage Werewolf** (1957)

Three recommendations of films not to see: **Don't Look Now** (1974) starring Julie Christie and Donald Sutherland; **The Thing (From Another World!)** (1951), starring James Arness at the top of his "Gunsmoke" fame; and **Zardoz** (1974), starring Sean Connery. These three are just barely watchable – only if you want to be disappointed should you experience them.

CIRCE LINK

Circe Link will entice, delight, and treat you to a sound she says comes from her "cosmic radio station." Circe was a self-taught fine artist before waking one morning from a dream with a song in her head. While never having written a song before, she penned three songs that day and discovered a new artistic path. Originally calling her music Cowboy Jazz, Link soon found there was so much more to her eclectic style. Circe's records range in genre and sound from Bob Wills to Bowie, from Patti Page to Patti Smith – essentially from ABBA to Zappa and everything in between. This broad diversity has yielded her a collection of songs that are at once charming and familiar, yet surprising and unique, often leaving melodies stuck in the listener's head for days.

With 10 records and over 90+ songs in her catalog, an Amoeba Records Homegrown Artist pick, the #1 spot in Jazz on Garageband.com for over two years, a Clear Channel "Emerging Artists" pick, film and TV placement credits that include Starbucks, Hanes, "Blades of Glory," "School of Rock," "Bittersweet," and "The Hills Have Eyes," among others, plus a successful tour in Japan as a back-up singer for The Monkees, Circe Link has proven her strengths and success as one of Los Angeles' most unique independent artists.

Circe writes, "Not many people know that I once had a big black Mohawk and painted my face nearly every day in big black eye makeup. So much so that other kids' parents often enjoyed reminding me it wasn't Halloween yet. I've also read more books on the occult and all things macabre than I can count, and I have in my possession a cherished collection of the complete *Man, Myth and Magic* encyclopedia set. While I'm not a fan of gore (I find it boring and distasteful) and I don't scare at all, this genre has some old beloved friends of mine in its ranks."

Website: www.CirceLink.com.

Circe Link's TERRORble Top 10 List of Horror Movies

The Exorcist (1973): It's on so many Top 10 all-time scary movie lists for a reason. And while I never found this film to be scary, I have seen it many times and have my very own copy for warm cozy nights by the fire. It's certainly one of the most quoted movies in my film quoting vocabulary: "Dimi, why you do dis to me..." is a favorite, to be sure.

Along with the wonderful Tubular Bells score, you will find actors perfectly playing their roles like mythological archetypes come to life. The profound subtext of existentialism from which Father Karras suffers, the heroic effort and defeat of Father Merrin, along with the internal feminist conflict that Chris MacNeil endures, is deep stuff and probably goes unmentioned by so many because of the extreme bombast of little Regan. I prefer the original edit and find the additional scenes superfluous. I also find the digital add-ons to be odd and out of context – no need to try and make this work of art compete with the extreme elements to which we have already become so inured. This film set the bar of excellence in the genre that likely may never be topped.

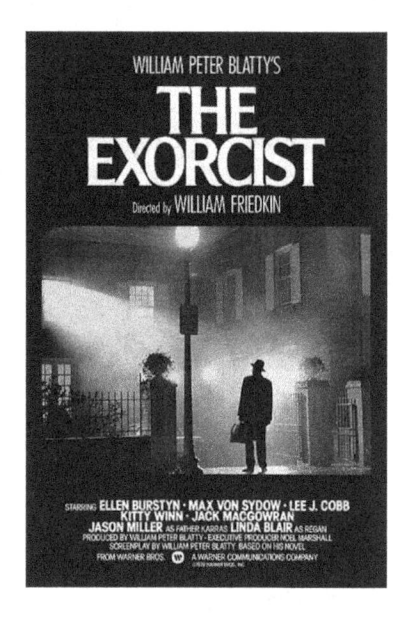

Halloween (1978): Many horror films of late seem to rely on blood more than plot, tempo, editing, and script. But this film is so wonderfully intense for its brilliant use of exactly those things. The stark simplicity, sparing use of gore, and the constant pressure of suspense forces the viewer's mind to squirm in a self-embellished anticipation that no film budget could possibly match. Enhancing all this mastery, director John Carpenter also wrote the music. Taking its influence from the Tubular Bells of **The Exorcist**, the score will raise the hair on the back of your neck all on its own. Few films have such a perfect pairing of music and picture as **Halloween**.

The Phantom of the Opera (1925): Arguably the most inventive actor of all time, Lon Chaney will thrill you to the bone in this macabre masterpiece. If this doesn't move you, then I suggest you are jaded beyond all hope and that you seek help. The early film work here uses light and shadow better than many modern films and the voyeuristic camera's eye allows us to see ghostly glimpses only slightly more clearly than the poor characters themselves. The scene where our leading lady creeps up upon the Phantom is a nice twist, I must say. I never fail to howl and shudder in morbid delight!

Rosemary's Baby (1968): First let me say…the fashion! Wanna know how to look absolutely chic while becoming the devil's consort? Just ask Mia Farrow while she's horking down that raw liver! Additionally, I love this film for its subtle creep, slightly buzzy disorientation, light-handed, clue-leaving camera work, mothball neighbors, and the sexy beast himself, Mr. Anton LaVey! This film is a classic and near and dear to me!

The Shining (1980): Any Kubrick is good Kubrick as far as I'm concerned and this epic astounds me every time. Having read the book, which has a notably different outcome that I prefer, I still love this film. The oppressive hand of doom invades every corner of this ominous environment. The space itself is a character that is always watching and waiting, almost narrating the rapid unraveling of a man's mind into paranoia and delusion. This is another film relatively lacking in gore, which is why when it is used, the intensity is so oceanic. I could go on about Nicholson and Duvall but I won't. You have heard the hype and it's all true. If you don't know already I entreat you to get into it, and freak.

An American Werewolf in London (1981): Sometimes you need a good dose of funny with your blood and guts and this film does that with aplomb! OK, so by today's standards the special effects look cheesy and dated, but the story is surreal and wonderful nonetheless. And the ever-so-hot Jenny Agutter is a delight to look at while she is tending her boy-wolf romance! Griffin Dunne is brilliantly snarky and David Naughton can do more than sell Dr. Pepper, people. He can eat your face off and do a very nice two-step!

Dracula (1931): I fell in love with Bela (and Boris – see below) at an early age and had their pictures on my walls when most of the kids were digging teen idols. The eyes, the eyebrows, the voice, the hand! Um…kind of dreamy. I much prefer the subtext of the Zombie narrative to the Vampire narrative that this film set in motion so long ago, which now so heavily dominates our modern culture. Basically, we are a bunch of puritanical prudes seeking release via blood metaphor instead of actual erotica. Go figure. But **Twilight** can eat dirt compared to this titanic treatment of sexual repression.

Frankenstein (1931): As I mentioned above, I had a thing for both Boris Karloff and Bela Lugosi as a little tot. So how could I not include this foundational film in my list? Written by Mary Shelley, this classic story never gets old no matter how many times it's remade. *Modern Prometheus* is the second half of the title for a reason and the story can be applied to every generation of human history. The story touches on feminism and humanism in a way the viewer/ reader is often unaware of. The film itself contains some of the most iconic imagery in cinema history and is a beautiful piece of shadow and light, set design, and acting even for its day. And if you don't think of this movie as scary, put yourself in the big ol' boots of the Monster.

Brotherhood of The Wolf (Le Pacte Des Loupes) (2001): While not typically "horror," I'll add this one to my list because it provides a great story, which seems to be a common thread for me in my choices. The visuals are breathtaking and the art direction is one of such detailed consideration that it's obvious a student of classic art history informed almost every shot. The creature that causes so much bloodshed and mutilation in this film is cleverly hidden for almost the entire first and second acts, making a rich and fertile ground for the viewers to plant nameless and faceless fears. Subtitles? *Merde!* Yes, it's better in French, so pony up and get out your glasses.

Psychomania (1973): Motorcycles, suicides, rock and roll, and undead revenge? I'm so in. This flick has more cheesy guitar riffs and bad dialogue than you can shake your mother's wand at, and that's certainly one of the reasons I love it. But I think the basic premise of narcissistic youths seeking paranormal powers and eternal life makes for a more obvious social narrative than your average Zombie exploit.

And my honorable mentions that don't quite fit into this category are: **The Silence of The Lambs** (1991), **Jacob's Ladder** (1990), **Psycho** (1960), **The Tenant** (1976), and **Aliens** (1986).

IAN LLOYD

"She was black as the night/ Louie was whiter than white." The song lyrics would have been a perfect horror happening if the "she" in the song was a witch or a vampire, but perhaps she was some evil seductress. Only the songwriter knows for sure.

Ian Lloyd's band The Stories had a #1 hit with this song, "Brother Louie," in 1973. The Stories' other Top 40 tunes included "I'm Comin' Home" (played as an anthem during the return of the Iranian hostages), "Mammy Blue," and "If It Feels Good Do It." The voice of The Stories was Ian Lloyd, who later sang with Foreigner and other acts through the years.

In 2009, Ian Lloyd released the CD *In The Land Of O-de-PO*, featuring the 2009 GMMA award for Best Rock Track, "O-de-PO," and an updated version of the classic hit "Brother Louie."

"Brother Louie" had a renewed life as the theme song music for "Louie," Louis C.K.'s loosely autobiographical FX sitcom, but it's the version by Ian Lloyd and The Stories that will live forever.

In 2015, Lloyd recorded a holiday song, "Everybody's Happy 'Cause It's Christmas Time," which was described as a sonic 'winter scene' – a mystically snowy celebration of grand proportions. All from a voice of grand proportions with a grand list of horror films.

He is currently recording and gigging in Europe.

Website: www.machinedreamrecords.com.

Ian Lloyd's Top 10 TERRORble Horror Movie Faves

Night of the Living Dead (1968): Still have trouble watching this movie. It's that scary!

Invasion of the Body Snatchers (1956): "They're Here Already" echoes in my head. Kevin McCarthy's defining moment (for me) on this classic.

Motel Hell (1980): Rory Calhoun on his tractor is etched in my memory cells forever! Breakfast sausages anyone?

A Nightmare on Elm Street (1984): Freddy Krueger's coming-out party. After seeing this film I voted never to fall asleep again.

Aliens (1979): Sigourney Weaver is sooo hot! A must see on the BIG screen. You can never have too many Aliens.

The Thing (1982): John Carpenter and Kurt Russell are a winning combo in the remake of this classic. (Also see **Escape from New York**.) One of the scariest aliens yet!

The Terminator (1984): Arnold Schwarzenegger is The Terminator. I'm sure the people of California would agree!

The Shining (1980): Snowed in for the winter with Jack Nicholson is scary enough. Add the brilliant writing of Stephen King with Stanley Kubrick's screenplay and go from there. We'll never forget the classic line, "Here's Johnny!"

Seconds (1966): Legend Rock Hudson gives a chilling performance in this shocker...He ROCKS! (sorry)

Shaun of the Dead (2004): Fantastic spoof of the zombie motif. Simon Pegg is my hero!

I cannot leave out my two favorite TV horror shows: "The Night Stalker" (1972 – Carl Kolchak) and "Millennium" (1996 – Frank Black). Buy the box sets, binge, and be prepared to not get up from the safety of your soft cushy couch...EVER!

DONNA LOREN
Beach Blanket Bingo Starlet

Pop culture icon Donna Loren is synonymous with the Swingin' '60s era of music, motion pictures, television, and fashion. The one-and-only Dr. Pepper Girl starred in five Beach Party films (**Muscle Beach Party**, **Bikini Beach**, **Pajama Party**, **Beach Blanket Bingo**, and **Sergeant Dead Head**). She was also a featured actress or dancer in ABC's "Shindig," "Batman," and "The Monkees." In 1965, Donna recorded *Beach Blanket Bingo* for Capitol Records, now a classic collectible LP and re-issued CD. As beautiful as ever and currently living in Hawaii, Donna re-emerged with a comeback album *Love It Away*, which will have listeners "Shakin' All Over" (search YouTube for her video of that song).

She also hosts her own incredible pop-culture podcast "Love's A Secret Weapon," based on her audio book. You can listen here: podcasts.apple.com/us/podcast/loves-a-secret-weapon-podcast/id1528902410.

You also can get an autographed copy of her book *Pop Sixties* on her website: www.DonnaLoren.net.

And now...with a groovy mini-skirted frug and drum roll...we present...

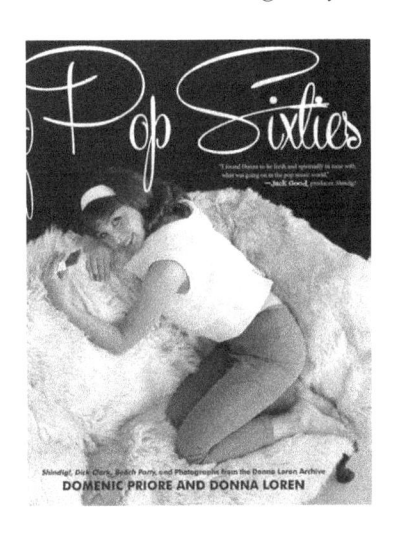

TERRORble Top 10 List by Donna Loren

One August afternoon in SoHo, claps of thunder exploded as I exited a building on Broadway. Mothers grabbed their children's hands and ran while drops of monsoon-size rain in a dark corridor terrified pedestrians as though Godzilla was coming. It felt like a scene in a Japanese Horror film. That is my #1 fave: **GODZILLA** (1954).

The Hand That Rocks the Cradle (1992) is a close second. Shattering glass falling from above is no Chicken Little story!

Definitely **King Kong** (1933).

Has to be **Mighty Joe Young** (1949).

Poltergeist (1982).

The scariest movie for me is still **The Exorcist** (1973).

I'm really more of a **Bambi** (1942) fan …to me the forest fire and his mother getting killed is frightening.

Dumbo (1941) is another one. Mothers being parted from their children is devastating.

Diabolique (1955).

Everything with Peter Lorre in it.

Not a film…but Marty Feldman's eyes.

KIMBERLY MAGNESS
Scream Queen Award Winner

Actress/ host/ model Kimberly Magness has been honored with the Scream Queen award and was listed on IMDb as one of the hottest actresses in horror movies. She was the lead actress in the brutal horror film **Devil's Grove**, and she also starred as the leads in Discovery ID's hit shows "Deadly Affairs," "I Married a Mobster," and "Scorned." Kimberly has modeled on the "Today Show," "Rachael Ray Show," and "E! News." In the past, she was a representative for the New York City Horror Film Festival, both as a judge and programmer.

She was in the Rolling Stones film **Shine a Light**, directed by Martin Scorsese, as was the author and editor of this book, Charles F. Rosenay!!! (AKA "Cryptmaster Chucky"), who played a backstage roadie who helps Ron Wood put on his robe at the end of the film.

Magness has performed off-Broadway in the murder mystery show "Murdered by the Mob" and was a lead in "Steel Magnolias." She was also one of the leads in the paranormal feature film thriller **The Manor**.

Photo Credit: Raven Adams

Judging by the photo, Magness was ahead of her time. She was wearing a surgical mask before the COVID-19 pandemic of 2020.

Upon submitting her list, Kimberly wrote, "Wahooo! Well, this was super hard to try and narrow down. I'm sure I'm leaving out some greats, but this is my Top 10 List of classic horror films that everyone should see!"

Website: www.kimberlymagness.com.

Kimberly Magness' Top 10 List of
Classic Horror Films Everybody Should See

The Exorcist (1973): In my opinion, the scariest movie of all time! I watched this for the first time when I was 10 years old, attending Catholic school, yadda yadda…you get it!

Rosemary's Baby (1968): A true horror classic! Really put Mia Farrow on the map.

What Ever Happened to Baby Jane? (1962): Two true Hollywood starlets as you've never seen them before, Bette Davis and Joan Crawford. Shows what show business can really do to you! ;);)

The Bad Seed (1956): This movie defines how little kids can be creepy. However, the curtain call at the end is quite possibly my favorite moment of the film!

Psycho (1960): Alfred Hitchcock is brilliant, and Anthony Perkins' performance is amazing. And who can forget the shower scene? I mean, c'mon!

The Shining (1980): Heeeeeere's Johnny! Even with the awful casting of Shelley Duvall, this movie still holds strong and stands the test of time! Redrum!

Frankenstein (1931): Boris Karloff portrays Frankenstein brilliantly! His interpretation and vision of Frankenstein has carried through to the current representation of him!

Play Misty for Me (1971): Beware of the crazy stalker woman! Before **Fatal Attraction** and **Misery**, there was this little gem!

Nosferatu (1922): The original vampire classic. The shadows alone are enough to give you the creeps!

The Birds (1963): Who ever thought to be scared of a bird? This movie proves that you can find the evil in almost anything and scare the crap out of us with what society knows as a gentle, harmless creature.

VINCE MARTELL
Vanilla Fudge Guitarist Likes Laughs with His Scares

Vince Martell is the legendary axeman of the '60s rock group Vanilla Fudge. By "axeman," we do not mean slasher film killer, we mean guitarist! His lead guitar work with the Fudge back in 1967 set the pace for other bands such as Led Zeppelin, Deep Purple, and Yes, among many others. In 1995, the editors of *Guitar Magazine* honored Vince's main riff on the hit "You Keep Me Hangin' On" as one of top five of The 50 Heaviest Riffs Of All Time.

Vince played his axe (sorry, guitar) on the *Garage Band Beatles* CD release and he continues to play out live with Vanilla Fudge, the Vince Martell Band, Rock Gold Trip, and other musical projects.

Thanks to Pat Horgan, we were able to get Martell's Top 10 List of favorite monster movies of all time – mostly comedies – and only one of them features some heavy scary riffs!

Website: www.rockersusa.com/vincemartell/main_right.htm.

Vince Martell's Mostly Monstrous TERRORble Top 10 List

Abbott & Costello Meet Frankenstein (1948): The classic, it doesn't get any better than this! Frankenstein, The Wolf Man & Dracula!

Abbott & Costello Meet The Mummy (1955): I always liked the Mummy!

Abbott & Costello Meet Dr. Jekyll & Mr. Hyde (1953): Boris Karloff was in this one, right? Love his movies.

Abbott & Costello Meet The Invisible Man (1951): I know, I know…I just like Abbott & Costello…and the Invisible Man…he was a boxer in this one, I think.

Scared Stiff (1953): My other favorites, Martin & Lewis…I think it was a remake of another one I like – **Ghost Breakers** with Bob Hope.

Bela Lugosi Meets a Brooklyn Gorilla (1952): Bela meets two guys who look like Martin & Lewis…good fun.

Dracula (1931): The greatest Dracula, Bela Lugosi.

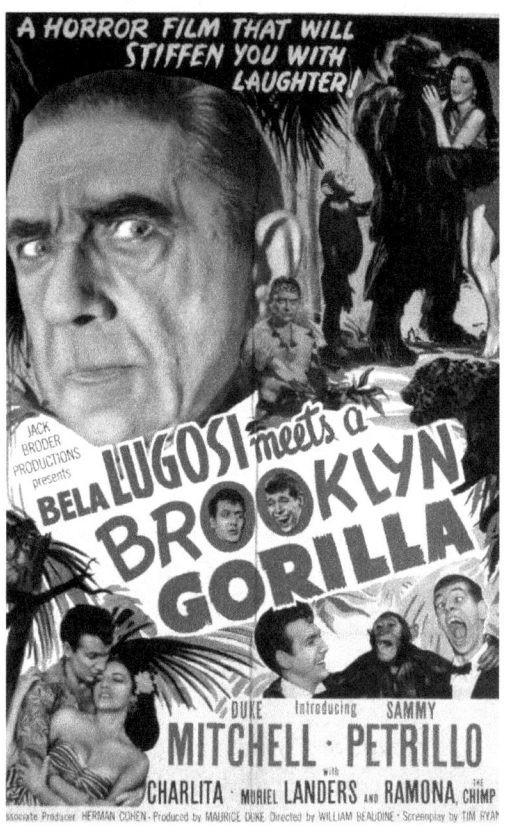

Frankenstein (1931): Boris Karloff, scary and sad as the monster.

The Wolf Man (1941): This might be my favorite. Lon Chaney Jr. as the Wolf Man, with Bela and Claude Rains, too…love it.

The Night Of The Living Dead (1968): In New York, when they first showed it on TV, they had in color on the bottom of the screen: "It's only a movie, it's only a movie"…scared a lot of people then…me, too!

ANTHONY MASI

Anthony Masi has made a huge impact on horror. He is the owner of MasiMedia and has written, directed, and produced content for Starz, the CW Network, CBS Studios, Anchor Bay Entertainment, Lionsgate, FEARnet, National Cinemedia, Shout! Factory, and Miramax. He is the producer of the horror genre's most successful epic cinematic television, DVD, and Blu-ray retrospectives, including "Halloween: 25 Years of Terror," "His Name Was Jason: 30 Years of Friday the 13th," and "Still Screaming: The Ultimate Scary Movie Retrospective."

Masi also produced and directed the 2014 television countdown "The 50 Best Horror Movies You've Never Seen," co-produced the horror film **Bread Crumbs**, wrote and directed the theatrically-released **Halloween: The Shape of Horror**, and was an interviewee in A&E's "Halloween: The Inside Story," alongside the likes of Jamie Lee Curtis and John Carpenter. In 2018, Anthony developed "The Black Rose Anthology" for the CW Network (CBS Studios) with Drew Barrymore's company, Flower Films.

Viewers of "Penn & Teller Fool Us" may recognize Masi, who performed his original magic under the name Anthony Asimov, a nod to sci-fi writer Isaac Asimov.

Website: www.MasiMedia.net

Anthony Masi's Favorite Top 10 TERRORble Moments in Creepy Kid Movies

Joshua (2007): The last few seconds of this fantastic movie directed by George Ratliff are subtle and explosive at the same time. You have a kid (played brilliantly by Jacob Kogan) sitting at a piano playing an eerie melody and singing along, and somewhere at the very end you come to the realization that something really horrific is going on. The thought creeps up on you, and then uncomfortably settles all around you like a chilling fog in the middle of nowhere. Up until this point, Joshua has been accused of doing some awful things in this movie, yet we really never see him do them so we wonder: is he guilty, or is it all in our minds? And what, if anything, has he been up to? The ending is one you won't forget, and for a film that didn't get a lot of attention, boy did those few seconds leave a huge impact.

Orphan (2009): When I saw this movie in theaters, I literally screamed at the ending and couldn't believe they had me! Esther is a kid that the movie poster warns us about way before we've even entered the theater. The tagline says, "There's something wrong with Esther." Well, with a tagline like that you'd better hope you don't figure out the twist ending in the first five minutes. Trust me... you won't! The twist in **Orphan** is as delicious as all of your favorite movie snacks, and then some. You know that feeling in **The Sixth Sense**, when the reveal happens and then suddenly in retrospect it changes the entire movie you THINK you've been watching into something else? Yeah, that's what happens here. And man is it fun! Esther is one mean little girl and she has a very dark secret.

Let the Right One In (2008): This Swedish (subtitled) film directed by Tomas Alfredson is outstanding in every way. Cinematically, it's gorgeous. The romantic story is beautiful and sad. It stars two child actors that wrap you around their fingers. And it's about vampires! What the movie does best is spin the familiar cinematic tropes about vampires in a devilishly different way. There is a scene at the end of the movie at a public pool that is one long take. The camera places you underwater with one of the actors, and "things" happen in the water in the background that will terrify and greatly satisfy you at the same time. This grim fairy tale won several major awards, don't miss it.

The Good Son (1993): Macaulay Culkin and Elijah Wood shine in this psychological thriller about a true child psychopath. Culkin's performance as the disturbed adolescent is excellent, but Wood plays off him with such great chemistry that it's difficult for me to think of this movie without thinking about both of them being equally important to the brilliance of the film. My favorite moment of the movie is its oh-so-talked-about-for-days controversial ending. I won't tip it here because I want you to see it! But it's one of those endings where you put yourself in the shoes of the person in the movie and wonder what YOU would do. And this one plays with your mind!

The Devil Within Her (1975): I could write volumes about this campy movie that's "so bad it's good!" Originally titled **I Don't Want To Be Born**, and starring Joan Collins (and Donald Pleasence!), this gem about a woman giving birth to the devil's spawn simply has to be on your viewing list. The weirdest shots in the movie are when the director is filming the baby in his carriage and its head momentarily gets replaced by a dwarf human's head in sporadic camera cuts, and it's so bizarre that you can't stop watching. And it happens a lot! This little baby does a lot of damage, but it's the amateurish directing and over-the-top acting that take center stage in this film that the critics at the British Horror Films website said: "There are some films that just defy description. **I Don't Want to Be Born** ranks very highly among them. The film is ... an out-and-out classic. And it was apparently made completely straight-faced. Quite how unbelievable that statement is can only be appreciated when the film is watched."

The Omen (1976): Director Richard Donner's film about yet another antichrist baby was executed far better than **The Devil Within Her**, and to this day remains one of the most stylish, unnerving, crazy horror films ever made. The Academy Award-winning score by Jerry Goldsmith is downright bone-chilling, and the ways people die in this movie make **Final Destination** look mild by comparison. In one kill, a huge sheet of glass slides off of a truck bed and decapitates someone in the street in broad daylight. The scene is so intense and well executed you'll never shake it from your mind, and you'll wonder if you'll ever have the courage to watch it again! Gregory Peck and Lee Remick bring their A-games, and little Damien (played by Harvey Stephens) was perfectly cast as the devilish toddler.

Them (2006): Directed by David Moreau and Xavier Palud, **Them** is a stylized and French-Romanian horror film that claims to be "based on real events," and it serves up a scary good time as soon as it opens with a mom and her daughter crashing their car in the middle of nowhere late at night. This is a horror movie so we know something bad is going to happen, and the scene is timed and executed so well that you'll find yourself screaming for mercy only ten minutes into the film. Trust me, it's a sign of good things to come because as the plot unfolds, the assailants aren't your run-of-the-mill hockey-mask-wearing weirdos with machetes. The story line offers something more intelligent, and gets you thinking about what evil is, and how it's harnessed by unexpected types of people.

The Strangers: Prey at Night (2018): With a storyline similar to **Them**, this film written by Bryan Bertino and Ben Ketai focuses on a single family facing the worst night of their lives at the hands of young assailants with a dread and hopelessness that will wrap around you like barbed wires. It's not easy to watch the film because your soul will be crushed when characters you love are forced to fight for their lives and lose in horrifically gruesome and sad ways. Wes Craven once said, "Horror movies don't create fear, they release it," and he was right. This film will bring you down, but it has an upside… when it's over you'll be glad you're alive, and you'll remember that nightmares in the form of movies are just chuckling phantoms that momentarily toy with your psyche and nothing more. Unlike the characters in the movie, you'll survive this dark and disturbed hell night and face another beautiful sunny day.

Grace (2009): Reports of fainting men during the screenings at the Sundance Film Festival were my introduction to Paul Solet's film about a blood-thirsty baby. Solet takes us into a dark and icky world of new motherhood, where the responsibilities of being a mother are sometimes stretched to unfathomable limits. This isn't a movie like **It's Alive** where the baby has fangs and claws, instead the baby's power comes from its ability to influence her mother into feeding her what she craves: the fresh blood of strangers. The poster shows a baby bottle partially filled with blood with a fly sitting on the nipple on top. Just looking at that image should give you an idea of the grimy style in which the movie is presented. You'll be nauseous, but you'll understand Grace. And it will be a beautiful thing.

Village of the Damned (1960): This is one trippy, inspired, over-the-top-but-played-straight sci-fi movie with a slew of creepy kids to fear. When the inhabitants of a quaint English village go unconscious for 24 hours, they awaken to realize that all of the women of child-bearing age are found to be pregnant. And when the kids are born, they wield killer psychic tendencies! If that doesn't sound like fun to you, you're dead inside! This film is sixty years old and still holds up tremendously well, and the images of these blonde littles kids with glowing hypnotic eyes will haunt you forever.

CHUCK MCCANN

Chuck McCann starred on live children's television programming in the New York market. You wouldn't think there are many things scarier than that! But many of his most memorable frights date back to his childhood films and radio years. He broke through in show business as a kids' television show host before working as a puppeteer, nightclub comic, movie actor, voice-over performer, and celebrity impersonator.

Fans of Laurel and Hardy know that Chuck did a perfect imitation of comedy legend Oliver Hardy. Along with actor Orson Bean, McCann founded Sons of the Desert, the international Laurel and Hardy fan club.

McCann created the voice of Sonny the Cuckoo Bird for General Mills' Cocoa Puffs TV commercials: "I'm cuckoo for Cocoa Puffs!" was all his!

Chuck McCann's film résumé includes **Play It As It Lays** (1972), **Herbie Rides Again** (1974), **Linda Lovelace for President** (1975), **Silent Movie** (1976), **Foul Play** (1978), **C.H.O.M.P.S.** (1979), **Ladybugs** (1992), **Storyville** (1992), **Robin Hood: Men in Tights** (1993), and **Dracula: Dead and Loving It** (1995). Yes, a Dracula movie under his belt.

In 1975, McCann starred in a wacky sci-fi comedy, teaming with Bob ("Gilligan's Island") Denver for the CBS family sitcom "Far Out Space Nuts." Along with Earl Doud and Sid and Marty Krofft, McCann created the slapstick series about two bumbling maintenance workers who inadvertently get launched into space.

Published in 2012, Chuck McCann's *Let's Have Fun Scrapbook* was filled with fun stories, memories, original photos, and a true lesson in the history of television. Chuck McCann, who brought countless laughs and joy to millions of kids, young and old, passed away in 2018.

Chuck McCann's TERRORble Top 10 List

Number 1 scariest: the original **The Thing (From Another World!)** (1951). Only my laundry man knew how frightened I was after I saw that one.

The 2 spot would have to go to Frankie (**Frankenstein,** 1931)...and Karloff! I had the pleasure of meeting him at N.B.C. What a thrill. He was bow-legged and much shorter than I thought.

For the 3 spot, I would have to say **Psycho** (1960). The set-up was sheer genius.

Lon Chaney Sr. in **The Phantom of the Opera** (1925) and **Hunchback** (1939) were two classics for the 4th and 5th spots.

For 6th spot – **The Beast with Five Fingers** (1946) frightened me as a kid. I always went slowly to the piano after seeing that.

The 7th spot – **The Wolf Man** (1941). It was always a hoot. I think Maria Ouspenskaya died smoking in bed. They called her the Grand Dutchess of horror films. And Jr. was a credit to Dad.

For the 8th spot, Karloff again as **The Mummy** (1932). But it wasn't films that scared me as much when I was a kid – it was the theater of the mind: RADIO. Remember your mother wouldn't let you go see **Frankenstein** but she would let you sit in the living room with the radio on and the lights down low listening to the "Quiet, Please" episode "The Thing on the Fourble Board" ("Quiet, Please" was a radio show, and this was Episode #60. It aired August 8, 1948.). I defy you to keep dry underwear listening to that or "Suspense" or "The Hitch-Hiker" or "Escape" or "Three Skeleton Key," a story about men trapped in a lighthouse surrounded by millions of hungry rats trying to find their way inside. RADIO was THEATER OF THE MIND. Your imagination could always cast the face and build the sets better than any Hollywood production could. Do you want to really get scared? Listen to some of those old shows and turn out the lights. I dare you.

But back to the matter at hand. Number 9 – **The Uninvited** (1944) with Ray Milland.

I enjoyed **The Cat and the Canary** (1939) as a kid. Both funny and scary. I would place that around 10.

Well, I guess that does it from this end. But remember, the mind is a tricky thing. It all depends at what time and circumstance that we are transported to our fears. You know it's fun to be safely frightened.

ANGIE MCARTNEY

Here is a name that is known worldwide, not just by Beatles fans. No, it's not Paul McCartney or his son James or any of his daughters (although a list from Stella McCartney may have proved to be quite *stylish*!). And no, it's not even Jesse McCartney. It's Angie McCartney, who was the wife of Paul McCartney's father, Jim.

Angela Lucia McCartney, born in Liverpool in 1929, was married to Paul McCartney's dad from 1964 to 1976.

She is an international entrepreneur based in California, but she's also a true appreciator of monster movies and a huge Vincent Price fan. Additionally, she was a Production Assistant on the Fox set of the Oscar-nominated **Aliens 3** (remember the film's tagline: "In 1979, we discovered in space no one can hear you scream. In 1992, we will discover, on Earth, EVERYONE can hear you scream.").

Your Mother Should Know: With Interruptions from Daughter Ruth is Angie McCartney's collection of stories about her life (and her daughter Ruth's life) as Paul McCartney's stepmother. The book includes stories and musings that are funny, romantic, sad, positive, inspirational, wise, witty, and simply fascinating. Now in her 90s, Angie takes you from her beginnings in Liverpool during World War II through her romance with Paul's father Jim in the midst of Beatlemania to life after The Beatles in Australia, Germany, Nashville, and Los Angeles.

Busier than most people a fraction of her age, Angie is the founder and head honcho of an organic tea company, with such flavors as 50 Shades of Earl Grey (if you're feeling naughtea), Strawberry Green Fields (forever), Blue Jay Blueberry (a black tea with organic blueberries), Liverpool Red (a Rooibos with Herbs de Provence – if South Africa and Southern France had a baby this would be it!), Golden Slumbers (a green tea with a cheeky little toasted puffy rice), Rockstar Rescue (a throat-soothing, aftershow tea), and recently they've expanded their inventory with bold new flavors: Penny Lane Peppermint, Abbey Road Apple, Maharishi Peach, and MopTop Maple.

Website: www.mrsmccartneysteas.com.

Angie McCartney's TERRORble
Top List of Favorite Fright Flicks

Stephen King's **The Shining** (1980): Jack Nicholson's performance still haunts me.

The Lost Boys (1987): I still like to watch this and follow through on the careers of the boys and Dianne Wiest. A classic.

The Omen (1976): I prefer the 1976 version to the more recent one.

M with Peter Lorre (1931): This Fritz Lang-directed movie still holds its spell with the amazingly creepy Peter Lorre holding viewers spellbound. Speaking of **Spellbound**, we need to include a Hitchcock classic…

Alfred Hitchcock's **The Birds** (1963): Tippi Hedren's performance was brilliant, and she is still as beautiful today. She runs Shambala, a wildlife preserve in Acton, California.

Rosemary's Baby (1968): Polanski's direction of this movie showed all aspects of horror, romance, and mystery.

Alien (all versions, 1979-2017): I worked as a Production Assistant on the third installment of the "Alien" series, which was the only one I watched at the rushes and the premiere. Shooting even started without a finished script. Upon completion, the studio dismantled and reworked it without director David Fincher's consent.

The Exorcist (1973): This great movie, based on an actual exorcism of a 14-year-old boy in 1949, garnered 10 Academy Award nominations. It had the tremendous cast of Ellen Burstyn, Max von Sydow, Lee J. Cobb, and of course, Linda Blair as the demonically-inhabited girl. An interesting note is that two cast members, Reverend O'Malley and Reverend Bermingham, played themselves.

Psycho (1960): I saw this with my first husband, Eddie Williams, on my first outing after the birth of my daughter Ruth. That night, after we had gone to bed, we heard screaming and someone pounding on our front door. Eddie ran downstairs and opened the door to a distraught young girl who had been attacked by a man behind our house. We brought her in and rang for the police, who took over. It was a night when we slept with all the lights on!

The Raven (1963): In addition to the classic Vincent Price movie, I have listened with great pleasure to James Earl Jones and Christopher Walken's spoken versions.

And all the other Vincent Price Movies!

ELAINE MCFARLANE
The Spanky List

Legendary folk/ rock singer Elaine "Spanky" McFarlane sang lead as the front-person in the '60s band Spanky & Our Gang, with such classic hits as "Sunday Will Never Be The Same," "Give a Damn," "Sunday Morning," and "I'd Like To Get To Know You."

Not to be confused with the Spanky and Our Gang comedies that became the Little Rascals (again, not the Young Rascals music group – sheesh, this could get confusing if you're not a pop culture fan), the folk-rock group's 1968 song "Give a Damn" was banned in several states because the word 'damn' was considered profanity. But more likely, the song was censored because it was a commentary on racial equality. It was also performed live on an episode of "The Smothers Brothers Comedy Hour," resulting in CBS' Standards and Practices division receiving numerous complaints about the song's title being used during 'family viewing hours.' One such complaint reportedly came from Richard Nixon (Tom Smothers, "Geraldo" interview, 1987). Ironically, "Give A Damn" would become John Lindsay's campaign song during his successful run for Mayor of New York.

After Mama Cass Elliot passed, Spanky McFarlane toured in her place with a revamped version of The Mamas & The Papas.

In 2010, Spanky was one of the Special Guests of Honor at "Rock Con:

Photo of Spanky McFarlane at the 2009 BEATexpo Beatles Convention in Stamford, Connecticut, produced by Charles F. Rosenay!!! ("Cryptmaster Chucky").

Weekend of 100 Rock Stars," where she was presented with a "Rock Con" "Icon" Award.

McFarlane has a beautiful soul and personality to go along with her lovely voice. Here is what Spanky wrote along with her choices: "Okay – here's my list, mostly classic 'horror' – not the slasher, Chucky, Saw, Friday the 13th, or Jason movies! Then again, no Christopher Lee either."

Spanky's TERRORble Top 10 List of Favorite Monster Movies

Invasion of the Body Snatchers (1956): Watch out for those alien pods! (I wasn't sure whether to choose this one or **The Day of the Triffids**.)

The Thing (From Another World!) (original from 1951): James Arness, the frozen north, and things that go bump in the night!

Creature from the Black Lagoon (1954): Is this the product of evolution? A monster movie from early in my life.

The Haunting (1963): Psychological terror always trumps slasher movies!

Kwaidan (1964, Japanese): Four classic Japanese ghost stories with a haunting soundtrack by classical composer Toru Takemitsu. What is real and what is imagined?

Rosemary's Baby (1968): Terrifying! Be careful whom you marry, ladies!

Psycho (1960): Who doesn't lock their bathroom door when showering after watching this classic Hitchcock film?

House of Wax (original from 1953, 3-D): A throwback to my youth. Vincent Price at his scariest (although I was also scared by **Abbott & Costello Meet Frankenstein**)!

The Birds (1963): Recently, I was in San Jose when a flock of crows suddenly started cawing and flying in crazy patterns, chasing a small black remote-controlled plane – I had to run for cover!

Carrie (1976): Stephen King and Brian De Palma combine a psychotic mother and bullying classmates to create gore and terror.

METAL PISTOL

Metal Pistol is a guitar-driven hard rock/ metal band with scorching guitars from Steven Stanley, female lead vocals/ keys by Sunny Lee and bassist Kelsey Kit, plus drums with strong pop-styled hooks. The band is based out of New York City/ Boston. Their debut album *Magnum Force* contains all original material and received strong airplay from internet radio, and Metal Pistol's fan base has been growing quickly. Craig Fenton, Jefferson Airplane's biographer, described Sunny Lee's vocals as sounding like "a cross between Pat Benatar and Cherie Currie (the Runaways) with plenty of individuality and clarity."

In the past, the band opened for the national act Otherwise in Syracuse, New York and also Scorpion Child at Webster Hall in New York City. Other gigs included The Bowery Electric in New York City and Copperfield's and the Cantab Lounge in Boston. Metal Pistol collaborated with Grammy-winning producer Tom Hambridge on their following album, mixed and mastered at Abbey Road Studios in London. The band released, as a single and music video, "Destruction in Action," which was followed by "Buried Alive." More recently, they've been touring extensively, playing colleges and universities.

A unique feature about the band is that they have a well-choreographed avant garde live stage act with model/ bassist Kelsey Kit. What they don't have is reasons for their choices, but it's a fine list nonetheless.

Thanks to Massachusetts Media Mogul Mastermind Joe Viglione.

Follow the band here: www.facebook.com/MetalPistol/.

Metal Pistol's TERRORble Top 10 List

Frankenstein (1931, with Boris Karloff)

The Blob (1958, original)

The Texas Chainsaw Massacre (1974, original)

Corridors of Blood (1958, also with Boris Karloff)

They Live (1988)

The Bride of Frankenstein (1935)

The Mummy (1932)

The Wolf Man (1941)

Dracula (1931, with Bela Lugosi)

The Exorcist (1973)

TED V. MIKEL
The Astro-Zombies

If you're fond of films such as **The Corpse Grinders** and **Blood Orgy of the She-Devils**, you may already be a fan of producer Ted V. Mikels. More likely, you never heard of them or him, but that's OK, most haven't.

The independent cult filmmaker, born Theodore Vincent Mikacevich in 1929, kicked off his career with 1955's **Snow Monsters**, but made his mark producing such titles as 1963's **Strike Me Deadly**, 1969's **The Astro-Zombies**, and 1973's **Children Shouldn't Play With Dead Things**. He had been responsible for over 70 films, and kept going until he passed in 2016.

Ted was a regular guest at horror conventions, where he was usually surrounded by a bevy of beautiful B-movie starlets.

When we asked him for his list of 10 favorite horror films or film-makers, Mikels couldn't come up with a list, writing "Charles: I love them ALL, and praises to the folks who made them." So instead, we asked Ted for a list of his own personal favorite films that he was involved in.

Ted V. Mikels' TERRORble Top 10 List of Ted V. Mikels Movies

The Cauldron: Baptism of Blood (2004)

Blood Orgy of the She-Devils (1973)

Strike Me Deadly (1963)

The Corpse Grinders (1971)

The Doll Squad (1973)

Mission: Killfast (1991)

Dimension in Fear (1998)

Heart of a Boy (2006)

Demon Haunt (2009)

Astro-Zombies M3: Cloned (2010)

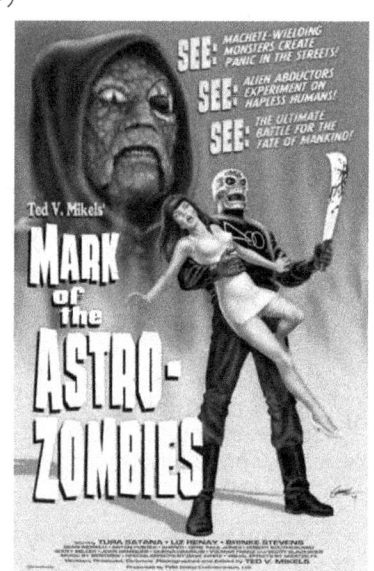

BILL MOSELEY
Chop Top's Top 10 Horror Scenes

He won our hearts (and probably cut a few out) as "Chop Top" in 1986's **The Texas Chainsaw Massacre 2**. Who would believe that one of our favorite horror stars, Bill Moseley, probably best known for his roles in Rob Zombie's **Halloween 2**, **House of 1000 Corpses**, **The Devil's Rejects**, and **3 From Hell**, is a Yale graduate?!

Other key roles among his 100+ credits include his take of Johnnie in Tom Savini's remake of **Night of The Living Dead**, where he got to echo that epic line "They're coming to get you, Barbara!"

Moseley, a musician in rock bands on the side, gets to do some singing as Luigi Largo in **Repo! The Genetic Opera**. He also starred along with Corbin Bernsen in the Bernsen-directed film **Dead Air**, which got a great deal of positive genre reviews but was hardly seen. In the film, an outbreak causes virus-crazed maniacs to run rampant in the streets. Hmmm – a virus outbreak? Could never happen!

A terrific guest at conventions, Bill Moseley is equally great at Top 10 Lists. He's not shy about including some key scenes he appeared in, and you gotta love any well thought-out list that mentions both **Attack of The Giant Leeches** and **Beast from Haunted Cave**.

Bill Moseley's TERRORble Top 10 List

The scene in **The Texas Chainsaw Massacre** (1968) when the girl in shorty-shorts stumbles into the "living" room full of chicken feathers and bone furniture and sees a large white chicken clucking in a small canary cage. When she tries to escape, Leatherface grabs her around the waist, carries her into the kitchen, and hangs her on a meat hook!

The scene in **House of 1000 Corpses** (2003) when Grampa (Dennis Fimple) and I are arguing while we're watching an episode of "The Munsters" and I'm throwing knives at Chris Hardwick. Big yuck yuck value for me!

In **The Texas Chainsaw Massacre 2** (1986), the radio station scene when DJ Stretch (Caroline Williams) meets my character, Chop Top, for the first time. She takes me on a very brief "tour" of the lobby, then tries to get rid of me. But I still want to hear the tape-recording of the chainsaw mayhem Bubba and I visited on some yuppies and their car the night before, so I back up Stretch in front of the record vault where Bubba springs out with his big ol' saw!

The scene in **The Innocents** (1961) where Deborah Kerr sees a ghost woman sitting on the water in the estate lily pond. Just a spooky, haunting image that has stayed with me all these years.

The grand finale of **Jaws** (1975) when Bruce the shark eats Robert Shaw with big, bloody chomps!

The spooky scene in **Carnival of Souls** (1962) where Candace Hilligoss dances with ghosts in the old Saltair Pavilion on the Great Salt Lake. Spooky scene, spooky organ/ calliope music.

The Kahiki Palms Motel scene in **The Devil's Rejects** (2005) where poor Kate Norby runs for her life wearing her dead husband's skinned face. She makes it all the way to the highway, only to be smacked down by a high-balling semi!

The ending of the original **Night of the Living Dead** (1968) where Ben, who has survived a night-long onslaught of zombies and crazy humans, is mistaken (?) for a zombie and shot between the eyes by a redneck posse. Director George Romero uses black and white stills to show the rednecks meat-hooking Ben's dead body and tossing it on a burn pile!

Any scene where we were told to put on our 3-D glasses during the original **13 Ghosts** (1960)! Dr. Zorba, I can still hear your ghastly breathing!

Toss-up between **Attack of The Giant Leeches** (1959) and **Beast from Haunted Cave** (1959), where captive humans are being sucked/ drained of blood by giant leeches and a giant spider. The actors really sold it, sobbing through weak protests as the filthy creatures had their way.

RICK MULLEN
The Zanti Misfits

What are Zanti Misfits? If you're a fan of "The Outer Limits," you already know the answer to this. If you're bassist Rick Mullen, it's one of your Top 10 choices.

Rick Mullen of Dutchess County, New York spent a decade playing bass guitar with Commander Cody (& the Lost Planet Airmen), best known for their huge hit "Hot Rod Lincoln." If you grew up on AM radio in the '70s, you'll never forget the line, "My Pappy said son you're gonna drive me to drinkin'/ if you don't stop drivin' that hot rod Lincoln." Released in 1971, this one-hit wonder is the most recognized version, even though it was recorded several times before. It was also the most successful version of "Hot Rod Lincoln," reaching #9 on the *Billboard* Hot 100 and #7 in Canada.

Mullen has done world tours with Don McLean and Van Morrison, concerts with Savoy Brown, Vince Martell (Vanilla Fudge), Benny Mardones, and many others. He brings his distinct style to any genre, effortlessly switching from electric 2 (yes, he made a 2 string bass), 4, 5 fretted/ fretless to acoustic/ electric upright bass. He was also the guitar tech for Richie Scarlet and The Lumineers.

In 2010, Rick Mullen was one of the many great special guest artists at New Jersey's "Rock Con: Weekend of 100 Rock Stars," held in the Meadowlands.

Rick – one of your choices was just so cool we had to include an image of it – yes, a Zanti Misfit!

Rick Mullen's TERRORble Top 10 List of Monster Movies (+ 1 Classic TV Show)

Vampyr (1932): Scared the crap out of me!

The Blob (1958): Steve McQueen!

Godzilla (1954): Love it, great for when I need to go to sleep.

Carnival of Souls (1962): 'Nuff said.

The Outer Limits (episode "The Zanti Misfits," 1963): "The Zanti Misfits" is an episode of the original "The Outer Limits" television show. It first aired on 12/30/63 during the show's first season.

The Atomic Submarine (1959): With veteran character actor Arthur Franz.

I Eat Your Skin (1971): Gotta love it for the title alone.

The City of the Dead (AKA **Horror Hotel**) (1960): Classic British horror with Christopher Lee.

Mark of the Vampire (1935): Classic American horror with Bela Lugosi.

Dracula (1931): Bela!

BILL MUMY

So many of us grew up with Bill Mumy. He made his mark early on as a child actor in "The Twilight Zone" (don't get that boy pissed!) and "Lost in Space" (which really turned into the Will Robinson/ Dr. Smith show). In the '90s, he returned to sci-fi in the show "Babylon 5."

We listened to his novelty records on Dr. Demento when Mumy was one-half of Barnes & Barnes ("Fish Heads") and we played them when we were in college radio, but that's just one side of his musical world – Bill is truly an accomplished musician who plays many instruments. He has recorded/ written songs with America, he's toured with Shaun Cassidy, and he even played in Rick Springfield's band in the film **Hard to Hold**.

Charles William Mumy Jr. (his full name), now in his 70s (!), is still recording, still acting, and also very busy doing voice-overs. As if this weren't all enough, he also authored many comic books.

A fan favorite for years, Mumy was quick to come up with a list of his favorite movies, and he didn't even include any of his own credits.

Website: www.billmumy.com.

Bill Mumy's TERRORble Top 10 Fear & Fantasy Films

The Day the Earth Stood Still (1951): The message still rings true. I was lucky enough to work with Michael Rennie on "Lost in Space" and Billy Gray was the best young actor ever, in my opinion. I'm happy to say he's a pal. My very fave sci-fi film of all time. Gort is so clean and simple yet full of power and strength and nobility.

Frankenstein (1931): The original. My grandfather, Harry Gould, was Boris Karloff's agent. Got him the Frankenstein gig. How cool is that?

Young Frankenstein (1974): Never ceases to crack me up. Cloris Leachman is too good. Teri Garr is turbo hot. Love the black and white. My favorite Mel Brooks project.

Godzilla (1954): The original Japanese version is a very strong anti-war, anti-nuclear statement. Bringing in Raymond Burr to make it work in America was a real good idea. The sound Godzilla makes is still bone-chilling. What a great tone! I've tried and failed several times to get a Les Paul electric guitar to sound like that on Barnes & Barnes albums.

King Kong (1933): An almost perfect film. The stop-motion animation is beyond brilliant. Kong resonates with soul. Glorious in defeat.

Dracula (1931): Why not? Bela Lugosi received cinema immortality with this one film. Much better than **Bela Lugosi Meets A Brooklyn Gorilla**. (Editor's note: Don't dare say that to Eddie Deezen!)

The Wolf Man (1941): Lon Chaney Jr. was perfect. You feel so sad for this guy who rips throats apart.

The Exorcist (1973): Scared the shit out of me for months, even after Linda Blair became a pal. Almost too real for me. Ellen Burstyn is great. Max von Sydow...wow. Turbo intense. Don't f— around with Ouija boards, kids!

Alien (1979): Who's gonna argue about it? Veronica Cartwright's so intense in this. Nasty-ass monster.

Freaks (1932, Todd Browning): "Gooble Gobble Gooble Gobble one of us...one of us..." Oh man...Sent me to the cornfield.

CHRISTIAN NESMITH

When we asked Christian Nesmith for his Top 10 List, we didn't even know that he contributed music to **The Hills Have Eyes**. When we asked him for his Top 10 List, a great list from him came through immediately!

Raised in a musical family, Christian was given the opportunity to learn and develop his playing from the moment he was able to reach the piano. A composer, guitarist, producer, and engineer, Christian has produced many independent artists and has placed songs in such films as **Blades of Glory**, **The Hills Have Eyes**, and **Lionheart**. He has toured with such artists as Air Supply, The Bangles' Debbie Peterson, and his girlfriend Circe Link.

The son of Mike Nesmith of The Monkees, Christian tours with The Monkees featuring his dad and Micky Dolenz, and continues to perform with Circe Link.

"Hope this is what you're looking for. Peace."

Website: www.christiannesmith.com.

Christian Nesmith's TERRORble Top 10 List

Alien (1979): **Alien** sits very securely in my #1 spot. Ridley Scott absolutely nailed this on all counts – direction, art direction, detail, creepiness, and suspense. And the look on Veronica Cartwright's face throughout the whole movie still gets to me.

The Exorcist (1973): If **The Exorcist** doesn't scare you, or at least get under your skin, you're probably dead.

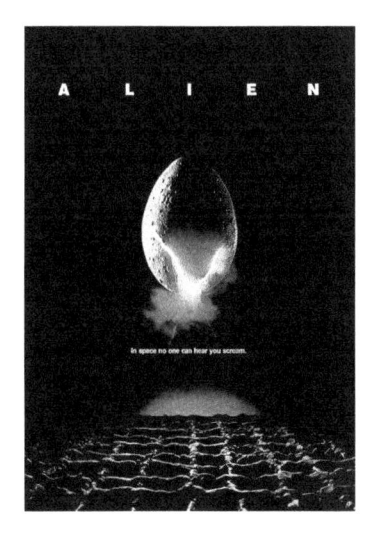

Carrie (1976): **Carrie** is amazing because of Brian De Palma's patience in building the suspense. And his use of split screen in the dance scene, while corny, is nevertheless effective. Not to mention Sissy's eyes when De Palma does the triple fast-cut/ zoom-in when John Travolta and Nancy Allen crash. Creeeeeeepy!

Jaws (1975): Jaws. 'Nuff said.

Aliens (1986)

Jacob's Ladder (1990)

The Tenant (1976)

Event Horizon (1997)

Evil Dead II (1987)

Hardware (1990)

Other than **Aliens**, the rest are not necessarily in order. **Aliens** has a special place in my heart. It was between that or **The Terminator** because both have the never-ending endings that keep you on the edge.

Jacob's Ladder, **The Tenant**, and **Event Horizon** messed with my head pretty bad, with the latter being a particular visual brain stain.

Evil Dead 2 must be on everyone's list. It is mandatory.

Lastly, **Hardware** is a guilty pleasure for me though I'll admit I first saw it in a chemically-altered mental state, very similar to that of the character Shades in the movie. "My heart feels like an alligator." So sue me.

ROBB ORTEL

Robb Ortel is an American artist and TV personality best known for his work as the in-house airbrush artist on the Discovery Channel's reality television show "American Chopper." His airbrushed artwork can be seen on hundreds of motorcycles all over the globe.

In 2011, Robb launched the "Robb Ortel" brand, creating Rott'n'Wear, a horror-themed clothing line, using iconic imagery in zombified form.

In 2015, Robb created a concept for a reality show to bring unknown "extreme" type art into the light. His show, "Art Attack," is an action-packed travelogue television series that features some of the most shocking, awe-inspiring, and physically demanding art forms in the world.

Each episode finds host Ortel traveling to two destinations to apprentice under two extraordinary artists.

Some of the amazing art on the cover of this book is by none other than Robb Ortel! Here is his incredible painting of Vincent Price.

Websites:
www.artattacktv.com/tv-show-1
facebook.com/ArtAttackTV
facebook.com/RobbOrtel

Robb Ortel's Top 10 (OK, 14) TERRORble List of His Favorite Scary Movies

The original **Halloween** (1978): It was the scariest movie I saw at the time it came out. I remember seeing it one night on HBO when I was a kid. Halfway through it, my mother told me and my brothers that the garbage had to be taken to the end of the driveway. I was the last one out the door and my older brothers were waiting outside to scare the crap out of me! Which they did!

Phantasm (1979): While watching this movie late one night with my brother, when I was about 10 or 11, we had to use the bathroom. We both went together and forgot to put the toilet seat back down. We continued watching and after about 10 minutes, the seat slammed down. We both jumped out of our seats and screamed. I think the Tall Man is one of the scariest characters in the film!

Salem's Lot (1979): I haven't seen the movie in years but I still have the image of the vampire crawling out of the basement room, up behind the unsuspecting guy. That scene is tattooed on my brain!

The Blair Witch Project (1999): Scariest movie I've seen in my adulthood. The way it was advertised and promoted, as footage found from a college film crew, made it all the scarier. I bought into the whole premise. Plus it was the first "first person" horror movie and it paved the way for a new style of filming.

Photo: Porcelain Money Studios

Paranormal Activity (2007): The movie was very well done. I actually like the entire franchise of movies.

Jeepers Creepers 1 and **2** (2001, 2003): Love these movies!

Nosferatu (1922): It's the all-time classic movie, crazy creepy. Everything about it is F**king creepy. Cinematic brilliance!!!

The original **Don't Be Afraid of the Dark** (1973): The one phrase "Sally, Sally, we want you…" sticks in my head.

Children Shouldn't Play With Dead Things (1972): I don't remember a whole lot about this movie except that it scared the living sh*t outta me!

Night of the Living Dead (1968): Another classic! First of its kind! Such a great movie I could watch over and over. George Romero is the sh*t!

The Descent (2005): Another one of my favorites as an adult. Those creatures were so badass and creepy as hell! The extra footage on the CD is hysterical! The creatures do a dance routine!

The Texas Chainsaw Massacre (1974): The original is crazy creepy. But I must admit I do love the remakes! All 150 of them!

Any Rob Zombie movie, especially **The Devil's Rejects** (2005). He picks very interesting people in his movies that are fascinating to see. Sid Haig is amazing to watch! I'd love to do a painting of him one day.

And of course…

"The Walking Dead" (series, 2010 -): My all-time favorite show on TV! I'm addicted to it.

BUTCH PATRICK
Eddie Munster

As a child actor, Butch Patrick played child werewolf Eddie Munster on the beloved monster comedy TV series "The Munsters." It was only on network television for two years, from 1964 to 1966, but Butch has remained a fan favorite for many years.

When "The Munsters" went off the air, Patrick's acting career didn't end. He guest-starred on numerous shows including "The Monkees," "I Dream of Jeannie," "Death Valley Days," "Gunsmoke," "Daniel Boone," "Adam-12," and "My Three Sons." He also had credits in such Disney films as **The One and Only**, **The Young Loner**, and **Way Down Cellar**. From 1971 to 1973, Patrick enjoyed a feature role on Sid and Marty Krofft's Saturday morning children's fantasy program "Lidsville."

Patrick recorded a few novelty records, including 1983's "Whatever Happened To Eddie?" with the flip side "Little Monsters," under the group name Eddie & the Monsters. His second single came 24 years later, "It's Only Halloween," a seasonal holiday tune released in 2007.

Patrick has remained in the genre field, continuing his popularity with fans who remember him fondly from "The Munsters." In 2002, Patrick co-hosted "Macabre Theater" with Natalie Popovich (AKA "Ivonna Cadaver"), a series that still airs on the Youtoo America Cable Network. He also made a cameo appearance in the 2005 retro-horror film **Frankenstein vs. the Creature from Blood Cove**, playing a man who had become a werewolf, speaking a line of dialogue in comical reference to "The Munsters."

He has made numerous convention appearances, including Comic Cons, horror shows, Halloween haunted attractions, Beatles conventions, and even Monkees conventions.

In 2008, Helen Darras wrote the biography *Eddie Munster AKA Butch Patrick* and in 2015, Patrick published his own *Munster Memories: A Mini Coffin Table Book*.

Butch Patrick was also a Special Guest of Honor on a past Dracula Tour vampire vacation to Transylvania (www.DracTours.com).

Thanks for the great list, Butch, but you left off all the films you were in.

Butch Patrick's TERRORble Top 10 List of Fave Fright Flicks

Psycho (1960)

Creature from the Black Lagoon (1954)

The Last House On The Left (1972)

The Shining (1980)

The Birds (1963)

Them! (1954)

Alien (1979)

The Texas Chainsaw Massacre (1974, the original)

Invasion of the Body Snatchers (1956, the original)

Frankenstein (1931, the original)

Butch Patrick alongside author Charles F. Rosenay!!! ("Cryptmaster Chucky") and his wife, Melissa Rosenay ("Cryptmastress Mel")

JON PROVOST
That Kid From "Lassie"

Jon Provost is a national treasure. The checked shirt and those jeans he wore for seven years as Timmy on "Lassie" hang in the Smithsonian next to Archie Bunker's chair. "Lassie" continues to air in 50 countries and Jon still receives letters and e-mails from fans of all ages around the world.

Provost was already a seasoned pro when he won the role of Timmy at age seven. During his career as a child actor and teen heartthrob, he worked with some of the biggest stars in Hollywood: Grace Kelly, Bing Crosby, Natalie Wood, Robert Redford, Rod Steiger, Anita Ekberg, Clint Eastwood, Kurt Russell, Kim Novak, Jack Benny, James Garner, and even Mr. Ed.

Throughout his career, Jon has received many awards and in 1994, he was honored with a star on the Hollywood Walk of Fame. He has earned a nationwide reputation as a philanthropist, giving his time to children's hospitals, animal shelters, and humane societies. For 25 years, he served on the Board of Governors for Canine Companions for Independence, which provides free service dogs to the handicapped. He is also an advocate for US military K-9 teams, recently signing 4,000 photos for war dog teams who served our nation in Afghanistan and Iraq.

Provost returned to television as Timmy all grown up in "The New Lassie" with Dee Wallace in 1990, and received a Genesis Award for Outstanding Television in a Family Series for a story he penned for the show focusing on the inhumane treatment of research animals.

Jon celebrated his 50th anniversary as Timmy with the release of his autobiography, *Timmy's In The Well*. He added the internet to his resume, directing and hosting short videos about dogs and cats for a Purina website. Recently, he shot a commercial for a large retail chain.

Of his many accomplishments, he is most proud of his children Ryan and Katie, and he is over the moon about his grandkids. Still a sought-after celebrity guest, Jon appears at fund-raisers, Comic Cons, celebrity signings, pet expos, and special events throughout the year.

Website: www.jonprovost.com.

Jon Provost's TERRORble Top 10 Monsters List

The Beast with Five Fingers (1946): The disembodied hand crawling around by itself trying to murder Peter Lorre and others in this creepy old mansion was a nightmare for me.

Pyscho (1960): I was terrified for months every time I took a shower.

The Bride of Frankenstein (1935): Elsa Lanchester totally freaked me out – that hair and her weird screeching. She scared the crap out of me.

Dracula (1931): "I vant to drink your blood." I still get chills. And when Bela Lugosi raised the corner of his cape, covered himself, turned into a bat, and flew away, it absolutely thrilled me.

The Phantom of the Opera (1925): The dark dungeon got to me…a place where no one could hear you scream. It was his domain and no one stood a chance against him if he got you down there.

2001: A Space Odyssey (1968): When Hal took over command of the space capsule and murdered the astronauts all while maintaining that soft, even tone…that movie is exactly why I will never get Alexa in my house.

The Exorcist (1973): I will never forget seeing it the first time: furniture flying across the floor to block the door was just the beginning. I was afraid the entire time: the head spinning, the horrible voice, Linda Blair's body floating above the bed. The Devil unleashing his power…and could this really happen? Somehow it wasn't out of the realm of possibility, which really made it so frightening.

Frankenstein (1931): The original with Boris Karloff is an amazing experience. It brought out such unexpected emotions in me. Here I thought I was going to see a monster movie. And yeah, he was scary and grotesque and he kills a kid, but I had such empathy for him! That had never happened to me before, a completely new experience. You understand why the villagers go after him, but you end up rooting for him to get away. I had the same experience in two other films:

The Hunchback of Notre Dame (1939): Charles Laughton, 1939. Spectacular sets. Maureen O'Hara as Esmerelda is beautiful. Quasimodo's ugliness frightened me but even as a child I knew that inside, he wasn't ugly at all. The flogging scene rips your heart out. He was cursed with these monstrous deformities and a love affair that was not going to end well…which is very similar in theme to my #1 Monster…

King Kong (1933): He's the king of them all for me…and not just because I knew him personally. He had everything: strength, power, this terrifying presence…and unrequited love. So much emotion showed in his face. It still holds up today. So, how did we meet? Free time at the studio was rare, but when I got it, I loved to explore. Desilu was the old RKO lot. I discovered where all the models and miniatures were stored. It was cool to see the planes and tanks and ships. I even found the plane used in **Back from Eternity**, which I shot at RKO in 1956. And then one day, I spotted him way up on a shelf in a back room. Kong. He was about 18" high and a little moth-eaten, but it didn't matter. If I ever wanted to impress a kid appearing on the show, I brought them to King Kong. It never failed.

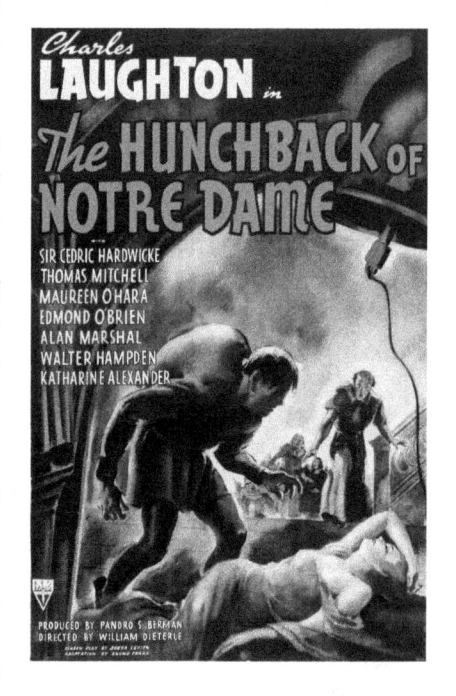

GARY PUCKETT

Gary Puckett and the Union Gap were one of the most successful musical groups of the 1960s. Literally a hit-making music machine, Puckett's unmistakable signature vocal garnered six consecutive gold records and Top 10 *Billboard* chart hits. Some of the best known were the following titles: "Young Girl," "Woman Woman," "Lady Willpower," "Over You," "This Girl Is a Woman Now," "Keep The Customer Satisfied," and "Don't Give In To Him."

Gary Puckett was much more than just a great voice. He has been a fan favorite for over five decades. He has never stopped touring and along the way, has played thousands of concerts, including a command performance for the President and Prince Charles at the White House.

Photo credit: Ron Elkman, USA Today

When asked to contribute to this book, Puckett wrote: "Here are some of my favorites. I grew up through the '50s so that's where I remember the films to be the scariest. There are many through the years since, some of which I will mention, but a child's mind is most impressionable. I was born in 1942."

Gary added, "I'm glad to be a part of this. Best of luck."

Website: www.garypuckettmusic.com.

Gary Puckett's TERRORble Top List of Favorite Scary Films

The Thing (From Another World!) (1951): Just scary for a nine-year-old.

The Day the Earth Stood Still (also 1951): I could just feel myself being melted by Klaatu Barada Nikto.

The War of the Worlds (1953): Orson Welles!

Them! (1954): The sound the giant ants made was excruciating!

Creature from the Black Lagoon (also 1954)

Invasion of the Body Snatchers (1956): Don't go to sleep!! Very creepy!

The Curse of Frankenstein (1957): Christopher Lee's other great portrayal back then.

The Blob, The Horror of Dracula, The Fly (1958): It was a very good year!

Psycho (1960): We saw this on my high school grad night out. We were all pretty frightened with this one.

A few later good ones for me...

The Exorcist (1973)

The Shining (1980)

Alien (1979)

The Texas Chainsaw Massacre (1974)

Carrie (1976)

Halloween (1978)

Jaws (1975)

GERI REISCHL
She Was Fake Jan, But She Met the Real Wolf Man

Geri Reischl is best known as a pop culture icon for being "Jan Brady" in "The Brady Bunch Variety Hour" TV series in the 1970s. Fans lovingly call her "Fake Jan." There is even her very own 'holiday' that is celebrated all over the world, called "Fake Jan Day," celebrated every year on Jan. 2nd with a Cheese Ball ("Fake Jan's" favorite food).

Reischl is also known for her horror roles in **Brotherhood of Satan**, **I Dismember Mama** (where she played "Little Annie"), and the 2012 psychological/ horror thriller **The Meat Puppet**, which won her a Best Supporting Actress award in the Downbeach Film Festival/ Atlantic City Cinefest, the very same Cinefest where the author of this book, "Cryptmaster Chucky"/ Charles F. Rosenay!!!, won the award for Best Supporting Actor for his role as Death in the film **Kvetch**.

As a singer/ dancer, Geri was part of Sammy Davis Jr.'s night club act, where she performed background vocals and danced with Sammy Davis Jr. onstage, doing two shows a night. Geri even performed for Elvis Presley. In 2011, she put out her first CD, *1200 Riverside*. Geri's signature solo from "The Brady Bunch Variety Hour" was re-recorded and put out as a CD single, "Fake Jan Sings For Real"/ "Your Song."

Geri still records and appears at conventions and special events.
Website: www.GeriReischl.com.

"Fake Jan" Geri Reischl's TERRORble Top 10 List

The Shining (1980): The whole premise of this movie is mind-blowing...and for the simple fact that it's a Stanley Kubrick movie starring Jack Nicholson. Whoa!

Carrie (1976): I remember three of my girlfriends and me going to see this right when it came out. All of us were on the edge of our seats. This one makes you think twice before you ever pick on or make fun of someone. We literally ran to my friend's gold Pinto when it was over. We were so FREAKED out. Oh...I screamed out loud at the end of the movie.

Frankenstein (1931): My favorite movies are in black AND white. Classics! You can't help but fall in love with Frankenstein, and Boris Karloff makes the movie.

Halloween (1978): I watched this movie by myself. Stupid idea. I hardly took a breath watching this and I flew three feet off the couch a few times. I guess I like to torture myself...LOL.

The Last House on the Left (1972): Just knowing this movie is based on a true story makes it even more scary. So many bizarre things take place in this movie that it becomes mind-boggling. I am not going into the woods!!! It was hard to watch sometimes...used one eye with my other one covered up...LOL.

The Haunting (1963): Julie Harris does an outstanding job in her role as Eleanor Lance. I think I'll pass on staying at "Hill House."

The Wolf Man (1941): Claude Rains – Lon Chaney Jr. Who would have ever thought that years later I would end up meeting Lon Chaney Jr. and hanging out with him at a studio while I was guest-starring on "The Bold Ones"?! It was 1970, I believe. What a very interesting man. He had a trunk with him. I was sitting on it. He came over to me and asked if I'd like to see what was inside. I said sure. He had different kinds of props in it. A hand, knives, hats...etc. So watching this movie was quite awesome, knowing I had met him. This is an all-time favorite of mine. I feel for the Wolf Man.

Invasion of the Body Snatchers (1978): This is a brilliant film that I daresay may even be a little underrated. Great cast, great performances, great script. The scream that Matthew lets out is just a crescendo of pure terror. I was glued to this movie.

Saw (2004): A good independent film. This movie totally upset my stomach. Lots of bloody and downright gross scenes. Watch out for the Jigsaw Killer. I didn't want to go into a bathroom for a very long time.

The Brotherhood of Satan (1971): I chose this one because I play the character "K.T." in this horror movie. It's been labeled a cult classic now. Strother Martin, L.Q. Jones, Ahna Capri, Charles Bateman, and Geri Reischl. This movie has a satanic format with some gore. Bloody body parts, kidnapping, Satanism. A diabolical plot concocted by a coven of elderly devil-worshippers who plan to use the children's bodies as receptacles for their own souls, enabling them to live again in younger bodies. Leaves you wondering how the children turned out.

DEBBIE ROCHON

It's always great to get Top 10 Lists from movie stars, especially from one of the great genre actresses, Debbie Rochon.

Debbie Rochon is an indie actress who has been in 200+ (mostly horror) films. Rochon started as a pre-teen in the cult punk rock classic "Ladies and Gentlemen: The Fabulous Stains!" in which she worked as an extra for three months. There began her cinematic journey. She worked her way up to leading lady status and continues to enjoy creating complex and off-kilter characters for the screen.

Debbie is as equally drawn to broad comedy as she is to deeply dramatic, horrifying horror roles. Readers may recognize such titles as **Mulberry Street**, **American Nightmare**, **Alien Vengeance**, **Slime City Massacre**, **Tromeo & Juliet**, **Citizen Toxie: The Toxic Avenger IV**, **Model Hunger**, **Doom Room**, **Bloody Ballet**, **Exhumed**, and so many more. Never heard of them? Well then, you have a lot of Rochon-bingeing to do!

Debbie has hosted four different radio shows in New York City, from terrestrial to satellite. She rocked a four-year run on SiriusXM hosting Fangoria Radio with Dee Snider and Tony Timpone.

Rochon has been one of the subjects of multiple books penned on genre films, has graced the cover of 45 magazines, and has written for dozens of genre publications since 1993.

Debbie submitted her list after the release of her film **Exhumed**. She wrote, "To celebrate the DVD release of **Exhumed**, a movie I am deeply proud of, I have made my Top 10 List based on my favorite black and white horror films!"

Website: www.debbierochon.com.

Debbie Rochon's TERRORble Top 10 Black and White Horror Favorites List!

Psycho (1960): The movie that would influence all slashers that would come after it. This movie has it all – great story, great atmosphere, and great horror.

Night of the Living Dead (1968): Another great film that would inspire decades of filmmakers to delve into the undead genre. Original, scary, and raw.

Cape Fear (1991): Robert Mitchum heads up a great cast in a disturbing and yet beautiful film of killer revenge.

In Cold Blood (1967): Based on true events from Truman Capote's novel, here we see Robert Blake in his best performance.

The Haunting (1963): Hill House was never as scary as in this 1963 classic. Use of atmosphere over actual gore and ghost shots proves how riveting filmmaking can be.

Carnival of Souls (1962): The movie that was said to inspire George Romero for his opus **Night of the Living Dead**, the imagery and eerie qualities Herk Harvey used make this picture memorable and disturbing.

Eraserhead (1977): This art house horror launched David Lynch's career and inspired Stanley Kubrick to demand his entire cast and crew watch this bizarre essay before shooting "The Shining," to "get them in the right mood."

The Night of the Hunter (1955): Another Robert Mitchum masterpiece of acting. Frightening, gorgeous black and white. Horrifying stories like this just aren't made anymore.

Invasion of the Body Snatchers (1956): This may be more of a sci-fi flick, but horrifying it is. Excellent performances, especially by Kevin McCarthy, who has a standout meltdown at the police station.

The Hitch-Hiker (1953): Ida Lupino's classic that really wasn't appreciated until many years after its release. A real fright due to its realism and was apparently based on a true story, according to the opening credits.

LADA ST. EDMUND
Not Boo!...Hullabaloo!

Lada St. Edmund has been a professional athlete in one capacity or another ever since the New York Metropolitan hired her at age 11. She was the youngest dancer ever in the ballet corps, which led to a career as a lead dancer in numerous Broadway shows including the original cast of "Bye Bye Birdie," "West Side Story," and "Promises, Promises."

For three years in the '60s, Lada was a featured go-go dancer on NBC-TV's "Hullabaloo" show, which led to appearances on Johnny Carson and Merv Griffin. She met all the great rock bands of the era, and there are amazing photos of Lada surrounded by The Beatles, The Rolling Stones, Herman's Hermits, The Beach Boys, and others. She even had a career as a singer, and shared the same stage with Frankie Valli and The Four Seasons.

She switched careers from dancer to stunt woman in the '70s, when she became the highest-paid stunt woman in Hollywood history, appearing in hundreds of movies and TV shows from "Smokey and the Bandit" to "Charlie's Angels." In 1974, she was the first human to successfully test and later lobby in Washington, D.C. for the air bag, which is now in every car in the U.S.

Lada was one of the Special Guests at a Beatles fan convention in Stamford, Connecticut known as BEATexpo 2010 and she was also an Honored Guest that same year at "Rock Con: Weekend of 100 Rock Stars" at New Jersey's Meadowlands.

Lada's focus changed gears again when she devoted her time to the highly-successful "Trim Kids" program, dealing with helping obese and out-of-shape children.

You can see vintage scenes of Lada on YouTube (then Lada Edmund, Jr.) dancing up a storm. Lada St. Edmund is a shining example of her beliefs: transforming obstacles into energy. Her bottom line: "Real People, Real Bodies, Real Simple!" She is the President of the Minor Miracles Foundation.

She gave us 11 choices instead of 10, and they're all great offerings, but we just wish she gave us some reasons or comments.

Website: www.facebook.com/Ladast.edmund.

Lada's TERRORble Top 10 (+1) List of Favorite Monster Movies

A Nightmare on Elm Street (1984)

Rosemary's Baby (1968)

Spawn (1997)

Constantine (2005)

Alien (1979)

Psycho (1960)

The Others (2001)

Carrie (1976)

Hellraiser (1987)

The Shining (1980)

Predator (1987)

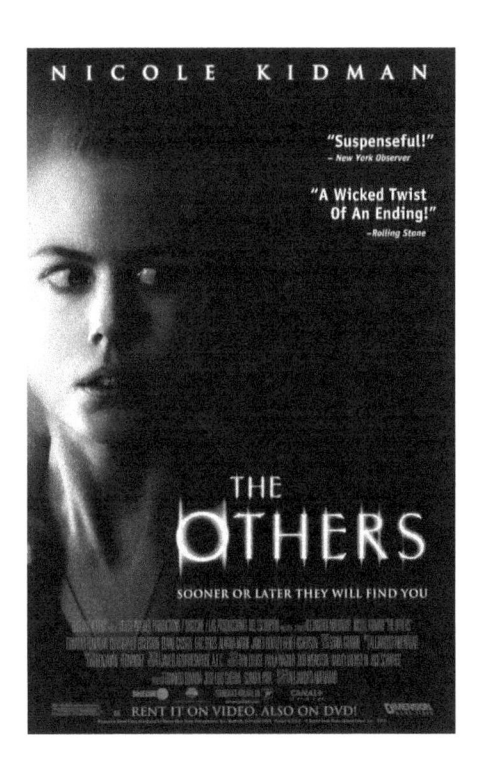

MITCH SCHECHTER
A Rip Chord

The Rip Chords were known for their 1964 million-seller smash hit "Hey Little Cobra" plus other chart hits "Three Window Coupe," "Here I Stand," "Gone," "409," and "Red Hot Roadster" from the beach movie **A Swingin' Summer** (produced by the team of Terry Melcher and Bruce Johnston, who also performed on the recordings). It was Bruce and Terry's voices that propelled "Hey Little Cobra" to the top of the charts! The original band disbanded in 1965 after touring the country, recording two albums for Columbia Records, and achieving four chart hits.

Bob Rush (who was planning to write a *Where Are They Now?* book) met original Rip Chords member Richie Rotkin in 1996, and in 1998 a new reformed band emerged with Richie Rotkin, Arnie Marcus, Bob Rush (Music Director 1998-2006), Mitch Schecter, Freddy Brog, and Larry Branca.

The "new" band performed on the PBS show "At the Drive-In," across the U.S. with countless '60s stars, and played multiple shows with Al Jardine and the Endless Summer Band, highlighted by a performance with Al Jardine in 2014 at Town Hall in New York City.

Fast forward to 2015, when the final line-up of the band included Richie Rotkin, Mitch Schecter (Music Director 2005-2020), Freddy Brog, Amy Lynne, Mike Kelly, Tony Tuttle, and Randy Bucksner.

The new band has recorded four new albums, and in 2016 was inducted into the Mid-America Music Hall of Fame in Iowa.

Mitch Schecter currently tours with a John Lennon tribute show, and definitely knows his horror films.

Website: www.theripchords.net

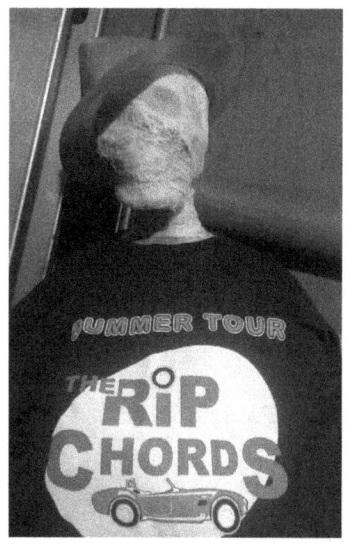

Mitch Schecter's TERRORble Top 10 List of Horror and Sci-Fi Films

The 4D Man (1959): Robert Lansing was the star of this film. After I saw this movie at the age of 8, I followed my Mom around the house for a year because I was so scared! I saw it recently and loved it...and got a few laughs from it as well.

The Mysterians (1957): This Japanese film had all of the amazing sets that are included in those films, and it scared me silly...especially when that giant space robot came out of the mountainside. Great early sci-fi.

The Exorcist (1973): I'm sure this is on everyone's list. I saw it recently on TV and it still gave me the creeps.

The Queen of Outer Space (1958): Gotta love Zsa Zsa Gabor. I think that planet was every male teen's dream! Except for the mangled queen, of course.

Forbidden Planet (1956): Leslie Nielsen, Walter Pidgeon, and Anne Francis...amazing. Still one of the best sci-fi films ever made.

The War of the Worlds (1953): Gene Barry was great in this film, as were the Oscar-winning effects. The best alien invasion film ever made...and a template for **Independence Day** and Jeff Goldblum's role in that film.

Close Encounters of the Third Kind (1977): Not horror, but great sci-fi...and kind of like the Yin to the Yang of **The War Of The Worlds**.

Star Wars: A New Hope (1977): OK I admit it...I'm a Star Wars Geek.

Invasion of the Body Snatchers (1956): The original film with Kevin McCarthy...so frightening when I first saw this as a kid. I still love watching this great film.

The Shining (1980): Jack Nicholson at his creepiest best...and one of Stephen King's best stories...even though King disliked this movie, I dug it.

FRED SCHNEIDER
Jaw-Dropping Bad Movies or Bad Lines from Movies

The B-52s are pop-rock heroes heavily rooted in New Wave and '60s rock and roll, as well as music from post-punk to dance. Formed by Fred Schneider, Kate Pierson, Cindy Wilson, Keith Strickland, and Ricky Wilson in Athens, Georgia, their positive, enthusiastic, slightly-oddball party band vibe gave the world hit songs such as "Love Shack," "Rock Lobster," "Roam," and "Private Idaho."

Even such studio albums as *Funplex* or their live album *With the Wild Crowd: Live in Athens* capture their almost-invincible sense of fun, performance power, and nostalgic high-wig energy.

For four decades, the B-52s have continued to play live shows, keep people dancing, and spread their musical joy. Our friend Fred Schneider gave a lot of thought to his favorite all-around "jaw-droppingly bad movies or lines from movies, in no particular order."

Website: www.theb52s.com.

Fred Schneider of the B-52s: TERRORble Top 10 List

Doris Wishman's **Dildo Heaven** (2002): Dildoes and a crazed-looking Peeping Tom make for a totally incomprehensible pleasure. Which leads to…

Another Wishman flick (her last), **Each Time I Kill** (2007), featuring yours truly. I thought I was really bad playing myself (!) on "The Guiding Light," but boy, am I terrible in this. Doris' script really was great, but then I saw the finished movie…God, her friends miss her, a true original!

The Creeping Terror (1964): Imagine a rug (literally) that eats a bunch of "helpless" kids at a teen dance, among other things.

Best line in a mediocre movie is from **Godzilla** (1985): "Professor, what makes you think Godzilla will head for Tokyo…?!!!"

Kronos (1957): A giant black box from outer space that sucks up electricity and grows bigger while it stomps on everything around. Scared me as a kid, but seeing it again…what was I thinking? As fake as can be!

Amityville: 3-D (1983): Basically just bad, but when the swordfish mounted on the wall comes loose and sails straight at the audience, it was great cinematic cheese.

I haven't seen these yet, but if they're as ridiculous as her books and records, **The Happy Hooker** (trilogy!) (1975-1980) should be really entertaining. And imagine, one stars Joey Heatherton!

Night of the Comet (1984): A comet streaks through the sky and everyone who is out and looks at it is turned to dust. Others inexplicably are turned into zombies. Besides the bad acting, it's impossible to concentrate on any plot because the bad '80s hairdos are hard not to stare at the whole movie.

Most people have forgotten Pia Zadora (who?) and her career (?) bankrolled by her billionaire hubby. In **The Lonely Lady** (1983), she's an 'actress' who has to sleep her way to the top (see, nothing ever changed in L.A. until the Me Too generation), and at the cheapest-looking awards ceremony, she accepts her award with (excuse the language) "That's the last cock I'll have to suck in Hollywood." Good line for someone to use at the Oscars.

Zombie Island Massacre (1984): I don't remember much about this piece of crap but it came out during the "snuff film" craze and it was rather sickening. It ran at a really sort of nice old theater on 42nd Street but afterwards you had to walk over puddles of throw-up.

JOHN SEBASTIAN

What do you do when somebody you've always admired gives a list but only gives two choices? That's right – two scary memories. When it's John Sebastian, founding member and original lead singer of the pop rock band The Lovin' Spoonful, you find a space for it! Especially considering how many celebrities never even bothered to submit one. The '60s group had a string of hits including "Do You Believe In Magic," "Summer in the City," "Daydream," "Did You Ever Have to Make Up Your Mind?," "You Didn't Have to Be So Nice," and "Darling Be Home Soon."

Sebastian, a singer/ songwriter/ guitarist/ harmonicist/ autoharpist from New York, wrote and sang the #1 song from 1976, "Welcome Back," the theme song for the TV show "Welcome Back, Kotter," which starred comedian Gabe Kaplan and a young actor named John Travolta.

Sebastian appeared at Woodstock, and even wrote the liner notes for a horror genre-related album's CD release, John Zacherle's *Monster Mash/ Scary Tales*.

A historic one-off reunion with some of the members of The Lovin' Spoonful was held in Los Angeles in early 2020, and our friend Elliott Easton (of The Cars, who also contributed his Top 10 List to this book) was part of the band.

John Sebastian still tours regularly.

Visit his website for tour info and updates: www.johnbsebastian.com.

John Sebastian's TERRORble Top 2 List of Scary Memories

Hi Charles,

For me there's no Top 10…there's only two.

At about five, I was taken to see **Peter Pan**… It was the original with Jean Arthur. The Hook part was played by BORIS KARLOFF!! Maybe my Mom's friendship with Vivian Vance had gotten us backstage after the show.

We were ushered into a dressing room where Mr. Karloff turned, still in full makeup, smiled, and in that voice, said, "Hello, J.B." (what I was called as a kid).

It took a minute to realize it wasn't still Captain Hook.

And here's another I almost forgot, Charles:

As a kid, I'd go to Philadelphia to visit my cousins. After dinner, we'd wait 'til Grandpa fell asleep, then switch the old television to **"The Shock Theatre (with "Roland").”** "Roland" was a late-nite ghoul/ host of what were just C-rated horror movies…but the fun was his break-ins for sly comments, a technique which would later be exploited by many imitators…and Beavis and Butthead. With every visit to my cousins, it was more "Roland," until he disappeared after getting too gruesome, we guessed.

But I called my cousin years later, because lo and behold, he reappeared during our adolescence as a New York afternoon dance show DJ/ host/ creature, complete with the same gruesome props and bad puns, except now his name was Zacherley, more resembling the real name of this actor/ creator, John Zacherle.

At some point The Lovin' Spoonful began lobbying to get on the show…which we did AND got asked back!

But even stranger was years later, while talking to Cameo/ Parkway (record label) reps about Zach's upcoming reissue of all his gruesome parody songs, they decided I was the guy to write his liner notes…which I did only a few years before his passing into some suitably gruesome, maybe slightly tacky afterlife.

Bless You Zach…you scared the hell out of us.

JS

WILLIAM SHATNER

Is it possible William Shatner's career spans 70 years!!??? Is it possible that we got a Top 10 List from Captain Kirk himself? Yes and yes indeed. Who can forget him in "T.J. Hooker," "Boston Legal," or that little-known sci-fi show "Star Trek"?

What can we tell you about William Shatner that you don't already know? Besides acting, he's produced, directed, written books, recorded albums, painted, launched comic books, hosted an interview show, been a chef, appeared at conventions, been spokesperson for Priceline, and has hosted charity horse shows. He is a Golden Globe and Emmy-winning actor, and there's even a religion inspired by him, "Shatnerology." Oh yes, and his face was the inspiration for the scariest mask ever, worn by Michael Myers in **Halloween**.

In this two-parter, first we give our TERRORble Top 10 List of William Shatner's Greatest Genre Contributions (we could've done a hundred of 'em!). Following this one we give you Bill's own Top 10 List – exclusively procured for us by Paul Camuso.

So first we start with what we feel were William Shatner's greatest contributions to fandom.

The TERRORble Top 10 List of William Shatner's Greatest Genre Contributions

"**Star Trek**" (1966), especially "The City on the Edge of Forever" (season 1, episode 28)

"**The Twilight Zone**" episodes "Nightmare at 20,000 Feet" (1963) and "Nick of Time" (1960)

"**The Outer Limits**" episodes "Cold Hands, Warm Heart" (1964) and "Wolf 359" (1964)

Incubus film (1966)

Kingdom of The Spiders film (1977) and **The Devil's Rain** film (1975), also starred Ernest Borgnine, Eddie Albert, Ida Lupino, and John Travolta.

His appearance on **"Saturday Night Live"** (season 12, episode 8, 1986) when he told his Trekkie fans to "Get a life!"

"TekWar" (series, 1994)

Tie: **"The Sixth Sense"** episode "Can a Dead Man Strike From The Grave?" (1972) and **"The Ray Bradbury Theater"** episode "The Playground" (1985)

Tie: His two appearances on the **"Alfred Hitchcock Presents"** show and his two appearances on **"Thriller."**

Interviewing Leonard Nimoy on his own show, **"Shatner's Raw Nerve"** (2009).

Bonus: Every time he was on Howard Stern.

WILLIAM SHATNER
Part two

William Shatner was born on March 22, 1931. The Canadian actor, recording artist, philanthropist, and author gained worldwide fame and became a cultural icon for his portrayal of James T. Kirk, Captain of the USS *Enterprise*, in the science fiction television series "Star Trek" from 1966 to 1969, "Star Trek: The Animated Series" from 1973 to 1974, and in seven of the subsequent "Star Trek" feature films from 1979 to 1994.

He has written a series of books chronicling his experiences playing Captain Kirk and being a part of "Star Trek" as well as several co-written novels set in the "Star Trek" universe. He has also authored a series of science fiction novels called "TekWar" that were adapted for television. He has an award-winning internet project about his adventures in life called "The Shatner Project" as well as a social media networking site, MyOuterSpace.com. Each spring, Shatner hosts the Hollywood Charity Horse Show, which benefits children's charities in the Los Angeles area and nationally.

Shatner also played the eponymous veteran police sergeant in "T.J.

Hooker" from 1982 to 1986. He has since worked as a musician, author, producer, director, and celebrity pitchman. From 2004 to 2008, he starred as attorney Denny Crane in the television drama "The Practice" and its spin-off "Boston Legal," for which he won two Emmy Awards and a Golden Globe Award. He turned to comedy to play the curmudgeonly father character Ed Goodson on the CBS television series "$#*! My Dad Says."

In 2019, the History Channel premiered "The UnXplained," a non-fiction series hosted and executive-produced by Shatner. The eight-episode, one-hour anthology series tackled subjects that have mystified mankind for centuries, from mysterious structures and cursed ancient cities to extraterrestrial sightings and bizarre rituals.

Thank you and may the Universe continue to bless you, William Shatner.
Special thanks to Paul Camuso.
Websites:
www.williamshatner.com
www.shatnerstore.com
Twitter.com/williamshatner

William Shatner's TERRORble Top List of Horror Films

Psycho (1960): The moment Mother turns to the camera.

Night of the Living Dead (1968): That stiff-legged walk towards the camera.

The Strangers (2008): Isolation and random acts of violence.

The Shining (1980): The hedge.

Halloween (1978): I loved the mask...looks familiar.

The Exorcist (1973): My head was spinning.

Jaws (1975): The shark that didn't work – did.

House of Wax (1953): Vincent Price and his honey voice.

The Silence of the Lambs (1991): Those staring eyes of Hannibal.

Aliens (1986): Sigourney Weaver and her T-shirt.

TIFFANY SHEPIS-TRETTA
Screen Queen Princess of Scream

Tiffany Shepis-Tretta is a Princess of Scream and a very popular convention guest, most notably at the Chiller Theatre Expo. She has been involved in filmmaking since the ripe old age of 12 and has appeared in numerous genre films since her debut in 1996's **Tromeo and Juliet**.

Some of her 100+ film appearances: **The Violent Kind, She Wolf Rising, The Frankenstein Syndrome, Live Evil, Night of the Demons, Dropping Evil, Zombies! Zombies! Zombies!, Chainsaw Cheerleaders, Bonnie & Clyde vs. Dracula, Shudder, Blood Oath, Nightmare Man, Dorm of the Dead, Corpses, The Deviants, Dead Scared, Devil's Moon, Ghouls, Bloody Murder 2: Closing Camp, Scarecrow, Ted Bundy, Citizen Toxie: The Toxic Avenger IV, Sharknado 2**, and so many others.

She loves blood and gore but detests violence. She has two Chihuahuas, named Vlad the Impaler and Boris Karloff. She was engaged to the late actor Corey Haim, and is currently working on several film projects, with others presently in pre- or post-production.

Best of all, she's a true fan of horror, and loves being in these films!

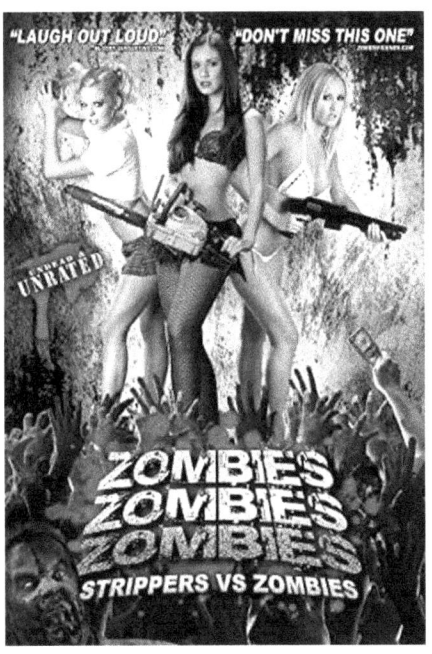

Tiffany Shepis' TERRORble Top 10 Favorite Horror Films (with the threat to deliver another 10 in the near future!)

Hellraiser (1987): Scary, gross, and 'cause Cenobites are just plain ol' bad-ass!

The Exorcist (1973): I have a daughter and I swear she was possessed a few times in her younger years. Little kids are SCARY.

Jaws (1975): Any movie that can make me think that there may be a shark in my pool…deserves a spot on this list.

A Nightmare on Elm Street (1984): Running up stairs that turn into quicksand?? Oh hell no, I'd just shoot myself.

Motel Hell (1980): 'Cause it's just awesome.

When a Stranger Calls (original, 1979): "Have you checked the children?" Children would be left, babysitter (me) running down the street. They did the stranger-watching-you thing loooong before "Scream" was ever thought of, and Carol Kane is crazy cool!

Trick 'r Treat (2008): 'Cause it's just plain old Halloween Fun.

Poltergeist (1982): The only movie that I still get creeped out by if I watch it alone.

The Last Exorcism (2010): I thought the ending was fantastic (cult stuff is cool) and I thought every performance was top-notch.

Waxwork (1988): 'Cause I enjoy most anything that was made in the '80s.

Bonus films: **The Hazing** (2004) – 'cause I'm in it, **Mountaintop Motel Massacre** (1983) – 'cause that bitch Evelyn who runs the motel is C R A Z Y! Last but not least, **Splice** (2009) – it was one of the smartest horror films I've seen.

JAMES LEE STANLEY

Stanley is an American folk-rock singer, songwriter, and humorist who tours constantly, sometimes performing up to 300 dates each year. He has performed with such diverse acts as Peter Tork of The Monkees, Stephen Stills, Nicolette Larson, Bonnie Raitt, and even comedians Robin Williams and Bill Cosby.

He has been hailed as one of the few all-time greats and undisputed geniuses among singer-songwriters. *Fi* Magazine listed his *Freelance Human Being* as one of the finest recordings of 1998 and one of the Top 200 Recordings of All Time (March 1999).

At the suggestion of John Densmore of The Doors, Stanley and collaborator Cliff Eberhardt took songs by The Doors and put a uniquely fresh spin on them, creating a remarkable album, *All Wood and Doors*. It's a follow-up to the critically-acclaimed *All Wood and Stones* (vintage Rolling Stones masterpieces composed by Mick Jagger and Keith Richards and reinvented by John Batdorf and Stanley). And to add further to an already remarkable recording, there was an all-star line-up of highly-regarded guest musicians including Timothy B. Schmit (The Eagles), Peter Tork (The Monkees), Paul Barrere (Little Feat), Laurence Juber (Paul McCartney & Wings), Scott Breadman (The

Photo of author Charles F. Rosenay!!! ("Cryptmaster Chucky") with James Lee Stanley, Special Guest of Honor at the Peter Tork Memorial Convention for Monkees Fans, February 8, 2020

Rippingtons, Lindsey Buckingham), Chad Watson (David Arkenstone, Janis Ian), and of course, John Densmore and Robby Krieger of The Doors.

He partnered with his best friend Peter Tork on several albums as Two-Man Band. In February of 2020, at the Peter Tork Memorial Convention for Monkees Fans in Connecticut, James Lee Stanley was the Special Guest of Honor, where he performed, met fans, was interviewed (by the author of this book), and accepted an official proclamation dedicating the date as Peter Tork/Monkees Day.

James Lee Stanley is a great guy with amazing talent. He should be more famous than he is! But he sure picked a lot of famous and great films for his Top 10 List.

Website: www.JamesLeeStanley.com.

James Lee Stanley's TERRORble Top 10 List of Scary Films

Night of the Living Dead (1968): I walked to the theater smoking a doobie, and then discovered the theater was six blocks further than I thought, so I sprinted the whole rest of the way to catch the film from the beginning. Sat down, the doobie kicked in like gangbusters, and that movie scared me to death. Right from the get-go. It never let up. A classic horror movie.

Them! (1954): The same kind of childhood scare. Atomic radiation mutating ants into GIANT ANTS. Fantastic.

Don't Look Now (with Donald Sutherland and Julie Christie, 1974): That film was so evocative to me and when that dwarf turned around and stabbed Sutherland with the scissors, I didn't think I would ever get my breath back.

Invaders from Mars (1953): I was a six-year-old boy when I saw that film. The horror of your own parents, the people you trust most, becoming zombies for the Martians was so horrifying to me. Then it appears to be a dream, and then the boy looks out the window and the ship goes behind the hill, just like the beginning of his dream. That was too great for my six-year-old mind. Loved it.

It Came From Outer Space (1953): That floating eyeball and the idea that they were just trying to get home, so it starts out scaring the caca out of me and then turns into this (for an eight-year-old) philosophical space story. Terrific.

The Sixth Sense (1999): The fact that all the clues are there from the get-go and you still don't know until the end that Willis is already dead. Knocked my socks off. Didn't scare me, but completely surprised me and there was enough horror in it for it to qualify for me as one of the very best horror films.

Creature from the Black Lagoon (1954): Loved the tension and the holding off of the actual sight of the monster, and what a monster it was. And I also was turned on by the leading lady. Got all damp and wiggly whenever she was on screen. Horror and sex. Can't beat it when you're a boy.

The Exorcist (1973): I was born and christened Catholic, though I never practiced the faith. But it all came back in an avalanche of horror as Satan possessed that little girl. Wow, I was so scared I slept with the lights on that night. And I was 26.

The Mummy (original Karloff black and white, 1932): The Mummy actually takes the woman into the swamp at the end and disappears into the water. She doesn't make it. I was so scared and horrified by that thing and I saw it on TV. Great black and white horror film.

Dracula (original Lugosi black and white, 1931): Bela Lugosi was so creepy, and back then vampires weren't disturbed or confused, they were pure evil, no question about it. They could come in on a moonbeam and suck the blood right out of you. Wow. I liked that so much more than what Anne Rice and her ilk have done to evil horror. Now it's sort of understandable and permissible. Clearly a commentary on what we really think of our leaders. They are slime and it's still okay. Sheesh!

KASIM SULTON

Singer/ songwriter Kasim Sulton is recognized and respected the world over for his music, and he is well-known for his work with other artists, including Todd Rundgren/ Utopia, Meat Loaf, Joan Jett, Hall & Oates, Patti Smith, Patty Smyth, Mick Jagger, and Celine Dion, to name a few. His level of involvement has ranged from playing bass, keyboards, and/ or guitar, to adding vocal harmonies, singing lead, and contributing as a songwriter – to producing entire albums, as he did with the Meat Loaf *VH-1 Storytellers* CD (1999).

Like many of the contributors to this book, Sulton was a Special Guest at the "Rock Con: Weekend of 100 Rock Stars" at the Meadowlands in New Jersey in 2010. There isn't much he hasn't done in his 35 years in the music industry.

Sulton's current releases and tour dates are available on his website: www.kasimsulton.com.

Thanks to super-publicity provider Ida Langsam of ISL Public Relations (www.islpr.com).

TERRORble Top 10 List from Kasim Sulton
(or, as he calls them, his Flick Pics)

Rosemary's Baby (1968): Not only a great film but…totally believable. Between Mia Farrow, John Cassavetes, and Ruth Gordon, you can't help but think it could happen. I still get the creeps every time I walk by the Dakota Apartments.

The Devils (1971): A little-known religious horror film from the '70s starring Oliver Reed and Vanessa Redgrave. There are scenes in this movie that are just too gruesome to watch.

The Exorcist (1973): What list would be complete without this one?

The Birds (1963): Crows, sparrows, pigeons, doves, they're ALL nuts. Never found out what made them that way, though.

House On Haunted Hill (1959): $10,000 if you can stay in this house overnight? Maybe in 1959 when the movie came out but today, you'd have to do a lot better than that. Vincent Price-less.

Abbott & Costello Meet Frankenstein (1948): Funny but actually scary, too. And Creighton Chaney (Lon Chaney Jr.)? He was fantastic.

Phantasm (1979): A cult classic. The Tall Man was beyond spooky and the spinning disk was enough to have you sinking in your seat.

Hell Raiser (1987): Clive Barker's book *The Hellbound Heart* was the impetus for the movie. The puzzle box always fascinated me and I'm also a sucker for fish hooks in skin. Pinhead is really a nice guy underneath it all.

Women in Cages (1971): Pam Grier at her finest! She does get a taste of her own medicine in the end.

Psycho (1960): Not much blood, not much gore but oh, what a nightmare of a hotel stay.

JONATHAN TIERSTEN

Jonathan Tiersten acted in the first **Sleepaway Camp** film (1983) at the age of 17, and he was back in **Return to Sleepaway Camp** (2008), also known as **Nightmare Vacation V** and **Sleepaway Camp V: The Return**. An accomplished composer and musician, Jonathan was the lead singer and guitarist in a band called Bambi's Apartment, and four of their songs were used in the independent film **Closing the Deal**. He fronted the band Ten Tiers, which recorded an EP called *Jonathan Tiersten and Ten Tiers* (2009). There is talk of future work with **Sleepaway Camp** star Felissa Rose (she has a production company that Jonathan will act and do soundtrack/ score work for).

Visit Tiersten's official website: www.jonathantiersten.com.

Jonathan Tiersten's TERRORble Top 10 Monster Movie List!

Eraserhead (1977): I saw this movie when I was in high school. Most people remember David Lynch for "Twin Peaks" and he has made some pretty bent movies since this, but none that have kept me up at night like **Eraserhead**. This masterpiece of sexual frustration is unparalleled.

Pet Sematary (1989): This is a beautiful looking movie. It looks like a family film, but unlike **Amityville Horror**, it lays the foundation so you care about these folks. Then the madness starts. The kid's face is terrifying and Fred Gwynne ("Herman Munster") as the old wise New Englander is just fantastic.

Open Water (2003): This film totally surprised me. I grew up spending summers on Martha's Vineyard (where most of **Jaws** was shot). That constant dread is probably my description of hell.

The Ring (2002): Modern horror that does not seem almost immediately dated is a rarity. Being set in the technological age makes this an impressive achievement. Think of **Scream** and **I Know What You Did Last Summer**. Those movies are laughable now. This movie is also pretty much gore-free, which is unusual for modern horror.

The Omen (1976): The cinematography is second only to **The Exorcist**. The shots in the rain. The cemetery scene. Our introduction to The Anti-Christ. We have loved him ever since, but never more. 666!

Hellraiser (1987): What else is there to say about this homage to acupuncture gone terribly wrong? I have met Doug Bradley several times (he is super nice) and that has done nothing to lessen my terror when watching this film.

The Shining (1980): The Overlook Hotel is actually based on The Stanley Hotel in Estes Park, Colorado. I live about 35 miles away. I have stayed in room #237. This movie is so terrifying on so many levels. Apparently Kubrick put Shelley Duvall through psychological torture and it really shows up on the screen. Nicholson was made for Kubrick like Peter Lorre for Hitchcock.

Rosemary's Baby (1968): Great actors. New York setting. Ruth Gordon won best supporting Oscar. If you haven't seen it, please do. It still works.

Psycho (1960): Anthony Perkins is brilliant! It probably hurt his career a little because he was so identified by this film from 1960. This set the standard for the macabre ever since.

The Exorcist (1973): Do not get the new cut of the film. It adds scenes that steal from the suspense. I had trouble sleeping for years after this film. Even now when I think about it, I get the creeps. It is just remarkable in every way. Lee J. Cobb is just awesome in the role as the detective, Jason Miller as Damien Karras, Ellen Burstyn overacting with so much panache, and the beautiful, innocent Linda Blair.

DANTE TOMASELLI
Another Dante's Inferno

Dante Tomaselli is a screenwriter, director, composer, and horror aficionado who has given us the films **Desecration** (1999), **Horror** (2002), **Satan's Playground** (2006), and **Torture Chamber** (2012).

The first feature, **Desecration**, was produced with the minuscule budget of $150,000. Yet it received instantaneous acclaim for its nightmarish visuals and unforgettable images. The supernatural chiller quickly established itself as a modern horror cult favorite.

FEARnet named Tomaselli one of their Favorite Underrated Horror Directors, calling his film projects "unique and eccentric."

In 2014, Tomaselli released his first audio CD of all-electronic horror music, *Scream in the Dark*, through Elite Entertainment and MVD Audio.

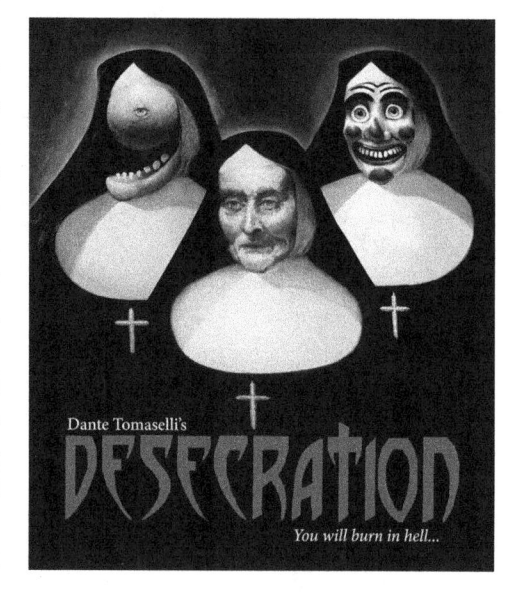

Two interesting bits of trivia: Tomaselli has utilized themes of Catholicism and Christianity in his work. Dante's cousin Alfred Sole directed the classic film **Alice, Sweet Alice** (1976).

Tomaselli has been a lifelong supernatural/ horror aficionado, and his well-thought-out film choices and descriptions can attest to this.

Website: www.enterthetorturechamber.com/.
Visit: www.facebook.com/people/Dante-Tomaselli/518554086.

Dante Tomaselli's Top 10 Underrated Horror Movies

Tourist Trap (1979): I discovered the sparkling horror jewel on TV in the early '80s. Growing up, this creative low-budget chiller was my addiction. I'd come home from school, close the blinds, and watch **Tourist Trap**. Witness dolls and mannequins mysteriously coming alive at an old tourist location in creepy rural America. The wildly imaginative film has a warm, lush score by Pino Donaggio that perfectly interlocks with the cold, twisted imagery. At the core, there's a bizarre and lonely man with a secret past. One by one, kids are turning to dolls. I love this macabre film.

The Brood (1979): Freaky and genuinely unnerving, David Cronenberg's "The Brood" came out when I was a kid. It was rated R and usually my mother took me to see practically every good horror movie. This film, however, was supposed to be "ugly" and "violent" and I was too young. Of course, that made me want to see **The Brood** even more. Soon I caught a late night viewing on cable and was hypnotized by its eerie power. It's actually a beautiful film, in a deep, dark, twisted way. In essence, **The Brood** is about domestic abuse and psychic violence and its never-ending cycle. Children of rage. Heavy stuff for a 10-year-old...and I've never been the same since.

Burnt Offerings (1976): Another '70s horror film centering on family violence. Karen Black is striking and enigmatic as the mother of the troubled clan, and Oliver Reed nails it as the disintegrating dad. I love the mood-drenched atmosphere, brooding music, and sprawling haunted mansion locale. The film's malevolent swimming pool jumps out as a show-stopper but the standout image has to be the grinning hearse driver! That sadistic, spine-tingling smile gave me serious night-mares.

The Sentinel (1977): I saw this religious horror shocker at a Drive-In. I was seven years old. My mother covered my eyes during certain scenes but I managed to take it in. Cristina Raines is outstanding as the cursed young model at the core of this ballsy and entertaining supernatural horror film. Her tragic character is doomed forever to be a guardian at the gates of Hell. Right down my alley. Even though I was very young, I owned the sinister cut-out paperback by Jeffrey Konvitz. I was attracted to the artwork and I'd illustrate the gothic title on my notebook and lunch box in the same lettered font as the cover art. That ominous brownstone building from the film still exists in Brooklyn Heights, New York. I've been there more than a few times.

231

Let's Scare Jessica to Death (1971): Jessica, newly released from a mental hospital, finds peace in the simple rural countryside. She's on the healing journey with her husband and his male friend. Once they arrive at their destination, a mysterious homeless woman appears, seemingly out of nowhere. Good-heartedly, Jessica instinctively invites the lady to stay. Big mistake. Jessica loses her husband to the bewitching seductress. Mostly she loses her sanity. Or was she ever sane to begin with? I love Jessica's whispering internal voices. Is this a portrait of schizophrenia or a ghost story? One thing is for sure, Jessica's descent into madness feels so achingly real.

Halloween 2 (1981): This sequel has aged really well. **Halloween 2** makes me feel alive and brings back memories. I was 11 years old when the film came out in theaters and was captivated by the advertisements on TV and in the newspaper. That poster! *"From The People Who Brought You 'Halloween'... More Of The Night He Came Home"*...In school and at home, I'd draw and paint the glowing pumpkin with the skull inside. I had the soundtrack and played it constantly. Aside from the original, the film contains the most visually arresting opening titles sequence ever. I put the opening credits on...and my brain releases serotonin. It has something to do with the pulsating theme music, too. The movie itself is not the dud many critics made it out to be. **Halloween 2** is well-made and entertaining, with beautiful Dean Cundey photography. The moody synthesizer soundtrack is electronic horror heaven.

The House with Laughing Windows (1976): An interior horror experience. A remote southern Italian village is the setting for this fever-dream mind-freak. Stefano has arrived at a strange rural town to restore the church's decaying painting of St. Sebastian. There seems to be the undercurrent of a conspiracy, something is just off. According to legend, the mysterious painter of the church's religious wall documented real death...and his paintings were actual murders. At the center of this ghoulish tale are the two sisters of the painter. These elderly women are absolutely chilling. I still dream about them. The voice-overs of their brother, the depraved artist, discussing colors and blood are deliriously unsettling. The unexpected conclusion to **The House with Laughing Windows** just might leave you stunned.

This Night I'll Possess Your Corpse (1967): This surreal, magical horror film is one of my favorites. Way ahead of its time, Coffin Joe creates a relentlessly bizarre nightmare world with no budget. It's such a personal experience. You feel the filmmaker's imprint 100%. I'm in awe of all the simple yet effective old-school horror effects. No CGI here. The film's colorful, eye-popping descent into the bowels of hell is worth the price of admission alone.

The Premonition (1976): I love ESP horror films and this unique low-budget gem is sorely underrated. Andrea is newly released from a mental institution. Aggressive and provocative, she's deemed an unfit mother by the government, so her young daughter has been placed in the care of foster parents. Now that Andrea is free...or loose...she wants her child back. Soon the innocent girl and her loving foster mother are stalked by the madwoman... psychically. Parapsychologists enter the scene and **The Premonition** turns into a fascinating tale of the occult. Richard Lynch gives a disturbing, ethereal performance as Andrea's psychotic boyfriend, a circus clown.

Shock (1977): Legendary Italian horror actress Daria Nicolodi stars in Mario Bava's final film, **Shock**. This very strange tale centers on an unstable woman confronting her hidden past. It seems Dora was a drug addict and had an extremely unhealthy relationship with her deceased husband. After a mental breakdown and electric shock treatments, Dora finds a new man, Bruno, and she and her son move back into the house where Dora and her late husband, Carlo, used to live. Soon her son is animated by the spirit of the angry, vengeful father. Eccentric and jittery, **Shock** delivers an intriguing horror tale. Is Dora going mad or is she haunted by the ghost of her drug-addled deceased husband? Or is it something else? Ambiguity is the essence of the plot.

VAMPY

Who or what is "Vampy?" Vampy is a Goth/ metal/ trance musician/ artist from the West Coast who also worked with rocker Buzzy Linhart (who also contributed a Top 10 List in this book). The esteemed Mr. Linhart produced new music from Vampy (sometimes know as Vampy & The Dead Star Band). Through PR wiz Joe Viglione, we were able to get a list of Vampy's Top 10 horror movies, which includes some obscure titles along with better-known classics. Vampy's music can be heard on www.reverbnation.com/vampyandthedeadstarband.

Vampy's TERRORble Top 10 Horror Movies

Nosferatu (1922): I considered Chris Lee's **Dracula** but had to go with **Nosferatu**. He didn't talk, best watched at dawn.

Dracula / Dracula (1931): Double feature: Brown and Mexican versions.

Andy Warhol's Frankenstein (1974): Andy Warhol version.

The Unknown (1927): This list could have more Lon Chaney Sr.

The Hunger (1983): Has the most meaning to my life. Seems every four years another ex-girlfriend is carried up to the attic.

The Picture of Dorian Gray (1945): In a shade of Dorian Gray I painted myself.

An Andalusian Dog (**Un Chien Andalou**) (1929): An image that stays forever.

Blood & Donuts (1995): For those who know Vampire movies, I recommend this.

The Hand (1981): This one wasn't my choice. It was the Hand's.

The Blood Countess (2008): Historically, right on.

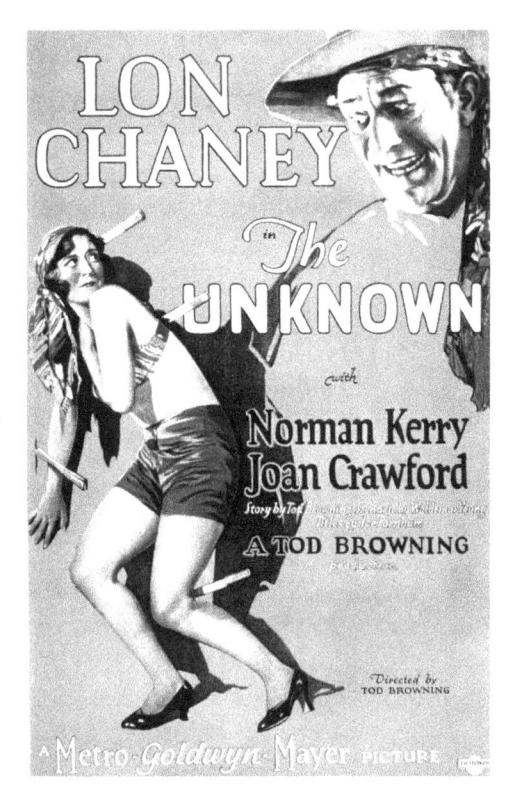

GARY VAN SCYOC
John Lennon's Bassist

Gary Van Scyoc has played bass and/ or recorded with John Lennon, Elephants Memory, Yoko Ono, Chuck Berry, Bo Diddley, Stevie Wonder, Mick Jagger, Jerry Garcia, Neil Sedaka, Keith Moon, Paul Simon, Howard Tate, Carl Hall, Benny Mardonas, La La Brooks (The Crystals), Gene Cornish (The Rascals), Mark Hudson, and others.

After hearing a tape of the band Elephants Memory, with Gary on bass, on Long Island radio station WLIR in late 1971, John Lennon showed up at the band's rehearsal studio and asked them to join his Plastic Ono Band. They merged into Plastic Ono Elephants Memory Band (P.O.E.M.). In 1972, John Lennon released the LP *Some Time in New York City*, which was produced by Phil Spector and backed by P.O.E.M. In 1972, Lennon and Elephants Memory performed at Madison Square Garden and recorded *Live in New York City* (released in 1986 on CD and VHS). In 1973, the band recorded *Approximately Infinite Universe*, a two-record set for Yoko Ono, with Lennon producing. John Lennon also produced the 1972 Apple release *Elephants Memory* that included Gary's songs "Wind Ridge," "Chuck and Bo," and "Baddest of the Mean." Gary appeared with the Lennons on "The Mike Douglas Show," "The Dick Cavett Show," "Dick Clark's Rolling Stones 25 Years," "Flipside," VH-1's "Legends" and "Behind the Music," as well as the motion pictures **Imagine** and **The U.S. vs. John Lennon**.

The last Elephants Memory release was *Angels Forever*, written by Van Scyoc on RCA in 1973. The song became the title track for the Hells Angels documentary film **Angels Forever** (1974).

Gary Van Scyoc was inducted to the Pittsburgh Music Hall of Fame in 2010. He was a Special Guest of Honor at the 2009 BEATexpo in Connecticut and at 2010's "Rock Con: Weekend of 100 Rock Stars" in the New Jersey Meadowlands.

Gary has written a book, *Shortcuts To Improving Your Bass Playing*, and created the curriculum for bass students at the Sam Ash Music Institute in Edison, New Jersey, while being the founder of Bass Styles Inc., a contemporary school for bass studies.

Van Scyoc released the album *Pop Goes The Elephant* in 2014, which is still available on his website: www.garyvanscyoc.com/.

Gary Van Scyoc's TERRORble Top 10 List

The original **The Day the Earth Stood Still** (1951): First saw it in the auditorium, my freshman year in high school, and didn't sleep for a week!

Creature from the Black Lagoon (1954) series including **Revenge of the Creature** (1955) and **The Creature Walks Among Us** (1956).

Rosemary's Baby (1968): While working with John and Yoko, I got a call from John that the Lennons were moving into the Dakota and I would be going there sometimes in the middle of the night to learn some of their new songs to record, which really freaked me out! Creepy!

The original **Night of the Living Dead** (1968): Awesome!

Psycho (1960): Thought about it in the shower for years.

Alien (1979): The alien popping out of a human chest was groundbreaking special effects for its time.

Frankenstein (1931): Imagine what it was like seeing this in 1931 – Amazing!

The Fly (1958): One of the most imaginative concepts ever.

The Exorcist (1973): I've never seen people so afraid in a theater, some just got up and left!

Jaws (1975): Again, people in the Manhattan Theatre were glued to their seats, including ME!

PHIL "FANG" VOLK

Phil "Fang" Volk is an American pop culture treasure, as well as a great rock and roll musician. He is best known as the bassist for '60s U.S. hitmakers Paul Revere & The Raiders. At one time, *Playboy* Magazine conducted a poll of readers' top favorite pop or rock bass players. Paul McCartney was #1; Phil "Fang" Volk was second. Not bad.

Volk was one of the Special Guests of Honor at "Rock Con: Weekend of 100 Rock Stars," which came together in 2010 at a Meadowlands, New Jersey hotel. The photo of "Fang" at "Rock Con" herein is courtesy of Danny Solazzi of the band The Characters. Shortly after that event, "Fang" recorded and released an incredible rocking version of Bob Dylan's classic "The Times They Are A-Changin,'" re-imagined for today's world of turmoil.

Phil resides in Las Vegas with his family and still plays shows on the West Coast. Most recently, he compiled a new CD anthology comprised of classic cuts and new recordings. The release is titled *Rocker*, and is available where recordings are sold, and also on Volk's website.

Website: www.philfangvolk.com/.

Below is Volk's list of 10 movies that he classifies as scary thrillers and/or bordering-on horror movie-type flicks.

"Fang" writes: "This is going to be a very eclectic list, so I've decided to make a few comments about each movie so you can understand my motivations and reasonings. I'm going way back to when I was a little kid, and what scared me back then, but probably wouldn't scare me today. I thought the commentary would add some insight about why I chose these films, plus give me an opportunity to offer you my personal 'back story' on these films, and perhaps even throw in a little humor in the reviews, just so people don't get bored reading it. Anyway, here we go..."

Phil "Fang" Volk's TERRORble Top 10 List for Horror Happenings

The Wizard of Oz (1939): This was the first movie I ever saw in a big theater and it scared the crap out of me. That Wicked Witch and those flying monkeys were terrifying! Hey, I was only *four years old* when my older brother Georgie, who was supposed to be babysitting me, decided to take me to the theater instead, on the handlebars of his bicycle (my folks had a few words to say to him when we got back)! Being in that big dark theater with all those crazy characters on the screen was not my idea of having a good time. I spent most of the time on the floor hiding under my seat. When that tornado picked up that house and that witch started laughing, I dove under my seat. My brother thought it was funny that I was so scared. Every time he put me back in my seat, some other freaky creature would appear on the screen, and down I went to the floor again! At the tender age of four, it was traumatizing, to say the least.

King Kong (1933): Animals gone wild...and in this case, a very large animal, capable of stepping on people and squishing them! My Dad was an actor at the time, and played a small role in the film as a policeman in New York City when the big gorilla went on his rampage. Unfortunately, he got squished, along with hundreds of other extras. It's a dirty job, but someone's gotta do it. I was proud of my Dad that he stood up to that awesome beast. He did what he could with his little six-shooter! Obviously, he needed a bigger gun, which brings me to my next scary film where they needed a bigger boat...

Jaws (1975): More animals gone wild...and not even a bigger boat could stop this 25-foot killing machine of a shark. Nothin' could slow down his wrath, mayhem, and murder! Why was this fish so pissed off? He obviously was the King of the Deep but he seemed to have a personal vendetta against one or all of the three R's: Roy Scheider, Richard Dreyfuss, and Robert Shaw. One of the best ensemble cast of actors ever assembled. "Hey, let me show you one of my scars!" But the best line was Shaw recounting a previous shipwreck of his old Navy cronies lost at sea: "If the cold embrace of the sea didn't get ya, then the sharkies would – and that's no lover's kiss!" Oddly enough, there was more suspense and terror when we didn't see the shark (which was not visible through most of the film), but our anticipation kept us on edge! Great movie-making by Spielberg...

Signs (2002): Speaking of "less is more," those mean-spirited aliens in this film had very little screen time, but they were still pretty scary anyway. It was obvious they had no intentions of being nice. Why was this movie scary? Well...the anticipation of being torn from limb to limb by these bad-ass critters, powerful aliens that we rarely got to see, but knew they were just outside our door, kept the plot edgy and moving forward in a sort of terrifying way. Excellent performances by Mel Gibson and Joaquin Phoenix protecting those two little kids, making us believe this was really happening to them. Good movie escapism! We took another couple with us to see this movie, and the woman said she didn't like scary movies, because they made her scream out loud. Since I was sitting next to her in the theater, the first time she screamed, I nearly "lost my cookies." She wasn't kidding. Her screams were bloodcurdling! Scarier than the movie itself.

Alien (1979): Speaking of creatures from other worlds, this film had a little bit of everything going for it, not the least of which was the incredible special effects. But obviously, the special effect we all remember the most is when John Hurt's chest burst open and a "baby alien" came out and scared the crap out of everybody. Hey, that puts new meaning in the word "emphysema"! Finally, when Sigourney Weaver realizes she's fighting a toothy, acid-breathing "Mother-Bitch," this movie ultimately becomes the cat fight from hell. Classic and unforgettable! Sigourney Weaver is truly a "mother-of-invention" here (Frank Zappa would've been proud). Her quick thinking and bravery, along with a very clever use of a futuristic fork-lift, saves the day for her and the little girl she discovers. I love happy endings.

Deliverance (1972): What can I say? After "Dueling Banjos," this movie kept you on the edge of your seat to the very end. Even during the final credits we get one more moment of terror, when that bloated hand comes floating to the surface of the lake. Hey, enough is enough, already. You're scarin' me! Those toothless, sadistic backwoodsmen were enough to scare anyone.

To this day, when I go backpacking or river-rafting, I get flashbacks, and find myself looking deep into the woods for signs of any unusual movements. Plus, I wear my stainless steel underwear just to be safe from perverts! This movie was terrifying, but so well done! This could happen to anyone...what a classic! Burt Reynolds has never been as strong in a part as he was in this one.

Cape Fear (1997): The Martin Scorsese film featuring Robert DeNiro as a psychotic stalker was truly an edgy thriller. As a Dad myself, I can only imagine what I might do to protect my family from such a monster. I've had stalkers come and go in my life – some benign, and some who were potentially dangerous – but the bottom line is: you never know when they're out there watching you or tracking your every move.

During the Raiders days on tour, I had a rather weird fan tracking me like that, and showing up at the most inopportune moments and causing me some grief. The worst episode came when the Raiders had a day off in New Mexico, and we decided to take a trip to Carlsbad Caverns, which ultimately takes you down through a cave over a mile below the surface of the earth. At the very bottom of the cavern they had a lunch area, where we all sat around some tables and had a bite to eat. All of a sudden, an announcement came over the intercom: "Emergency phone call for Phil Volk!" My heart nearly stopped as I tried to process that gloomy message, and walked toward the one telephone they had down there a mile underground. I was literally shaking, thinking something terrible had happened to a family member. The only person who knew we were going to the Caverns was the hotel manager where we were staying. I thought something bad may have happened to my parents, and my siblings were urgently trying to reach me. When I picked up the phone and said, "Hi, who is this?," the voice on the other end said, "Hi Fang, this is your favorite fan, Linda Wacko...I just wanted to see how you were doing...etc..." I was so angry at her for doing this. I cursed her out. She threatened to send some of her boyfriends to find me and kill me. How did she know where I was? Why did she say it was an emergency? Why did they connect her? Why, why, why??? Stalkers are real. Be glad if you don't have any of them tracking you, but then again, you never know...This movie is kind of like that.

The Illustrated Man (1969): This was a very strange movie, with a very strange storyline and a very strange and troubled main character. When you talk about someone being sinister, mysterious, and a little left of center, Rod Steiger is the man. This movie was riveting and very edgy. Here's a man with a body full of tattoos and a crazy, scary story for every one of them. Be careful not to stare! It's not polite...it's not safe either! I think that because of this movie, I've never gotten a tattoo on my body. In fact, I've never seen this movie again, but it did leave a lasting impression on me...hey, no pun intended...

The Birds (1963): Once again, animals gone wild!!! This time it's our not-so-friendly winged creatures! Hey listen, when I was a little boy, I was attacked by a flock of geese and it wasn't very funny. In fact, it was very scary for me and obviously, it didn't feel very good, either. I know some people who use geese as "watchdogs" to protect their property. They can be pretty aggressive, in fact downright mean-spirited. Such was the case in this movie: the birds began to swarm and eventually became very mean and dangerous and of course, deadly! This kind of aggressive and carnivorous bird behavior is even mentioned in the Book of Revelation where it describes birds feasting on the dead carcasses of humans! Maybe Alfred Hitchcock was onto something here...maybe the movie is prophetic!

Psycho (1960): What can I say? This movie scared everybody. It set a new standard for horror movie thrillers. Being in black and white made it even more ominous and threatening. Having the main character knocked off halfway through the film may have seemed odd at first, but director Alfred Hitchcock realized that fear resides in the mind, and the psychological thriller that followed was even more tense and mind-bending then any shower scene gore. Anthony Perkins was so calm on the surface, but underneath there raged a very troubled monster with a lot of secrets. I was in college in the early '60s when I saw this film. I went alone, late at night, not really knowing what to expect. To this day, I don't think I've ever felt that kind of horrific terror in a movie theater before...well, of course, with the exception of **The Wizard of Oz** *when I was only four years old...*

There you go. That's my story, and I'm sticking to it.

EERIE VON
"I Von to Suck Your Blood"

Eerie Von was the drummer for a band with the great name Rosemary's Babies from 1980 to 1983. He is better known as the original bassist for the metal band Danzig and before that he played in Samhain.

Along with being one of the coolest horror-themed monster music rock artists ever, Eerie also worked on *The Misfits* box set (out on Caroline Records), he has released his own CDs, and he has published a best-selling book. Here is the media info on his 2009 book *Misery Obscura: The Photography Of Eerie Von (1981-2009)*: "From the deepest depths of punk rock's 1970s primordial wastelands, through the stygian goth swamps of the 1980s, and on into the blood-stained arenas of 1990s heavy metal, Eerie Von witnessed it all. Beginning as the unofficial photographer for punk legends The Misfits and later taking charge of the bass guitar as a founding member of underground pioneers Samhain and metal gods Danzig, the evil eye of Eerie Von's camera captured the dark heart of rock's most vital and bleeding-edge period, a time when rock and roll was not only dangerous, but downright menacing. Eerie Von's lens has documented everything from The Misfits' humble beginnings in Lodi, New Jersey to the heights of Danzig's stadium-rock glory alongside metal superstars Metallica. As well as an essential visual document of music history, Eerie's road stories of triumph and damnation bring to life an era the likes of which will never again be seen."

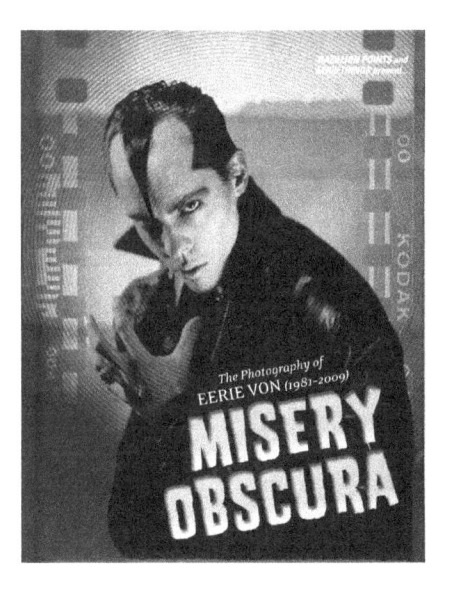

Website: www.facebook.com/eerievon/.

Eerie Von's TERRORble Top 10 List of Films

The Black Cat (1934, Karloff/ Lugosi): I stole Karloff's hairstyle for my own in Samhain.

Carrie (1976): Saw it at the Drive-In when I was 11. Blood, and spooky religious stuff.

The Bride of Frankenstein (1935, Karloff): The Monster speaks. Great Sequel.

Rosemary's Baby (1968): Named my first Band after it. There's that Devil thing again.

Hellraiser (1987): Hell, Damnation, and great Monsters.

The Phantom of the Opera (1925, Lon Chaney Sr.): The Phantom is my all time Fave Monster.

Night of the Living Dead (1968): So many nights at the Midnight Movie House. Great Film.

The Texas Chainsaw Massacre (1974): So Scary Real.

The Omen (1976): Anything that deals with Hell and the Devil pretty much makes my list.

Angel Heart (1987, Mickey Rourke/ Robert De Niro): De Niro as the Devil, Voodoo, Lisa Bonet? Damn.

DEBORAH VOORHEES

Voorhees is a legendary name in horror history. But enough about Jason. Or his Mom.

Deborah Voorhees played Tina in the fifth **Friday the 13th** film, 1985's **Friday the 13th: A New Beginning** (billed as Debisue Voorhees). If anyone thought she was cast because of her last name, Voorhees, they'd be very wrong. She has been a filmmaker, director, writer, journalist, editor, teacher, Hollywood B-scream starlet, and even a Playboy Bunny – which has given her much fodder for her filmmaking.

Her film roles include **Avenging Angel** (1985), **Appointment with Fear** (1985), **Innocent Prey** (1989), and as a witch, **Billy Shakespeare** (2014). She was also on the TV series "Dallas" (1982-1985).

Of all the jobs Voorhees has ever done, she loves filmmaking the most. Her Voorhees Films, originally founded in 2010, is releasing **13 Fanboy**, about an obsessed fan who stalks the real-life actresses from **Friday the 13th** with the intent to kill. She has several other film projects in the works: **The List** (a horror comedy), a horror film, a family sci-fi, a ghost story, two romantic comedies, a western, a thriller, and a couple more horror films.

Website: www.voorheesfilmsproduction.com.

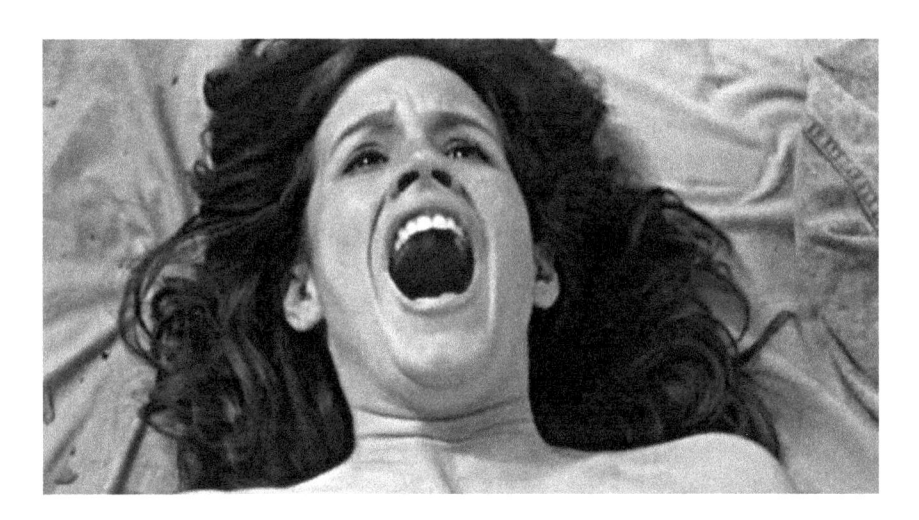

Deborah Voorhees' Unnumbered TERRORble List

Horror films that grab me have strong characters that I get emotionally attached to. If I don't get involved with the characters, I won't care about the film.

I love dark comedies that make me laugh and cringe, thriller/ horror films that cause me to clutch my theater chair, supernatural predatory films, creature features from the monster's perspective, and human killers with multi-layered personalities, where on some level I can sympathize with their plight.

My first two picks for dark comedies are Mel Brooks' horror spoof of Mary Shelley's *Frankenstein*, the black-and-white masterpiece **Young Frankenstein** (1974), and Edgar Wright's comedy horror **Shaun of the Dead** (2004), starring Simon Pegg. Both films are beautifully shot, have a great story, and make me laugh.

Films that keep me clutching my theater seat are Mike Flanagan's **Hush** (2016), which revolves around a deaf writer who is stalked by a masked killer, and **A Quiet Place** (2018), directed by John Krasinski and starring Emily Blunt. Both films are unrelenting. The latter's birthing scene is the most intense scene in a horror film. I didn't take a deep breath until the final frame on either film.

The supernatural horror films from director James Wan **Insidious** (2010), starring Lin Shaye as paranormal investigator Elise Rainier, and **The Conjuring** series (2013-2020), with paranormal investigators Ed and Lorraine Warren, are among my favorites. Both series keep me guessing and on the edge of my seat.

What Lies Beneath (2000), starring Michelle Pfeiffer and Harrison Ford, is another favorite ghost story. It's a subtle story about a wife being haunted. The film masterfully draws the audience in without relying heavily on special effects and jump scares. It's just a terrific scary ghost story with characters to care about. The twists and turns make **The Others,** starring Nicole Kidman, another favorite ghost story.

The two that lure me into the mind of a killer are Martin Scorsese's thriller **Cape Fear** (1991), starring Robert De Niro, Nick Nolte, and Jessica Lange, and William March's horror thriller **The Bad Seed** (1956), starring Patty McCormack as the darling Rhoda. The latter is my all-time favorite horror film. It has a fantastic story and a horrifying villain that can rival any monster out there. Eight-year-old Rhoda Penmark's first kill is the boy who wins the penmanship pin, a pin she covets. There's nothing scarier than a pig-tailed blonde little girl who will kill for a penmanship pin.

DICK WAGNER
Welcome To His Nightmare

Dick Wagner was a world-renowned and respected rock guitarist/songwriter best known for his work with Alice Cooper and Lou Reed. One of the best-known songs written by Wagner was the hit "Only Women Bleed" from the Alice Cooper album *Welcome to My Nightmare*.

He was also very proud of his work on the *Welcome to My Nightmare II* album. Alice Cooper said, "We'll put some of the original people on it..." Names that Alice mentioned were Slash, Neil Smith, Dennis Dunaway, Steve Hunter, and, of course, Dick Wagner.

Wagner also played lead guitar or wrote songs for Aerosmith, Lou Reed, Burton Cummings, KISS, Meat Loaf, Steve Perry, Ringo Starr, Etta James, Peter Gabriel, Rod Stewart, Tina Turner, Air Supply, Hall & Oates, Roy Orbison, Jerry Lee Lewis, Little Richard, and many more.

There's a reason that Dick Wagner's fans and friends called him "The Maestro of Rock." Dick's guitar playing was both wild and fluid. His songwriting, guitar playing, and musical arrangements were uniquely rockin', majestic, and orchestral. Listen back to his monumental arrangements on Lou Reed's live album *Rock 'N' Roll Animal*. He took Reed's Velvet Underground songs and turned them into ravishing and passionate arena rock.

Wagner was prolific not only in the tangible realm of what we can see and hear, but in the boundless energy of his spirit, which will never die. He was a fighter but in the end his body couldn't keep up with his spirit, and so he laid to rest. Dick said in 2013, "Love is in the air. Breathe deep." Take Dick's advice into your own hearts, and embrace all the passion and beauty in the world.

His creativity and passion will live on forever in the legacy he has left for us, in his music and his words.

Dick Wagner The Maestro of Rock: www.facebook.com/groups/maestroofrock

Dick Wagner's personal Facebook page: www.facebook.com/wagnerrocks

Dick Wagner's TERRORble Top 10 Horror Films

The original **Dracula** (1931): I was between five and seven years old when my Grandfather took me to the matinee, Saturday afternoon, the Ritz Theatre, Oelwein, Iowa. It was a double feature of **Dracula** and **Frankenstein**. At that very young age, I learned what the word fear was all about. I never forgot.

The original **Frankenstein** (1931): See **Dracula**.

The Thing (From Another World!) (1951): Demonic space vegetable creature, entombed for ages in ice, gets loose in an Antarctic science lab and scares the crap out of me and many others, until he's undone by electrical charge. Too much, too young. Scary!!

The Creeper (2012): Frighteningly ugly second story man, murderer… comes in through the living room window to kill beautiful blonde woman. Plot foiled, creeper arrested. Butt cheeks relaxed.

Se7en (1995): Serial killer bases kills on the seven deadly sins, ends up delivering head of detective's young wife placed in a box, to detective, after his arrest. Great movie. Chilling ending…I was old enough.

Parasomnia (2008): Written and directed by my friend William Malone, it's a story about the love between a comatose girl and a young disturbed man, conflicted by the interference of a raging serial killer hellbent on having the comatose girl for himself. Excellent pacing with hypnotic 1960s Bossmen soundtrack. A must-see, rounding out the list…

House on Haunted Hill (1959)

Psycho (1960)

"Dexter" (series, 2006)

"True Blood" (2008)

BEVERLY WASHBURN
Spider Baby

Spider Baby isn't usually on anyone's Top 10 List, but in this case it deserves to be. The child actress in this film, Beverly Washburn, has quite an on-screen resume. As a child, she was already in more genre productions than many actresses play in their entire careers. Fans of the Lon Chaney Jr. film **Spider Baby**, which also featured horror icon Sid Haig, will recognize the name Beverly Washburn from her role as the young Elizabeth.

Her first uncredited role was as six-year-old Walda Kowalski in the 1950 film entitled **The Killer That Stalked New York**. She appeared once on NBC's original "Star Trek," playing the role of Lieutenant Arlene Galway in the 1967 episode "The Deadly Years." In 1951, Washburn appeared in the theatrical film **Superman and the Mole Men**, which was thereafter edited into two half-hour segments. These became the first two episodes of the TV series "The Adventures of Superman," starring George Reeves. She portrayed the character Lollie Harrod in the 1961 episode "Parasite Mansion" of Boris Karloff's NBC suspense series "Thriller," and also appeared in an episode of "One Step Beyond."

Her biography is *Reel Tears: The Beverly Washburn Story* and it was published by BearManor Media.

Beverly loves to hear from fans of **Spider Baby**, adding "That film was so much fun for me and working with Lon Chaney was amazing. **Spider Baby** was one of my favorite films and I'm always so touched when people receive it in such a positive way."

Special thanks to the wonderful Auntie B's lovely niece Shannon for arranging this article.

Beverly Washburn's TERRORble Top 10 Favorite Fright Flicks

Psycho (1960): Alfred Hitchcock was a brilliant filmmaker and the shower scene was frightening.

Young Frankenstein (1974): Mostly because I love what Mel Brooks does.

The Wolf Man (1941): How can you not love Lon Chaney Jr.? Very cool movie

The Shining (1980): Jack Nicholson is amazing and I thought it was very well done.

Invasion of the Body Snatchers (1956): I think Kevin McCarthy is wonderful and I was fortunate enough to get to work with him on a TV show. Excellent OLD scary film.

Abbott & Costello Meet Frankenstein (1948): OK, just silly, but who doesn't want to laugh? I worked with Lou Costello on an episode of "Wagon Train" and it was the only dramatic role he ever did. He was the nicest man ever.

Rosemary's Baby (1968): Creepy and scary.

What Ever Happened to Baby Jane? (1962): Wonderful acting, wonderful cast, and damn scary!

The Howling (1981): Scaaaarrryy!

Carrie (1976): Sissy Spacek is an amazing actress and it was REALLY scary.

OK...dare I add number 11? And is it too tacky to name my own movie?! Yep, that would have to be **Spider Baby** (1967). Very low budget, very tongue in cheek, and very campy. And Lon Chaney Jr. sang the theme song, too! How cool is that?

JANE WIEDLIN
"We Got the (Monster) Beat!"

Who doesn't know and love The Go-Go's? Jane Wiedlin, together with lead singer Belinda Carlisle, formed The Go-Go's, and most of their songs were written or co-written by Jane (including the classic "Our Lips Are Sealed"). The Go-Go's went on to enormous success, becoming the first-ever all-girl group to write all their own songs, play their own instruments, and become immensely popular doing it. Jane continues to write, record, and perform, and *Rolling Stone* Magazine called her solo album *Kissproof World* a "solo tour de force by an entrepreneur, an actress, and rock goddess."

As Wiedlin puts it, "Unless you are living under a rock (and that actually sounds kinda cool), you know that Go-Go's activity has really ramped up. We had the Broadway Musical 'Head Over Heels,' which ran for six months. Now the show is being produced all over the country in smaller theaters. Pretty cool. The latest news is that the documentary **The Go-Go's** premiered at Sundance Film Festival. It's getting rave reviews from audience members and critics alike." Her Top 10 List deserves rave reviews as well.

For more information on Jane, visit www.JaneWiedlin.com.

And now...with a New Wave drum roll...we present...

Jane Wiedlin's TERRORble Top 10 Rockin'/ Horror Films List

The Blob (Steve McQueen, 1958): When I was a little kid, they used to show teenage horror movies from the '50s on TV on Saturdays, and this one left quite the impression. I ADORE the whole genre of "the kids are the only ones that know what's really going on, but those danged adults JUST WON'T LISTEN!"

Psycho (1960): This is the first horror movie I remember seeing, and to this day, I cannot handle shower curtains being closed. I'm serious!

The Birds (1963): Just thinking about this movie makes me want to cover my eyeballs! I can't believe I saw this film as a small child!

Godzilla (all, starting in 1954): I spent my childhood watching Godzilla movies. I love that the Japanese were never very clear-cut on whether he was good or bad. He was...complicated, like every good leading man. And I was totally in love with Baby Godzilla!

Invasion of the Body Snatchers (1956, 1978): I recall both the original (with the great Kevin McCarthy) and the remake (with the great Donald Sutherland). This movie reminds me of recurrent nightmares I've had, where the bad news is relentless and unstoppable. Really just an incredibly depressing story, when you think about it.

The Shining (1980): If there is anything creepier than your husband/father going postal on you while you are stuck in an ultra-charming but secluded hotel, I can't think of it. Of course, "REDRUM" became a personal mantra of mine for YEARS afterward.

Dead Ringers (1988): Maybe not strictly horror, but certainly super-horrifying. I know I'm a weirdo, but I find this movie super sexy. The whole good twin/ bad twin thing is mesmerizing, especially with the red hot Jeremy Irons as its star.

Videodrome (1983): I love the druggy, surreal feel of this movie, and the way fantasy and reality become so entwined it's impossible to tell which is which. And Debbie Harry is so gorgeous in it!

Buffy the Vampire Slayer (1992): What a TOTALLY AWESOME idea to make a bouncy blonde cheerleader a kickass vampire assassin!! Most original horror film premise of the 1990s. Also turned me into a lifelong Joss Whedon worshipper.

Shaun of the Dead (2004): I think this movie, and Simon Pegg, are absolutely brilliant! The Everyman vibe that Pegg brings to the film as the star and the screenwriter, to me, makes it the best horror movie of this millennium (so far!).

ASHLEY C. WILLIAMS
Human Centipede

There are two actresses named Ashley Williams, but only one of them, Ashley C. Williams, has the horror credentials. A native of Boston, Massachusetts, this Ashley will always be ingrained in the hearts of horror fanatics for her role as Lindsay, the middle member of the human centipede in the infamous motion picture **The Human Centipede**. Anyone who ever watched the 2009 film will never forget it.

Williams' follow-up genre role was Piper in 2010's suspense drama **Empty**. In 2014, she had the title role in the horror film **Julia** as a rape victim pursuing revenge, and she also appeared in **Hallow's Eve**.

Ashley co-founded and acted as Vice President of a company named Mind The Art Entertainment, which produces new work in all art mediums in the New York City area. If she didn't do anything else in the film world, she would be a hero for being in **The Human Centipede**.

Ashley C. Williams' TERRORble Top 10 Fave Monster Movies

Pan's Labyrinth (2006): Directed by the greatest man in the world, Guillermo del Toro. I have to work with him someday. This film is hauntingly beautiful. All his movies are.

The Devil's Backbone (2001): Again, directed by my hero Guillermo. This film is super scary, but so well made. I love the story, and ghost movies are the best cause you can't see them! Ahhh!

Quarantine (2008): Directed by John Erick Dowdle. This film scared the hell out of me. The way the film was shot with just a handheld and no one could see was just brilliant...

Jaws (1975): Directed by Steven Spielberg, who is also a hero of mine. This classic was one of the first scary films I saw, still love it, and still get scared when I go into the ocean...

Shaun of the Dead (2004): Directed by Edgar Wright. I LOVE British humor. This film, the way it's directed, is just brilliant. If this film was made in America, it would not have been as funny.

20,000 Leagues Under the Sea (1954): Directed by Richard Fleischer. This film is such a classic, another amazing one...when I first saw this, that giant squid freaked me out!

Alien (1979): Directed by the great Ridley Scott. Aliens creep me out. I can say so many awesome things about this film, it was just so well acted, so gross, so amazing, so well done!!

Jurassic Park (1993): Directed by Steven Spielberg. Oh Spielberg, I love you so. This film was the first-ever PG-13 movie I ever saw and I was so excited. I loved it and still love watching it to this day. Those T-Rexes were sooo scary!!!

Daybreakers (2009): Directed by Michael Spierig and Peter Spierig. I think this is the best vampire film I have seen. It was so well directed and the story was stellar. I loved the idea.

The Nightmare Before Christmas (1993): Directed by Henry Selick. Ah, Tim Burton. I love his work. This classic I love singing along to, and always watch it over the holidays...it's last but definitely not least!!

BARRY WILLIAMS

He starred in the Syfy movie **Bigfoot** in 2012 (along with Danny Bonaduce of "The Partridge Family") and was the "Marsh Man" in the 2018 film **Flea**. Those are just two of his approximately 50 credits in an over-50-years career in show business. We can agree, however, that the world knows Barry Williams best as Greg Brady, the eldest son in the much-loved TV sitcom "The Brady Bunch" (1969-1974). Before that, as a kid he appeared on a 1967 episode of "The Invaders."

Williams wrote *Growing Up Brady: I Was a Teenage Greg* back in 1992, which actually stayed on *The New York Times*' bestsellers' list for half a year.

Williams toured in the Broadway show "Pippin," which was just the first of his 85 stage productions. He played concerts with The Monkees as Davy Jones' and Micky Dolenz' opening act, and he was one of the Special Guests at the Davy Jones Memorial National Monkees Convention after his friend Davy passed away. For six years, he starred in "70's Music Celebration" in Branson, Missouri, which featured songs and comedies from the '70s.

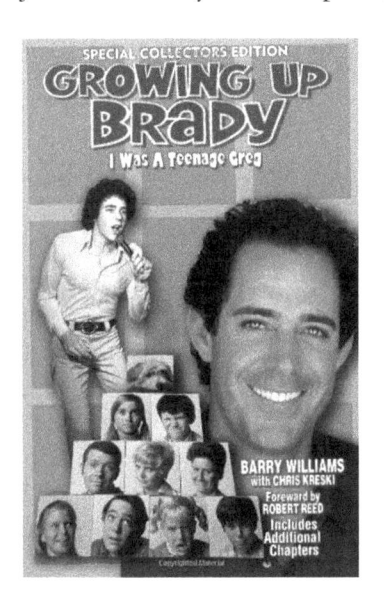

Actor/ singer/ pop culture personality, and all-around good guy, Barry Williams was not only prompt when asked for a list of his favorite genre films, he came through with a great, well-thought-out selection.

Website: www.barrywilliams.com / www.barrywilliamsofficial.com.

Thanks to Ann Reinke, Jodi Blau Ritzen, and Phyllis Paganucci.

Barry Williams' TERRORble Top 10 List

Double Jeopardy (1999): The enjoyment of this film does not come from wondering how it's going to turn out, because Paramount Studios tells the audience before the movie even starts that Ashley Judd's character has been framed for killing her husband ("Libby Parsons is in jail for a crime she didn't commit!," the trailer exclaims right off the bat). Libby correctly suspects that her no-good husband has betrayed and framed her, and is still very much alive. A fellow inmate informs her that since she has already been tried and convicted for her husband's murder, she can't be tried for the same crime twice. Therefore – in theory, at least – she could walk up to him in broad daylight and shoot him in front of a million people without fear of punitive consequences. Not exactly what I'd call sound legal advice. Nevertheless, the relationship between Libby and her gruff, hard-nosed, man-of-few-words parole officer (played by Tommy Lee Jones) makes the movie interesting...that, and the immortalization of Ashley Judd's beauty at the age of 31, even in a prison jumpsuit.

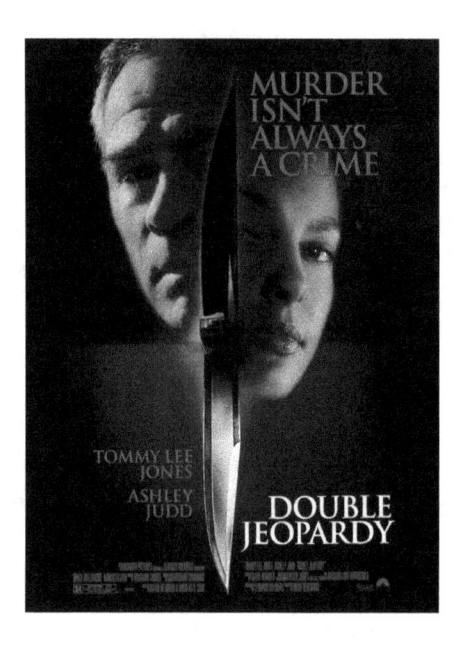

A Time to Kill (1996): Based on John Grisham's first novel. Best film adaptation that I've seen of Grisham's body of work to date. An all-star cast that includes Samuel L. Jackson, Sandra Bullock, Kevin Spacey, Donald Sutherland, Kiefer Sutherland, Matthew McConaughey, and my girlfriend Ashley Judd (when she was only 28) among its luminaries. The film opens with the stomach-churning rape of a 10-year-old black girl by two rednecks in a pickup truck; unwilling to wait for justice (or the likely lack thereof), the girl's father, Carl Lee Hailey (Jackson), kills the rapists in broad daylight on their way to a court hearing, crippling a deputy in the process. What father of a little girl in this world could pretend not to understand the motivation for Hailey's crime? McConaughey plays the attorney willing to take the case amidst a climate of racism, hate, and mistrustfulness, and the still-prevalent presence of the KKK in the "new" South. A morality-play storyline not without its flaws, but well written and featuring terrific performances that make the film ultimately very compelling.

Fright Night (1985): This is a cult classic, full of nods to traditional vampire lore and the black-and-white Hammer, Hitchcock, and Bela Lugosi films of bygone days. (What's especially interesting about that is the fact that **Fright Night** was released at a time when slasher films were all the rage, amidst the seemingly endless **Friday the 13th** and **A Nightmare on Elm Street** installments of the 1980s.) Roddy McDowall is spot-on as Peter Vincent (his moniker is, of course, a combination of the names Peter Cushing and Vincent Price), a man who was once an industry icon and star of old-school horror films, but is now reduced to hosting a TV show called "Fright Night," a campy, low-budget weekly horror film review that is unapologetically shot at a fake graveyard. Charley Brewster, the teenaged hero, must enlist Vincent's help after his attempts to convince his mother, his girlfriend, and the police that new neighbor Jerry Dandridge is a vampire fall hopelessly flat...and what's more, the audience knows that Jerry is on to Charley's meddling from very early on, which builds a palpable tension. The scene where Jerry wanders through Charley's house whistling "Strangers In The Night" before attempting to kill him for the first time has a creepily special charm. Stylishly written and with equal parts humor and terror, **Fright Night** is still a unique horror movie genre hit more than 25 years later.

Rear Window (1954): The ultimate scary movie, if for no other reason than the girl you're watching it with will have to move in close for comfort. Possibly Hitchcock's most masterful thriller. The viewer is so completely drawn into the deceptively simplistic storyline that from the beginning, watching the film feels less like a movie and more like you're actually spying on the neighbors. Jimmy Stewart is superb, and it is his "everyman" quality that helps us to identify with him and become such immediately willing accomplices to his naughty voyeurism, despite the fact that we know it's probably not such a good idea. Grace Kelly is at her smoking hot finest and so affable that at times, we want to throttle Stewart's character for not having the good sense to put down the damn binoculars and take her to bed, already. Riveting from the first scene to the last.

Cape Fear (1991): A fine example of Martin Scorsese's brilliance as a director, this remake shines with a complexity that the 1962 original couldn't have imagined. In this updated version, there are no real heroes, everyone is flawed, and there is an imminent danger lurking beneath the surface of every scene. Robert De Niro, as Max Cady, is a man just released from a 14-year prison sentence for the rape and assault of a young woman, and he wants revenge against Sam Bowden (Nick Nolte), the public defender who represented him at trial and who knowingly concealed a piece of evidence that might have lessened his sentence. Cady is a villain "wronged" (in his mind); Bowden is a pseudo-hero who has transgressed (although the audience would be hard-pressed to disagree with Bowden's tactics in light of Cady's obvious sadism and the brutality of his crimes). Juliette Lewis gives one of her best performances as the displaced 16-year-old daughter strangely intrigued by Cady's evil darkness and implied sexuality; naturally she is drawn to whatever would unnerve and bother her parents (whom she deeply resents) the most. Jessica Lange is subtle but powerful as the alcoholic, long-suffering wife who has tolerated too many of her husband's infidelities and her willingness to sacrifice herself becomes a pivotal moment in the story's climax.

Gregory Peck, Robert Mitchum, and Martin Balsam have cameos in the film; all three actors appeared in the 1962 original. Clever and delightfully disturbing.

Presumed Innocent (1990): Excellent cast, edge-of-your-seat suspenseful storyline, and an unexpected, mind-blowing twist (which, of course, I can't tell you about because it would be a total spoiler and ruin the surprise). Harrison Ford rocks the role of Rusty Sabich, an assistant state's attorney assigned to the murder case of an attractive and highly sexually-charged female lawyer who worked in his office. It is quickly revealed that not only was Rusty shagging her, but so was Rusty's boss (whoops!)…who also happens to be the guy who assigned him specifically to the case. From there, the accusations fly and legal gymnastics ensue; with so many wobbly defenses and questionable (at best) alibis, the viewer's answer to the "did he do it?" question vacillates until the very end. An intricate, complex, and tangled web for the audience to unravel. Based on a best-selling novel. A highly engaging, intelligent, psychological thriller.

The Fugitive (1993): Slick, great acting and directing, action-packed, and taut with tension from beginning to end. Inspired by the TV series of the same name, the film elevates the theme of an innocent man unjustly accused to a whole new complex (and much more exciting) level. Harrison Ford is Dr. Richard Kimble, a well-respected Chicago surgeon who returns home late one night to discover that his wife has just been beaten to death by an unknown one-armed man; a brief struggle takes place with the assailant, who then flees, vanishing as if without a trace. Dr. Kimble's story of the intruder is dismissed in the courtroom and he is sentenced to death, but he manages to escape during a collision between his prison bus and a train…one of the best action scenes in cinematic history. The electrifying crash sequence is reason enough to watch this film, although the movie as a whole is very satisfying. Leading the manhunt for Kimble is a Deputy U.S. Marshal (Tommy Lee Jones), whom the audience simply knows as "Deputy." The cat-and-mouse game is an impressive tactical display as well as a full-fledged adrenaline rush up until the moment the credits start rolling.

The Silence of the Lambs (1991): There's no shortage of creepy elements in this film, based on a novel by Thomas Harris; it has everything from kidnapping to cannibalism, dismembered body parts in jars, beheadings, a figure spying unseen with night vision goggles, unnaturally large bugs, and a psychopath who likes to skin his female victims. Add to that one who likes to eat his victims, plus persistently low lighting and a sense of terror that pervades even the most seemingly-innocuous scenes, and you have the recipe for why this story sticks with you long after you finish watching. But unless you have lived under a rock your whole life, you've already seen this movie and I don't need to go any further with plot analysis. One thing stands out above the others in a long list of what makes this a truly unforgettable cinematic experience, and it is Anthony Hopkins' chilling embodiment of brilliant, unhinged psychiatrist and mass murderer Dr. Hannibal Lecter. Don't watch this one alone, unless you're big on having nightmares.

Se7en (1995): Another ultra-creepy, excellent film with a twist you'll never forget. Two detectives – one newly-appointed to the precinct (Brad Pitt) and the other on his last case before retirement (Morgan Freeman) – investigate a series of murders that at first appear to be unrelated. But as the body count rises, it becomes clear that the victims have been chosen because the killer believes them to be guilty of committing one of the Seven Deadly Sins. Each successive crime scene discovered by the police becomes more gruesome and disturbing, and the message more darkly foreboding; the viewer feels a strong sense of unease long before the killer's awful "masterpiece" is actually revealed. Kevin Spacey delivers an eerie, solid performance as a total nut job. Chilling.

Bigfoot (2012): Featuring Danny Bonaduce, Alice Cooper, Sherilyn Fenn, Bruce Davison, and ME (!) plus a spectacular fight against a legendary behemoth monster…what more could you possibly want? OK, maybe for the setting to be somewhere tropical instead of the beautiful but cold state of Washington, so that all of the girls were living in their bikinis. I could agree with that. Even though our location definitely wasn't bikini weather, this is still a get down, good time movie. If you want to be severely disturbed or have the s@%! scared out of you, then go watch **Psycho** or **The Exorcist**. Or check out any news channel for yet another dismal take on the fiscal cliff. Otherwise, if you're looking to have fun…then get comfortable with a big bag of popcorn and a hot date, turn this one on, and get ready for a happy ending.

DAVE WINFIELD
Top 10 List from a Baseball Hall of Famer

We pride ourselves on having printed Top 10 Lists from some wonderful people. We've had movie stars, authors, singers, musicians, horror icons, convention producers, film-makers, and Rock and Roll Hall of Famers. As we reach the end of this collection, we're proud to present a list from another Hall of Famer, but this one's an athlete who would be known to anyone who has ever followed baseball.

Slugging baseball superstar Dave Winfield played in the Major Leagues for 22 years, with such teams as the New York Yankees, San Diego Padres, California Angels, Minnesota Twins, Cleveland Indians, and Toronto Blue Jays. The slugging outfielder was loved wherever he played, and was an All-Star 12 times. He was voted into the Hall of Fame in 2001.

Dave Winfield was one of the first active athletes to establish a charitable foundation. From its humble beginnings in 1975 to an internationally-acclaimed substance abuse prevention program, the David M. Winfield Foundation, with a $4 million endowment (funded primarily by Winfield), provided services to underprivileged youth, families in need, and the cities in which he played.

After his playing career, Winfield spent years as a sports analyst on ESPN, and he served as the Special Assistant to the Executive Director of the Major League Baseball Players Association.

There weren't many pitchers Dave faced that scared him, but there are some films that still give him the creeps.

Dave Winfield's TERRORble Top 10 List
of Hall of Fame Horror Films

Psycho (1960): Hitchcock, the master. I knew some people who wouldn't go near a shower (though I'm not too sure it had anything to do with this movie).

The Birds (1963): Another Hitchcock, and don't think I didn't think about this one in Toronto in 1983. (*Editor's note*: Winfield accidentally killed a seagull while throwing a ball between innings of a game between the New York Yankees and the Toronto Blue Jays in 1983.)

When A Stranger Calls (1979): The original, because it scares my wife.

Rosemary's Baby (1968): The Dakota, Roman Polanski, it has all the elements.

The Exorcist (1973): I was unaware of some of the activities in hell prior to this one.

Shaun of the Dead (2004)

The Omen (1976)

Aliens (1986)

The Shining (1980): Jack Nicholson gone crazy... there's a stretch.

The Next Voice You Hear (1950): Which isn't exactly a horror movie, but it scared me when I was a kid.

ROBERT ZAPATA
Cannibal and The Headhunters

The name alone conjures scenes of black and white horror films where you didn't know which was scarier – the Headhunting Cannibals or the slow-walking voodoo zombies. But in the mid-'60s, they were a hot band.

Robert Zapata is the band leader and trademark owner of Cannibal and the Headhunters for over half a century. In 1965, the band exploded onto the scene with a great beginning. Within a few months of the group's conception, they were the opening act for the Rolling Stones, The Righteous Brothers, and The Beach Boys. Three months after the Rolling Stones concert, Paul McCartney asked Cannibal and the Headhunters to be one of the opening acts on The Beatles' second American tour, from August 15 through August 31, 1965. Their biggest charting hit was "Land of a Thousand Dances."

"Cannibal" passed away in 1996, but Zapata carries on the band's tradition by continuing to perform, mostly with other acts from the '60s and '70s.

His list represents some of his favorite movie moments "that were some of the best I think of – from when I was a kid – that I still enjoy today."

Robert Zapata's Favorite Top 10 TERRORble Horror-Terror Scary Films

The Phantom of the Opera (1925): Now this movie is a silent horror film starring Lon Chaney that left a lot to the imagination. Living in the catacombs of an opera house, the deformed Phantom is on a mission to make the woman he loved a star. In the scene where the Phantom is sitting at the organ and when he turns his head to show his face to me...that was the scariest movie moment as a young kid.

There are three movies that are my all-time best. The first is **Frankenstein** (1933), starring Boris Karloff as Frankenstein, based on a story written by Mary Shelley when she was 18 years old. She published the story in January 1818, when she was 20 years old! To think of a scientist that would create a person from body parts is crazy, but when I saw this movie, the thought of it made me wonder how the monster would look and walk. But when they made the monster talk and smoke later on, I did not care for that. The grunting is what works for the monster.

Second all-time best is **The Wolf Man** (1941), starring Lon Chaney Jr., written by Curt Siodmak, and produced and directed by George Waggner. I remember this line from the movie: "Even a man who is pure in heart and says his prayers by night may become a wolf when the wolfsbane blooms and the autumn moon is bright." Lon Chaney Jr., who plays Larry Talbot, is the best wolfman ever! The special effects were amazing back then – to transform from man to beast and back again to man was the part of the movie everybody waited for. The silver bullet was the wolfman's way to end his misery.

My third all-time best is **The Mummy** (1932), starring Boris Karloff. It's a romantic horror classic directed by Karl Freund with a story by Nina Wilcox

Putnam and Richard Schayer. Another great performance by Boris Karloff, playing an Egyptian mummy who seeks out a lost love and tries to make her his again. King Karloff was the right choice to play the Mummy – he had the walk with no talking at all and you knew what he was thinking. I have always been a lover of Egyptian movies. This made me like Egypt even more; hope to visit there some time.

1953 gave us **House of Wax**, starring Vincent Price, Frank Lovejoy, and Phyllis Kirk. Price plays a man who has a disfigured face and runs a broken-down wax museum. He starts filling his museum with waxed corpses from people that his partner brings (played by Charles Bronson). I've never seen Charles Bronson play a character like this; he goes out to murder people so they can be waxed and displayed in the museum.

Dracula (1931): Starring Bela Lugosi as Count Dracula, the well-known supernatural horror film directed and co-produced by Tod Browning with a screenplay written by Garrett Fort, as adapted from the 1897 novel *Dracula* by Bram Stoker. The pool of actors from back in the 1930s was some of the best in this genre. Bela Lugosi was so perfect for the part – that face! His eyes! When his eyes stared at someone, you knew what was coming next...a bite in the neck. Bela Lugosi is the one and only Dracula that goes down in history as the BEST.

The Exorcist (1973): Starring Linda Blair, Ellen Burstyn, and Max von Sydow. Directed by William Friedkin, this movie is based on actual exorcisms. In the movie, Linda Blair plays a girl who is possessed by spiritual entities. It's the devil who takes over her body. Before we know it, she is tossing around the bed like a doll. The young Linda Blair played it well. This film was very well done. It was so scary and frightening that it actually made you jump. With this film, we actually saw a 50% increase in the number of exorcisms performed between the early 1960s and the mid-1970s, and a lot of people were praying more after they saw this movie.

The Birds (1963): Starring Rod Taylor, Tippi Hedren, and Jessica Tandy. A brilliant horror thriller directed by Alfred Hitchcock, based on the story by Daphne du Maurier. It's kind of a love story between Rod Taylor and Tippi Hedren, surrounded by the attacks of birds on a small town called Bodega Bay, California. The scene of a massive amount of birds attacking a school and killing the teacher (played by Suzanne Pleshette) was unforgettable. Seeing the birds kill a neighbor and poke out his eyes was definitely scary for a bird movie. Talk about "Angry Birds!"

It (2017): Starring Bill Skarsgard, Jaeden Martell, and Jeremy Ray Taylor. This movie takes place in Derry, Maine, where a clown who goes by the name of Pennywise is a blood-hungry, shape-shifting evil that comes out of the sewer every 27 years. He's hungry for the town's children. This modern-day scary movie had me on the edge of my seat and just made it harder for people to like clowns.

King Kong (1933): Starring Fay Wray, Bruce Cabot, and Robert Armstrong, directed and produced by Merian C. Cooper and Ernest B. Schoedsack. The movie starts with Robert Armstrong as Carl Denham, on the lookout for a girl on the streets of New York to travel to a mysterious island to film some wildlife. They take a long voyage and come to a place where the fog is heavy and thick. Once the fog clears up in the morning, they take a small boat to Skull Island. There are no natives to be seen anywhere. But they are there! One look at Ann Darrow and the natives want her for a sacrifice to the Great Ape. As it turns out, the ape falls in love with her and doesn't kill her. We all know the rest. One of my all-time best beasts.

"CRYPTMASTER CHUCKY"

The author of this book does most of his acting in a haunted attraction called "FrightHaven." There, he greets guests, reads them the rules of the haunt, injects a little humor to give them a sense of false security, and then ushers them into Connecticut's largest, scariest, and greatest indoor haunted attraction, where they are accosted by actors/ monsters of all shapes, colors, and sizes. Anyone who has ever worked in the haunt industry knows how much fun it is to scare! The haunt is curated by fright fanatic and scare expert Bobby Arel with help from Cara Canelli, an amazing cast of scare-actors, and a behind-the-scenes crew that makes up the "Fright Family."

It's located in Stratford, Connecticut, and can be found on the web at www.FrightHaven.com.

As a demonic clown in the Fright Haven Haunted House (Stratford, CT)

"Cryptmaster Chucky," better known as Charles F. Rosenay!!!, is much more of an actor than his haunted house fright family may realize. As a child, he appeared on Bozo the Clown's kiddie television show in New York, where he was chosen to do a commercial for Ronzoni spaghetti. However, his first-ever film credit came in 1982, but not as an actor. Charles supplied rare audio material for the 1982 documentary film **The Compleat Beatles**, and his name can be seen when the credits scroll at the end. His first credited acting role, though, was in the vigilante revenge thriller **A Gun for Jennifer**, a 1997 film release directed by Todd Morris and starring Deborah Twiss. Weirdly enough, Charles only auditioned for this film and was never in it. That's right, despite having his name as a credited actor (it's also included on his IMDb listing), he never appeared in the film, nor shot any scenes for it!

He was an extra, playing a student, in the 1990 film **A Girl's Guide**, which aired on the USA Network's "Night Flight" programming schedule in the '80s and then disappeared. So did Charles – from films, that is. Instead of spending time auditioning for films or actually getting on-screen work, Rosenay!!! was too busy organizing theme tours to Liverpool for Beatles fans, to Transylvania for horror/ Dracula buffs, publishing a magazine on The Beatles, DJing/ MCing full time, producing conventions, and, oh yes, ultimately taking care of his elderly parents.

But the acting bug bit again in the next decade. Charles appeared in the New York-shot short film **Shadayim** as an Uncle (2006), was cast as a news reporter in the made-for-TV mini-series "The Bronx is Burning" (2007), and was a teacher in the teen comedy **All Screwed Up** (2009). Also in 2009, in what is probably his favorite non-horror role, he played Elton John in HBO's musical comedy series "Flight of The

"The Bronx is Burning," and so is the scalp after having to wear that period hairpiece for a day of extra work.

Conchords." It was the seventh episode of Season Two ("Prime Minister"), which first aired March 1, 2009 on HBO. Rosenay!!! was one of two Eltons (the other was actor/ comedian Patton Oswalt), and the same episode also guest-starred Art Garfunkel. He recalls the phone conversation from the casting director: "Is this Charles?" "Yes." "Have you ever played Elton John?" "Yes." "OK, you have the role." Rosenay!!! never took acting lessons, but he was always told to say "yes" no matter what they asked. No, he hadn't played Elton John, aside from lip-syncing "Crocodile Rock" at parties. But he pulled it off and it was a blast!

In 2010, Rosenay!!! played a rehab group member in "This Wretched Life" and portrayed "Death" in Austin Case's Yale-produced black comedy **Kvetch**. His portrayal of a grim reaper – complete with Yiddish accent – won him the Best Supporting Actor Role in the Atlantic City Cinefest/ Downbeach Film Festival, where the film itself won an award for Best Comedy Short.

Rosenay!!! shared screen time with actor Fran Kranz (**The Cabin in the Woods**) as a sometimes-topless cult member in a comedy that was shot years earlier but finally released in 2018, **The Truth About Lies**. Colleen Camp and Jonathan Katz also appeared in the film.

Charles was an extra in some of Gorman Bechard's films: **Disconnected**, **Galactic Gigolo**, and **Psychos in Love**, and he had a recurring role in the raunchy comedy web-series "Winners," playing the bumbling Dad. He was also an extra (in outdoor Manhattan scenes alongside Ben Stiller and Kristen Wiig) in the big-budget theatrical release **The Secret Life of Walter Mitty** (2013), a bar patron in HBO's **The Deuce** (2017), and a cameraman in HBO's **Vinyl** (2016), which was produced by Martin Scorsese and Mick Jagger.

Speaking of Scorsese and Jagger, Rosenay!!! also appeared in the Rolling Stones' film **Shine a Light**. At the end of the 2008 concert film, when the Stones come off the Beacon Theatre stage, you can see Charles as a backstage roadie putting a robe on Ron Woods. It was a great thrill for Charles to be directed by Martin Scorsese, especially when Robert De Niro came to visit the set. When the live concert movie came out, Charles and a few friends went to see the premiere, and they all burst into a standing ovation when Charles came on the screen – to the complete confusion of the rest of the movie theater audience.

To close out this book, the author is delighted to include his favorite horror roles (none of which were mentioned above).

Thank you for reading all the previous lists herein. Now go catch up on watching the films mentioned in this book that you haven't seen!

"Cryptmaster Chucky's" Favorite TERRORble Top 10 Horror Film Roles

Pink Eye (2008): It's an American horror film directed by James Tucker. The movie is set in a run-down asylum where drugs are tested, in a small town in upstate New York. I got to play one of the disturbed patients who tries to attack the hero at one point, but he kills me instead – with a crowbar up through my head. The stills and rushes from the film were so much better and scarier than the released film! It's too bad because

Scene from "Pink Eye"

I ad-libbed at one part and I really freaked everyone out by creepily walking backwards in the background of one scene.

The Sadist (2013): It was amazing seeing this on the big screen when it had its theatrical motion picture premiere in 2015 (even though it was in Waterbury, Connecticut and not Hollywood). I got to play the father of the lead (Frank Wihbey) in the beginning of the film, and pretty much played myself. The movie, directed by Jeremiah Kipp from Big Caper Films, turned very dark and sinister thereafter, with horror legend Tom Savini as the sadist. It was originally going to be called "The Swine." The only thing better than being cast as the dad in the film was seeing (and hearing) the film's official trailer.

The Sadist (trailer): My voice is the first voice you hear in the trailer. That was almost as exciting as being in the film itself! It's the only time I made it into a film's trailer/ preview/ coming attraction! You can find it on YouTube.

Dead Survivorz (2017): I had fun with this one. It's a grade-Z zombie film shot on a shoestring budget. I got production designer credit because it was filmed in my haunted house in Connecticut, but I also had free rein to play a crazed coroner alongside my buddy and fellow DJ Lew Bundles (real name Dave Gallo). We had a blast learning the lines at the shoot, and improvising as we went. Unfortunately, the film was re-shot in 2018 (on a sneaker-string budget) with other actors. I was called in to do a scene but I don't think it made the cut. But I have the footage with my manic scenes from the original shoot, which is hysterical to watch. I'm on an antique rotary phone when a zombie I was ready to dissect wakes up.

I was also cast as a hotel desk clerk by the same filmmaker, Michele Plunkett, in her 2018 suspense short, **The Dark Passenger**. For that, I wanted to spice up the brief scene I was in and make him a demented character with some visual props. She wanted me to play it straight, which I did, but it was boring and a waste of some comic relief that I could've added to a droll role. Plunkett has a lot of talent as a filmmaker and camera-person; I look forward to seeing where her potential leads.

Welcome Mats (2010): This was my first film for Douglas A. Plomitallo of ScaredStiff.TV, and the beginning of a great friendship and working relationship. It's also a great memory for several reasons: Firstly, it's a clever plot with a nice ending. Secondly, it also starred Analisa Robertson. Thirdly, I got to be a vampire! Fourth, and most importantly, I was able to get two of my kids in the film – my daughter Lauren (who was 11 at the time) and my older son Harrison (who was five). They were so young!

All I can add is one word… "FEEEEED!"

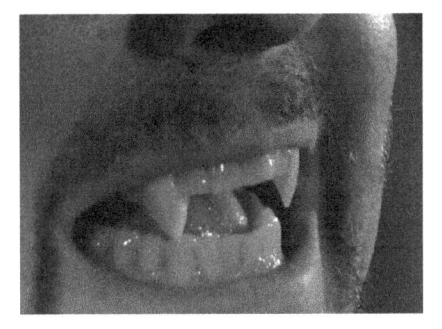

The Confessional (2011): My next adventure for Plomitallo was in a rather unique and experimental film combining live actors with CGI-ish animation in a hybrid mash-up. When a guy, played by the always-excellent George Walsh, survives the zombies and comes into the church confessional to spill his heart out to the priest, he has no idea that the priest is actually one of the zombies he's trying to escape from. Yes, I'm the zombie priest! Similar to **Welcome Mats** in that I only appear briefly right at the end, but it's a strong showing. I particularly liked the make-up work on my teeth.

The Zombie Chronicles (2013): I had to learn a lot of lines for Plomitallo in this multi-part series, but it was worth it. He probably got the best acting out of me ever, and I also came up with the great line in Part One of the trilogy, "Forgive me father...," that is recited by actor Jason Kulas right before he kills me. I may have been speared up the neck in **Pink Eye**, but it wasn't half as cool as being blown away by a single gunshot right to the head. I still can't get over how realistic it looks (not so much in the photos). In another of his productions, **The Confes-**

In the car driving home after "The Confessional" shoot

sional, Douglas cast me as a zombie priest, but here as a former priest. I guess he realized I was a religious guy (just the wrong religion)! What's also cool is that the scene is reprised, albeit in atmospheric black and white, as part of the intro to the second chapter of this series. You could watch the whole series on YouTube, or just find the one episode by searching "ScaredStiff Zombie Chronicles Part 2 Odyssey."

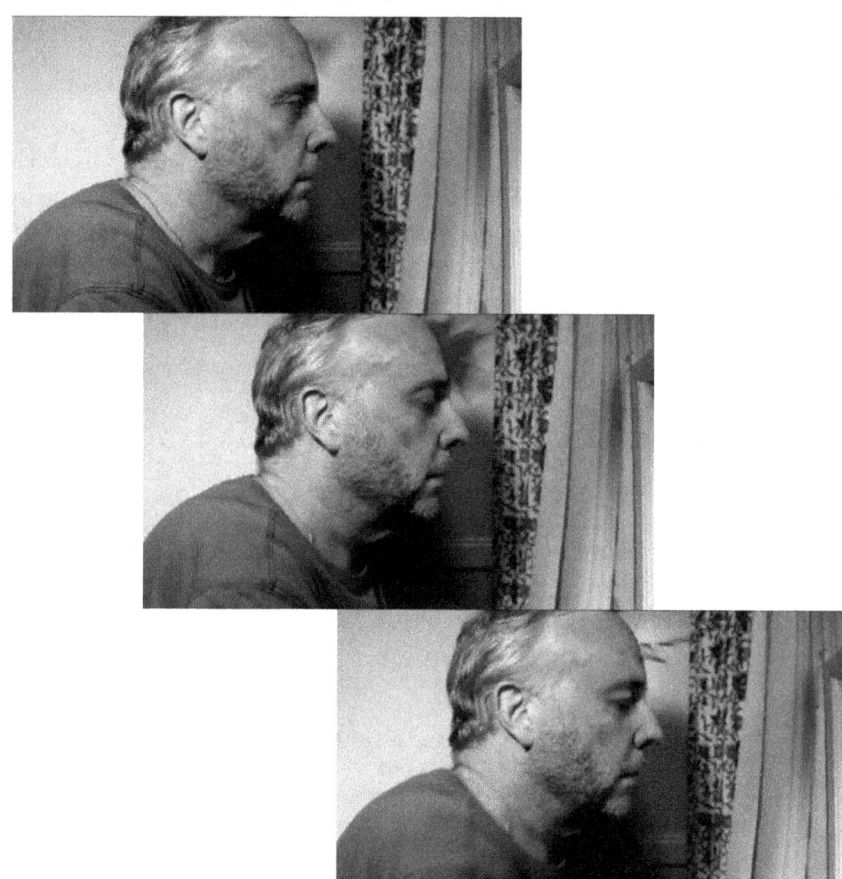

Tiny's Halloween 3 (2012): Yes, it's the third sequel, as there were a number of these. Another Douglas Plomitallo production, Tiny is his personal Freddy Krueger/ Michael Myers/ Jason Voorhees, but in clown form. Every Halloween, Tiny is on the hunt for candy, and bad things happen to those who deny him. Tiny is sort of an anti-hero. Surprisingly, I don't die in this one! Bonus points: both my older son Harrison and younger son Ian got to be in a trick-or-treat scene together. Even though they're my sons, I was cast as their grandfather.

The author's sons, Harrison Rosenay and Ian Rosenay, are out trick-or-treating in "Tiny's Halloween 3."

Halloween House (2017): In between two of these "Tiny" films, I got to do another Scared-Stiff.tv production, filmed in Fright Haven, my haunted attraction. I play the henchman, and I really had fun with this one. Yes, of course I was killed in it (huge gunshot holes in the throat), but before biting the bullet (literally), I got in some tasty lines and flexed some acting chops, working with ace Connecticut actor Joe Nemchek, a huge fellow Beatles fan who also chewed up the scenery beautifully.

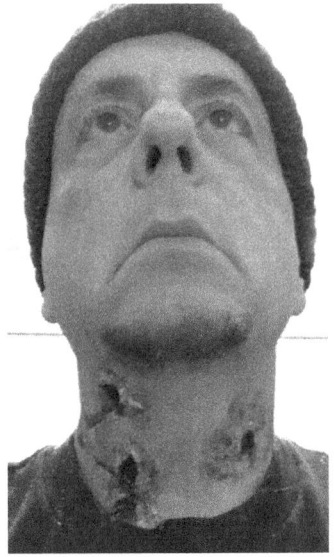

I felt as if this was a warm-up for me, to hopefully soon have a lead role in one of Plomitallo's projects, and the whole production seemed like a precursor to...

Tiny's October 31st (2019): Oh, I loved this one. Plomitallo finally trusted me with the lead, and I think I shined in a dark role. Here, I got to play Anthony Carvoni, the heartless owner of a haunted attraction, with free rein to camp it up. This was also filmed at Fright Haven, with some of my haunt actors as extras, plus guest appearances by professional wrestler Tommy Dreamer and actress/ model Monique Dupree. It's a tour-de-farce with some excellent effects, cool lighting, amazing camerawork, a smart and solid script, a lot of great acting, a tremendous crew (shout out to Fred and Jose – let's talk about horror films again soon), a cameo by Lou Bundles, and yes, in case you were wondering, I do get killed again (by stapler this time!). Thank you, Douglas. Thank you, Tiny!

Two scenes from ScaredStiff.TV's award-winning "Tiny's October 31st" Horror Short. Photos by Jose Lopez Jr.

I appreciate you reading my list, and all the lists herein.
Now go catch up on watching the films mentioned that you haven't seen!

Thank you, readers.
Cheers and Chills,
Charles F. Rosenay!!! (AKA "Cryptmaster Chucky")

Websites:
www.BookOfTop10HorrorLists.com
www.DracTours.com
www.GHOSTours.com
www.ParaConn.org
www.FrightHaven.com
www.ToursAndEvents.com.

Email:
BookofTop10HorrorLists@gmail.com

THE ULTIMATE TERRORBLE TOP 10 LIST

Now we present the "ultimate" list – the films that were selected the most times by our esteemed celebrities in this book:

The Exorcist (1973) – 34 votes

Psycho (1960) – 32 votes

The Shining (1980) – 30 votes

Frankenstein (1931) – 28 votes

Dracula (1931) – 21 votes

Jaws (1975) – 19 votes

Night of the Living Dead (1968) – 19 votes

Alien (1979) – 18 votes

Rosemary's Baby (1968) – 18 votes

The Wolf Man (1941) – 16 votes

INDEX OF FILMS

Below are the titles of all the films (as well as books and plays) followed by the celebrities who included them in their lists.

Abbott & Costello Meet Dr. Jekyll and Mr. Hyde (1953): Vince Martell
Abbott & Costello Meet Frankenstein (1948): Michael Dante, Eddie Deezen, Elliott Easton, Little Anthony Gourdine, Vince Martell, Kasim Sulton, Beverly Washburn
Abbott & Costello Meet the Invisible Man (1951): Vince Martell
Abbott & Costello Meet the Mummy (1955): Vince Martell
After.Life (2009): Debbie D
Albino Farm (2009): Bianca Allaine
Alfred Hitchcock Presents (series, 1955): Bev Bevan
Alfred Hitchcock Presents episode **The Glass Eye** (1957): William Shatner
Alfred Hitchcock Presents episode **Mother, May I Go Out to Swim?** (1960): William Shatner
Alien (1979): Ed Asner, Mark Bego, Corbin Bernsen, Bev Bevan, Ron Dante, Micky Dolenz, Gloria Gaynor, Little Anthony Gourdine, Frank Jeckell, Angie McCartney, Bill Mumy, Christian Nesmith, Butch Patrick, Gary Puckett, Lada St. Edmund, Gary Van Scyoc, Phil "Fang" Volk, Ashley C. Williams
Alien: Covenant (2017): Angie McCartney
Alien: Resurrection (1997): Angie McCartney
Alien 3 (1992): Angie McCartney
Aliens (1986): Tim Atwood, Steve Cuden, Sharon Farrell, Brute Force, Circe Link, Ian Lloyd, Angie McCartney, Christian Nesmith, William Shatner, Dave Winfield
An American Werewolf in London (1981): Sybil Danning, Circe Link
The Amityville Horror (1979): Pete Best, Beverly Bremers, Gloria Gaynor
Amityville 3-D (1983): Fred Schneider
Anaconda (1997): Tim Atwood
An Andalusian Dog (Un ChienAndalou) (1929): Vampy
Andy Warhol's Frankenstein (1974): Vampy
Angel Heart (1987): Eerie Von
Animal Farm (book, 1945): Julia Baird
Astro-Zombies M3: Cloned (2010): Ted V. Mikels
The Atomic Submarine (1959): Rick Mullen
Attack of the 50 Foot Woman (1958): Elliott Easton
Attack of the Giant Leeches (1959): Bill Moseley
Audition (1999): Michael Hein
Back to the Future (1985): Micky Dolenz
The Bad Seed (1956): Laurie Jacobson, Kimberly Magness, Deborah Voorhees
Bambi (1942): Clay Cole, Murray Langston, Donna Loren
Basket Case (1982): Dean Friedman
Basket Case 2 (1990): Dean Friedman
Basket Case 3 (1991): Dean Friedman

Beast from Haunted Cave (1959): Bill Moseley
The Beast with Five Fingers (1946): Chuck McCann, Jon Provost
The Beatles episode **A Hard Day's Night** (cartoon series, 1965): Eddie Deezen
Beauty and the Beast (1946): Brute Force
Bela Lugosi Meets a Brooklyn Gorilla (1952): Eddie Deezen, Vince Martell
Ben (1972): Clay McLeod Chapman
Beverly Hills Vamp (1989): Eddie Deezen
Beyond Re-Animator (2003): Dean Friedman
Bigfoot (2012): Barry Williams
The Birds (1963): Corbin Bernsen, Beverly Bremers, T. Graham Brown, Ruth Buzzi, Michael Dante, Kimberly Magness, Angie McCartney, Elaine Spanky McFarlane, Butch Patrick, Kasim Sulton, Phil "Fang" Volk, Jane Wiedlin, Dave Winfield, Robert Zapata
The Black Cat (1934): Sara Karloff, Eerie Von
The Blair Witch Project (1999): Pete Best, Robb Ortel
The Blob (1958): Tony Bramwell, Clay McLeod Chapman, Sharon Farrell, Don Grady, Frank Jeckell, Metal Pistol, Rick Mullen, Gary Puckett, Jane Wiedlin
Blood & Donuts (1995): Vampy
The Blood Countess (2008): Vampy
Blood Orgy of the She-Devils (1973): Ted V. Mikels
Bram Stoker's Dracula (1992): Mark Bego
The Bride of Frankenstein (1935): Tony Bramwell, Ron Dante, Deana Demko, Elliott Easton, Sharon Farrell, Greg Hawkes, Irwin Keyes, Metal Pistol, Jon Provost, Eerie Von
Bride of Re-Animator (1990): Deana Demko, Dean Friedman
Brokeback Mountain (2005): Murray Langston
The Brood (1979): Dante Tomaselli
The Brotherhood of Satan (1971): Geri Reischl
Brotherhood of the Wolf (Le Pacte Des Loups) (2001): Circe Link
Buffy the Vampire Slayer (1992): Jane Wiedlin
Burnt Offerings (1976): Michael Hein, Dante Tomaselli
Cape Fear (1991): Debbie Rochon, Phil "Fang" Volk, Deborah Voorhees, Barry Williams
Carnival of Souls (1962): Bill Moseley, Rick Mullen, Debbie Rochon
Carrie (book, 1974): Bev Bevan, Frank Jeckell
Carrie (1976): Tony Bramwell, Frank Jeckell, Elizabeth Leiknes, Elaine Spanky McFarlane, Christian Nesmith, Gary Puckett, Geri Reischl, Lada St. Edmund, Eerie Von, Beverly Washburn
The Cat and the Canary (1939): Chuck McCann
The Cauldron: Baptism of Blood (2004): Ted V. Mikels
Children Shouldn't Play With Dead Things (1972): Michael Hein, Robb Ortel
Child's Play (1988): Deana Demko
The City of the Dead (1960): Rick Mullen
Close Encounters of the Third Kind (1977): Mitch Schecter
The Confessional (2011): Charles F. Rosenay!!! ("Cryptmaster Chucky")

The Conjuring (2013): Deborah Voorhees
The Conjuring: The Devil Made Me Do It (2020): Deborah Voorhees
The Conjuring 2 (2016): Deborah Voorhees
Constantine (2005): Lada St. Edmund
The Corpse Grinders (1971): Ted V. Mikels
Corridors of Blood (1958): Metal Pistol
The Crawling Eye (1958): Dean Friedman
The Crazies (2010): Beverly Bremers
Creature from the Black Lagoon (1954): Mark Bego, Freddy Boom Boom Cannon, Walter Egan, Don Grady, Greg Hawkes, Buzzy Linhart, Elaine Spanky McFarlane, Butch Patrick, Gary Puckett, James Lee Stanley, Gary Van Scyoc
The Creature Walks Among Us (1956): Gary Van Scyoc
The Creeper (2012): Dick Wagner
The Creeping Terror (1964): Fred Schneider
Creepshow (1982): John Amplas
Cujo (1983): Tim Atwood
The Curse of Frankenstein (1957): Tony Bramwell, Gary Puckett
The Curse of the Werewolf (1961): Ron Dante
Dark Shadows (series, 1966): Debbie D
Darkness Falls (2003): Gloria Gaynor
Dawn of the Dead (1978): John Amplas, Karen Black, Kevin Clement, Irwin Keyes
Day of the Dead (1985): John Amplas
The Day of the Triffids (book, 1951): Joe R. Lansdale
The Day the Earth Stood Still (1951): Micky Dolenz, Bill Mumy, Gary Puckett, Gary Van Scyoc
Daybreakers (2009): Ashley C. Williams
Dead of Night (1945): Forrest Ackerman, Kevin Clement
Dead Ringers (1988): Jane Wiedlin
Dead Survivorz (2017): Charles F. Rosenay!!! ("Cryptmaster Chucky")
The Dead Zone (1983): Walter Egan
Death of a Ghost Hunter (2007): Debe Branning
Deep Blue Sea (1999): Clay McLeod Chapman
Deliverance (1972): Phil "Fang" Volk
Demon Haunt (2009): Ted V. Mikels
Den (2001): Michael Hein
The Dentist (1996): Corbin Bernsen
The Descent (2005): Robb Ortel
The Devil Within Her (1975): Anthony Masi
The Devils (1971): Kasim Sultan
The Devil's Backbone (2001): Ashley C. Williams
The Devil's Rain (1975): William Shatner
The Devil's Rejects (2005): T. Graham Brown, Kevin Clement, Bill Moseley, Robb Ortel
Dexter (series, 2006): Dick Wagner
Diabolique (1955): Ruth Buzzi, Don Grady, The Amazing Kreskin, Donna Loren

Dildo Heaven (2002): Fred Schneider
Dimension in Fear (1998): Ted V. Mikels
Dr. Jekyll and Mr. Hyde (novella, 1886): Julia Baird
Dr. Jekyll and Mr. Hyde (1941): Clay Cole
The Doll Squad (1973): Ted V. Mikels
Don't Be Afraid of the Dark (1973): Robb Ortel
Don't Go in the Woods (1981): Bianca Allaine
Don't Look in the Basement (1973): Michael Hein
Don't Look Now (1974): Buzzy Linhart, James Lee Stanley
Double Jeopardy (1999): Barry Williams
Dracula (book, 1897): Julia Baird, Joe R. Lansdale
Dracula (1931): Forrest Ackerman, John Amplas, Pete Best, Karen Black, Freddy Boom Boom Cannon, Ron Dante, Walter Egan, Brute Force, Little Anthony Gourdine, Greg Hawkes, The Amazing Kreskin, Circe Link, Vince Martell, Metal Pistol, Rick Mullen, Bill Mumy, Jon Provost, James Lee Stanley, Vampy, Dick Wagner, Robert Zapata
Drag Me to Hell (2009): Sybil Danning
Dumbo (1941): Donna Loren
Dune (1984): Brute Force
Each Time I Kill (2007): Fred Schneider
The Elephant Man (1980): Brute Force
The Entity (1982): Donna Hamblin
Eraserhead (1977): Debbie Rochon, Jonathan Tiersten
E.T. (1982): Karen Black
Event Horizon (1997): Christian Nesmith
The Evil Dead (1981): Dinky Dawson
Evil Dead II (1987): Christian Nesmith
The Exorcist (1973): Tim Atwood, Corbin Bernsen, Bev Bevan, Debe Branning, Beverly Bremers, T. Graham Brown, Ruth Buzzi, Kevin Clement, Steve Cuden, Ron Dante, Micky Dolenz, Walter Egan, Sharon Farrell, Bobby Hart, Laurie Jacobson, Irwin Keyes, Circe Link, Donna Loren, Kimberly Magness, Angie McCartney, Metal Pistol, Bill Mumy, Christian Nesmith, Jon Provost, Gary Puckett, Mitch Schecter, William Shatner, Tiffany Shepis, James Lee Stanley, Kasim Sulton, Jonathan Tiersten, Gary Van Scyoc, Dave Winfield, Robert Zapata
Fallen Angels (2007): Ruth Buzzi
Fatal Attraction (1987): The Amazing Kreskin
Fear in the Night (1972): Tony Bramwell
Fido (2006): Dean Friedman
Flash Gordon (1936): Brute Force
The Fly (1958): Little Anthony Gourdine, Don Grady, Murray Langston, Gary Puckett, Gary Van Scyoc
The Fly (1986): Tim Atwood
Forbidden Planet (1956): Micky Dolenz, Buzzy Linhart, Mitch Schecter
The Forest (1983): Bianca Allaine
The Fountainhead (1949): Barbara Leigh

The 4D Man (1959): Mitch Schecter

Frankenstein (book, 1818): Julia Baird

Frankenstein (1931): Forrest Ackerman, John Amplas, Pete Best, T. Graham Brown, Freddy Boom Boom Cannon, Debbie D, Michael Dante, Ron Dante, Eddie Deezen, Sharon Farrell, Little Anthony Gourdine, Greg Hawkes, Frank Jeckell, Irwin Keyes, The Amazing Kreskin, Buzzy Linhart, Circe Link, Kimberly Magness, Vince Martell, Chuck McCann, Metal Pistol, Bill Mumy, Butch Patrick, Jon Provost, Geri Reischl, Gary Van Scyoc, Dick Wagner, Robert Zapata

Freaks (1932): T. Graham Brown, Ron Dante, Bill Mumy

Friday the 13th (1980): Gloria Gaynor

Friday the 13th Part VI: Jason Lives (1986): Clay McLeod Chapman

Fright Night (1985): Barry Williams

From Beyond (1986): Dean Friedman

The Fugitive (1993): Barry Williams

Galaxy of Terror (1981): Michael Hein

Get Smart episode **Rebecca of Funny-Folk Farm** (series, 1970): Ed Asner

Ghost Story (1981): Jack Ketchum

Ghostbusters (1984): Clay McLeod Chapman, Brute Force, Jack Ketchum

Ghostbusters 2 (1989): Clay McLeod Chapman

Godzilla (1954): Eddie Deezen, Donna Loren, Rick Mullen, Bill Mumy, Jane Wiedlin

Godzilla (1985): Fred Schneider

Gog (1954): Frank Jeckell

The Good Son (1993): Anthony Masi

The Great American Snuff Film (2003): Michael Hein

Grace (2009): Anthony Masi

Gremlins (1984): Dinky Dawson

Grizzly (1976): Bianca Allaine

Halloween (1978): Tim Atwood, Pete Best, Steve Cuden, Deana Demko, Donna Hamblin, Jack Ketchum, Murray Langston, Elizabeth Leiknes, Circe Link, Robb Ortel, Gary Puckett, Geri Reischl, William Shatner

Halloween (2007): Sybil Danning

Halloween House (2017): Charles F. Rosenay!!! ("Cryptmaster Chucky")

Halloween II (1981): Dante Tomaselli

Hamlet (play, 1599-1601): Julia Baird

The Hand (1981): Debbie D, Vampy

The Hand That Rocks the Cradle (1992): Donna Loren

The Happy Hooker (1975): Fred Schneider

The Happy Hooker Goes Hollywood (1980): Fred Schneider

The Happy Hooker Goes to Washington (1977): Fred Schneider

Hardware (1990): Christian Nesmith

The Haunting (1963): Kevin Clement, Elliott Easton, Laurie Jacobson, Elaine Spanky McFarlane, Geri Reischl, Debbie Rochon

The Haunting of Hill House (book, 1959): Joe R. Lansdale

The Hazing (2004): Tiffany Shepis

Heart of a Boy (2006): Ted V. Mikels

Hellraiser (1987): Dean Friedman, Lada St. Edmund, Tiffany Shepis, Kasim Sulton, Jonathan Tiersten, Eerie Von
The Hitch-Hiker (1953): Debbie Rochon
Horror of Dracula (1958): Tony Bramwell, Walter Egan, Barbara Leigh, Gary Puckett
The Horror of Party Beach (1964): Greg Hawkes
House of 1000 Corpses (2003): T. Graham Brown, Irwin Keyes, Bill Moseley
House of Wax (1953): Clay Cole, Ron Dante, Elaine Spanky McFarlane, William Shatner, Robert Zapata
House on Haunted Hill (1959): Mark Bego, Pete Best, Debe Branning, Kevin Clement, Elliott Easton, Greg Hawkes, Barbara Leigh, Kasim Sulton, Dick Wagner
The House with Laughing Windows (1976): Dante Tomaselli
The Howling (1981): Sybil Danning, Ron Dante, Jack Ketchum, Beverly Washburn
The Howling II (1986): Sybil Danning
Hulk (2003): Brute Force
The Hunchback of Notre Dame (1939): John Amplas, Eddie Deezen, Brute Force, Irwin Keyes, Chuck McCann, Jon Provost
The Hunger (1983): Jack Ketchum, Vampy
Hush (2016): Deborah Voorhees
I Am Legend (book, 1954): Joe R. Lansdale
I Bought a Vampire Motorcycle (1990): Dean Friedman
I Drink Your Blood (1970): Sybil Danning
I Eat Your Skin (1971): Rick Mullen
I Was a Teenage Werewolf (1957): Sybil Danning, Walter Egan, Murray Langston, Buzzy Linhart
The Illustrated Man (1969): Phil "Fang" Volk
In Cold Blood (1967): Debbie Rochon
The Incredible Shrinking Man (1957): Elliott Easton
Incubus (1966): William Shatner
Innocent Blood (1992): Jack Ketchum
The Innocents (1961): Kevin Clement, Bill Moseley
Insidious (2010): Deborah Voorhees
Interview with the Vampire (1994): Mark Bego
Invaders from Mars (1953): Micky Dolenz, James Lee Stanley
Invasion of the Body Snatchers (1956): Karen Black, Debe Branning, Walter Egan, Sharon Farrell, Gloria Gaynor, Little Anthony Gourdine, Ian Lloyd, Elaine Spanky McFarlane, Butch Patrick, Gary Puckett, Debbie Rochon, Mitch Schecter, Beverly Washburn, Jane Wiedlin
Invasion of the Body Snatchers (1978): Geri Reischl, Jane Wiedlin
The Invisible Man (1933): Freddy Boom Boom Cannon, The Amazing Kreskin
Island of Lost Souls (1932): Brute Force
It (2017): Donna Hamblin, Robert Zapata
It Came From Outer Space (1953): Don Grady, Buzzy Linhart, James Lee Stanley
It's Alive (1974): Karen Black
Jacob's Ladder (1990): Circe Link, Christian Nesmith

Jaws (1975): Tim Atwood, Corbin Bernsen, Debe Branning, Beverly Bremers, T. Graham Brown, Steve Cuden, Gloria Gaynor, Donna Hamblin, Jack Ketchum, Murray Langston, Elizabeth Leiknes, Bill Moseley, Christian Nesmith, Gary Puckett, William Shatner, Tiffany Shepis, Gary Van Scyoc, Phil "Fang" Volk, Ashley C. Williams
Jekyll & Hyde: The Musical (2001): Steve Cuden
Jeepers Creepers (2001): Deana Demko, Robb Ortel
Jeepers Creepers 2 (2003): Robb Ortel
Joshua (2007): Anthony Masi
Junior Bonner (1972): Barbara Leigh
Jurassic Park (1993): Ashley C. Williams
Just Before Dawn (1981): Bianca Allaine
Killer Klowns from Outer Space (1988): Clay McLeod Chapman
King Kong (1933): Forrest Ackerman, Eddie Deezen, Bobby Hart, Laurie Jacobson, Donna Loren, Bill Mumy, Jon Provost, Phil "Fang" Volk, Robert Zapata
King Kong (1976): Debe Branning
King Lear (play, 1605-1606): Julia Baird
Kingdom of the Spiders (1977): William Shatner
Kronos (1957): Fred Schneider
Kwaidan (1964): Elaine Spanky McFarlane
The Last Exorcism (2010): Tiffany Shepis
The Last House on the Left (1972): Debe Branning, Elliott Easton, Butch Patrick, Geri Reischl
The Last Winter (2006): John Amplas
Legend (1985): Deana Demko
Legend of the 7 Golden Vampires (1979): Tony Bramwell
Leprechaun (1993): Dinky Dawson
Leprechaun 2 (1992): Dinky Dawson
Leprechaun 3 (1995): Dinky Dawson
Leprechaun 4: In Space (1997): Dinky Dawson
Leprechaun Part 5: Leprechaun In The Hood (2000): Clay McLeod Chapman, Dinky Dawson
Leprechaun 6: Back 2 tha Hood (2003): Dinky Dawson
Let The Right One In (2008): Anthony Masi
Let's Scare Jessica to Death (1971): Dante Tomaselli
The Lodger (1944): The Amazing Kreskin
Logan's Run (1976): Debbie D
The Lonely Lady (1983): Fred Schneider
Lord of the Flies (book, 1954): Julia Baird
The Lost Boys (1987): Angie McCartney
Lost Horizon (1937): Debbie D
Lost in Space (series, 1965): Debbie D
Love At First Bite (1979): Brute Force
Lucky (2004): Steve Cuden
Lust for a Vampire (1971): Tony Bramwell

M (1931): Laurie Jacobson, Angie McCartney
Ma Barker's Killer Brood (1960): Don Grady
Macbeth (play, 1606-1607): Julia Baird
Madman (1982): Bianca Allaine
The Man with the Golden Arm (1955): Don Grady
Maniac Cop 2 (1990): Clay McLeod Chapman
Mark of the Devil (1970): Elliott Easton
Mark of the Vampire (1935): Rick Mullen
Martin (1978): John Amplas
Mighty Joe Young (1949): Donna Loren
Millennium (series, 1996): Ian Lloyd
Misery (book, 1987): Bev Bevan
Misery (1990): Steve Cuden, Don Grady
Mission: Killfast (1991): Ted V. Mikels
Monkeyshines (1988): Dean Friedman
The Monster Squad (1987): Clay McLeod Chapman
Motel Hell (1980): Bianca Allaine, Michael Dante, Dean Friedman, Ian Lloyd, Tiffany Shepis
Mother's Day (1980): Debbie D
Mountaintop Motel Massacre (1983): Tiffany Shepis
The Mummy (1932): Forrest Ackerman, Freddy Boom Boom Cannon, Chuck McCann, Metal Pistol, James Lee Stanley, Robert Zapata
My Bloody Valentine (1981): Clay McLeod Chapman
The Mysterians (1957): Mitch Schecter
The Next Voice You Hear (1950): Dave Winfield
Night of the Comet (1984): Fred Schneider
Night of the Creeps (1986): Michael Hein
Night of the Demon (1980): Bianca Allaine
The Night of the Hunter (1955): Debbie Rochon
Night of the Living Dead (1968): John Amplas, Corbin Bernsen, Kevin Clement, Walter Egan, Sharon Farrell, Brute Force, Dean Friedman, Laurie Jacobson, Irwin Keyes, Ian Lloyd, Vince Martell, Bill Moseley, Robb Ortel, Debbie Rochon, William Shatner, James Lee Stanley, Gary Van Scyoc, Eerie Von, Ross Wilson
The Night Stalker (series, 1972): Ian Lloyd
The Nightmare Before Christmas (1993): Ashley C. Williams
A Nightmare on Elm Street (1984): Pete Best, Dinky Dawson, Gloria Gaynor, Donna Hamblin, Elizabeth Leiknes, Ian Lloyd, Lada St. Edmund, Tiffany Shepis
A Nightmare on Elm Street Part 3: Dream Warriors (1987): Clay McLeod Chapman
A Nightmare on Elm Street Part 4: The Dream Master (1988): Clay McLeod Chapman
Nosferatu (1922): Elliott Easton, Irwin Keyes, Kimberly Magness, Robb Ortel, Vampy
Oliver Twist (1948): Ed Asner
The Omen (1976): Pete Best, Steve Cuden, Anthony Masi, Angie McCartney, Jonathan Tiersten, Eerie Von, Ross Wilson, Dave Winfield
Open Water (2003): Jonathan Tiersten

Orphan (2009): Anthony Masi
Othello (play, 1603-1604): Julia Baird
The Others (2001): Lada St. Edmund, Deborah Voorhees
Outbreak (1995): Don Grady
The Outer Limits episode **Cold Hands, Warm Heart** (1964): William Shatner
The Outer Limits episode **Wolf 359** (1964): William Shatner
The Outer Limits episode **The Zanti Misfits** (series, 1963): Rick Mullen
Pan's Labyrinth (2006): Deana Demko, Ashley C. Williams
Paranormal Activity (2007): Robb Ortel
Parasomnia (2008): Dick Wagner
Pet Sematary (1989): Mark Bego, Clay McLeod Chapman, Donna Hamblin, Jonathan Tiersten
Peter Pan (musical, 1950): John Sebastian
Phantasm (1979): Robb Ortel, Kasim Sultan
The Phantom of the Opera (1925): Forrest Ackerman, Circe Link, Chuck McCann, Jon Provost, Eerie Von, Robert Zapata
The Picture of Dorian Gray (1945): The Amazing Kreskin, Vampy
Pink Eye (2008): Charles F. Rosenay!!! ("Cryptmaster Chucky")
The Pit and the Pendulum (short story, 1842): Julia Baird
The Pit and the Pendulum (1961): Elliott Easton
Pitch Black (2000): Brute Force
Plan 9 from Outer Space (1959): Walter Egan, Greg Hawkes
Planet of the Apes (1968): Brute Force
Play Misty for Me (1971): The Amazing Kreskin, Kimberly Magness
Poltergeist (1982): Pete Best, Dinky Dawson, Donna Loren, Tiffany Shepis
Predator (1987): Little Anthony Gourdine, Lada St. Edmund
The Premonition (1976): Dante Tomaselli
Presumed Innocent (1990): Barry Williams
Pretty Maids All in a Row (1971): Barbara Leigh
Pretty Woman (1990): Murray Langston
Prince of Darkness (1987): Dinky Dawson
Psycho (book, 1959): Joe R. Lansdale
Psycho (1960): Ed Asner, Mark Bego, Corbin Bernsen, T. Graham Brown, Ruth Buzzi, Kevin Clement, Steve Cuden, Ron Dante, Sharon Farrell, Little Anthony Gourdine, Frank Jeckell, Sara Karloff, The Amazing Kreskin, Circe Link, Kimberly Magness, Chuck McCann, Angie McCartney, Elaine Spanky McFarlane, Butch Patrick, Jon Provost, Gary Puckett, Debbie Rochon, Lada St. Edmund, William Shatner, Kasim Sultan, Jonathan Tiersten, Gary Van Scyoc, Phil "Fang" Volk, Dick Wagner, Beverly Washburn, Jane Wiedlin, Dave Winfield
Psychomania (1973): Circe Link
Pumpkinhead (1988): Bianca Allaine, Deana Demko
Q (1982): Dean Friedman
Quarantine (2008): Ashley C. Williams
The Quatermass Experiment (British series, 1953): Bev Bevan
The Quatermass Xperiment (1955): Tony Bramwell

The Queen of Outer Space (1958): Mitch Schecter
A Quiet Place (2018): Bev Bevan, Deborah Voorhees
The Raven (1963): Angie McCartney
The Ray Bradbury Theater episode **The Playground** (1985): William Shatner
Re-Animator (1985): Dean Friedman
Rear Window (1954): Barry Williams
Red Planet Mars (1952): Walter Egan
The Relic (1997): Deana Demko
Repulsion (1965): Ron Dante, Jack Ketchum
Return of the Living Dead 3 (1993): Deana Demko
Revenge of the Creature (1955): Buzzy Linhart, Gary Van Scyoc
Ring (1988): Ross Wilson
The Ring (2002): Elizabeth Leiknes, Jonathan Tiersten
Rituals (1977): Bianca Allaine
The Road (book, 2006): Steve Cuden
The Rocky Horror Picture Show (1975): Beverly Bremers
Rosemary's Baby (1968): Debe Branning, Beverly Bremers, Ruth Buzzi, Michael Dante, Gloria Gaynor, Laurie Jacobson, Jack Ketchum, Circe Link, Kimberly Magness, Angie McCartney, Elaine Spanky McFarlane, Lada St. Edmund, Kasim Sulton, Jonathan Tiersten, Gary Van Scyoc, Eerie Von, Beverly Washburn, Dave Winfield
The Sadist (2015): Charles F. Rosenay!!! ("Cryptmaster Chucky")
The Sadist (trailer, 2015): Charles F. Rosenay!!! ("Cryptmaster Chucky")
'Salem's Lot (book, 1975): Frank Jeckell, Joe R. Lansdale
Salem's Lot (1979): Mark Bego, Robb Ortel
Saturday Night Live, season 12, episode 8 (1986): William Shatner
Saw (2004): Elizabeth Leiknes, Geri Reischl
Scared Stiff (1953): Eddie Deezen, Vince Martell
Scream (1996): Beverly Bremers
Seconds (1966): Ian Lloyd
Secret Window (2004): Debe Branning
The Sentinel (1977): Dinky Dawson, Dante Tomaselli
The Serpent and the Rainbow (1988): Michael Hein
The Servant (1963): Buzzy Linhart
Se7en (1995): Gloria Gaynor, Elizabeth Leiknes, Dick Wagner, Barry Williams
Shatner's Raw Nerve episode with **Leonard Nimoy** (2009): William Shatner
Shaun of the Dead (2004): Ian Lloyd, Deborah Voorhees, Jane Wiedlin, Ashley C. Williams, Dave Winfield
The Shawshank Redemption (1994): Steve Cuden
The Shining (book, 1977): Frank Jeckell, Joe R. Lansdale
The Shining (1980): Tim Atwood, Corbin Bernsen, Pete Best, Bev Bevan, Beverly Bremers, Ruth Buzzi, Sybil Danning, Dinky Dawson, Sharon Farrell, Gloria Gaynor, Don Grady, Greg Hawkes, Laurie Jacobson, Frank Jeckell, Elizabeth Leiknes, Buzzy Linhart, Circe Link, Ian Lloyd, Kimberly Magness, Angie McCartney, Butch Patrick, Gary Puckett, Geri Reischl, Lada St. Edmund, Mitch

Schecter, William Shatner, Jonathan Tiersten, Beverly Washburn, Jane Wiedlin, Dave Winfield
Shock (1977): Dante Tomaselli
Shocker (1989): Clay McLeod Chapman
The Shock Theatre (with Roland,1957): John Sebastian
Signs (2002): Phil "Fang" Volk
The Silence of the Lambs (book, 1988): Joe R. Lansdale
The Silence of the Lambs (1991): Corbin Bernsen, T. Graham Brown, Ruth Buzzi, Michael Dante, Elizabeth Leiknes, Circe Link, William Shatner, Barry Williams
Sinister (2011): Donna Hamblin
The Sixth Sense (1999): Micky Dolenz, Don Grady, James Lee Stanley
The Sixth Sense episode **Can A Dead Man Strike from the Grave?** (1972): William Shatner
Snakes on a Plane (2006): Tim Atwood
Something Wicked This Way Comes (book, 1962): Joe R. Lansdale
Son of Frankenstein (1939): Greg Hawkes
Son of the Invisible Man (2009): Murray Langston
Sorry, Wrong Number (1948): Ruth Buzzi
Spawn (1997): Lada St. Edmund
Species (1995): Jack Ketchum
Spider Baby (1967): Beverly Washburn
Spirits of the Dead (1968): Karen Black
Splice (2009): Tiffany Shepis
The Stand (book, 1978): Steve Cuden, Joe R. Lansdale
Stand By Me (1986): Steve Cuden
Star Trek series (1966): William Shatner
Star Trek episode **The City on the Edge of Forever** (1967): William Shatner
Star Wars (A New Hope) (1977): Micky Dolenz, Mitch Schecter
Strait-Jacket (1964): Buzzy Linhart
Strange Things Happen at Sundown (2003): Michael Hein
The Strangers (2008): William Shatner
The Strangers: Prey at Night (2018): Anthony Masi
Strike Me Deadly (1963): Ted V. Mikels
The Student Nurses (1970): Barbara Leigh
The Stuff (1985): Dean Friedman
Suspiria (1977): Kevin Clement
Taste of Fear (1961): Tony Bramwell
Teenage Exorcist (1991): Eddie Deezen
TekWar (series, 1994): William Shatner
The Tenant (1976): Buzzy Linhart, Circe Link, Christian Nesmith
The Terminator (1984): Karen Black, Steve Cuden, Ian Lloyd
The Texas Chainsaw Massacre (1974): Karen Black, Metal Pistol, Bill Moseley, Robb Ortel, Butch Patrick, Gary Puckett, Eerie Von
The Texas Chainsaw Massacre 2 (1986): Bill Moseley
Theater of Blood (1973): Beverly Bremers

Them (2006): Anthony Masi
Them! (1954): Butch Patrick, Gary Puckett, James Lee Stanley
They Live (1988): Metal Pistol
The Thing (1982): Dinky Dawson, Sharon Farrell, Ian Lloyd
The Thing (From Another World!) (1951): Bev Bevan, Brute Force, Little Anthony Gourdine, Bobby Hart, Irwin Keyes, Buzzy Linhart, Chuck McCann, Elaine Spanky McFarlane, Gary Puckett, Dick Wagner
13 Ghosts (1960): Elliott Easton, Bill Moseley
This Island Earth (1955): Micky Dolenz
This Night I'll Possess Your Corpse (1967): Dante Tomaselli
Thriller episode **The Grim Reaper** (1961): William Shatner
Thriller episode **The Hungry Glass** (1961): William Shatner
A Time to Kill (1996): Barry Williams
Tiny's Halloween 3 (2012): Charles F. Rosenay!!! ("Cryptmaster Chucky")
Tiny's October 31st (2019): Charles F. Rosenay!!! ("Cryptmaster Chucky")
Tourist Trap (1979): Dante Tomaselli
Trailers from Hell (series, 2007): Joe Dante
Trick 'r Treat (2008): Tiffany Shepis
True Blood (2008): Dick Wagner
28 Days Later (2002): Elizabeth Leiknes
20,000 Leagues Under the Sea (1954): Frank Jeckell, Ashley C. Williams
The Twilight Zone (series, 1959): Bev Bevan
The Twilight Zone episode **Nick of Time** (1960): William Shatner
The Twilight Zone episode **Nightmare at 20,000 Feet** (1963): William Shatner
The Twilight Zone episode **Time Enough at Last** (1959): Karen Black
2001: A Space Odyssey (1968): Jon Provost
Ultra Man (1972): Debbie D
Unearthly Stranger (1964): Karen Black
The Uninvited (1944): Barbara Leigh, Chuck McCann
The Unknown (1927): Vampy
Us (2019): Laurie Jacobson
Vampyr (1932): Rick Mullen
Van Helsing (2004): Mark Bego, Barbara Leigh
Village of the Damned (1960): Anthony Masi
Videodrome (1983): Jane Wiedlin
Wait Until Dark (1967): Mark Bego
The Walking Dead (series, 2010-): Robb Ortel
The War of the Gargantuas (1966): Donna Hamblin
The War of the Worlds (1953): Micky Dolenz, Frank Jeckell, Gary Puckett, Mitch Schecter
War of the Worlds (2005): Donna Hamblin
Waxwork (1988): Tiffany Shepis
Welcome Mats (2010): Charles F. Rosenay!!! ("Cryptmaster Chucky")
Wendigo (2001): John Amplas
Werewolf Women of the SS (2007): Sybil Danning

What Ever Happened to Baby Jane? (1962): Corbin Bernsen, Laurie Jacobson, Kimberly Magness, Beverly Washburn
What Lies Beneath (2000): Deborah Voorhees
When a Stranger Calls (1979): Tiffany Shepis, Dave Winfield
White Heat (1949): Brute Force
Willy Wonka & the Chocolate Factory (1971): Dinky Dawson, Donna Hamblin
Wishmaster (1997): Deana Demko
The Wizard of Oz (1939): Tim Atwood, Debe Branning, T. Graham Brown, Sara Karloff, Phil "Fang" Volk
The Wolf Man (1941): Pete Best, Freddy Boom Boom Cannon, Debbie D, Sybil Danning, Michael Dante, Ron Dante, Little Anthony Gourdine, Barbara Leigh, Buzzy Linhart, Vince Martell, Chuck McCann, Metal Pistol, Bill Mumy, Geri Reischl, Beverly Washburn, Robert Zapata
Women in Cages (1971): Kasim Sultan
Wrestlemaniac (2008): Irwin Keyes
Wuthering Heights (1939): Barbara Leigh
Young Frankenstein (1974): Eddie Deezen, Greg Hawkes, Bill Mumy, Deborah Voorhees, Beverly Washburn
Zardoz (1974): Buzzy Linhart
The Zombie Chronicles (2013): Charles F. Rosenay!!! ("Cryptmaster Chucky")
Zombie Island Massacre (1984): Fred Schneider
Zulu (1964): Ruth Buzzi

INDEX OF CONTRIBUTORS

A

Ackerman, Forrest	13
Allaine, Bianca	14
Amplas, John	16
Asner, Ed	18
Atwood, Tim	20

B

Baird, Julia	23
Bego, Mark	33
Bernsen, Corbin	35
Best, Pete	37
Bevan, Bev	39
Black, Karen	41
Bramwell, Tony	45
Branning, Debe	47
Bremers, Beverly	49
Brown, T. Graham	51
Buzzi, Ruth	54

C

Cannon, Freddy "Boom Boom"	56
Chapman, Clay McLeod	58
Chick, Mother	61
Christy, Richard	64
Clement, Kevin	67
Cole, Clay	69
Cuden, Steve	71

D

D, Debbie	75
Danning, Sybil	79
Dante, Joe	81
Dante, Michael	83
Dante, Ron	87
Dawson, Dinky	89
Deezen, Eddie	91
Demko, Deana	93
Dolenz, Micky	95
Dunaway, Dennis	97

E

Easton, Elliott	100
Egan, Walter	103

F

Farrell, Sharon	105
Force, Brute	108
Friedman, Dean	111

G

Gaynor, Gloria	116
Gourdine, Little Anthony	118
Grady, Don	120

H

Hamblin, Donna	123
Hart, Bobby	125
Hawkes, Greg	127
Hein, Michael	129

J

Jacobson, Laurie	131
Jeckell, Frank	135

K

Karloff, Sara	137
Ketchum, Jack	139
Keyes, Irwin	141
Kreskin, The Amazing	143

L

Langston, Murray	149
Lansdale, Joe R.	151
Leigh, Barbara	154
Leiknes, Elizabeth	157
Linhart, Buzzy	159
Link, Circe	161
Lloyd, Ian	165
Loren, Donna	167

M

Magness, Kimberly	169
Martell, Vince	171
Masi, Anthony	173
McCann, Chuck	177
McCartney, Angie	179
McFarlane, Elaine	182
Metal Pistol	184
Mikels, Ted V.	186
Moseley, Bill	187
Mullen, Rick	189
Mumy, Bill	191

N

Nesmith, Christian	193

O

P

Ortel, Robb	195
Patrick, Butch	198
Provost, Jon	200
Puckett, Gary	203

R

Reischl, Geri	205
Rochon, Debbie	208
Rosenay!!!, Charles F.	267

S

St. Edmund, Lada	210
Schecter, Mitch	212
Schneider, Fred	214
Sebastian, John	216
Shatner, William	218
Shepis, Tiffany	221
Stanley, James Lee	223
Sulton, Kasim	226

T

Tiersten, Jonathan	228
Tomaselli, Dante	230

V

Vampy	234
Van Scyoc, Gary	236
Volk, Phil "Fang"	238
Von, Eerie	243
Voorhees, Deborah	245

W

Wagner, Dick	247
Washburn, Beverly	249
Wiedlin, Jane	251
Williams, Ashley C.	253
Williams, Barry	255
Winfield, Dave	261

Z

Zapata, Robert	263

CPSIA information can be obtained
at www.ICGtesting.com
Printed in the USA
BVHW052228220921
617294BV00001B/102

9 781629 337654